MUSIC FOR LOVE

The Music Party (Thomas Gainsborough)

MUSIC FOR LOVE

An Anthology of
Amateur Music-Making

edited by

CHRISTOPHER DRIVER

WEIDENFELD & NICOLSON, LONDON

For 'viola wives'
and other partners

Introductory material and selection © 1994 by
Christopher Driver

First published 1994

Typeset at Create Publishing Services Ltd,
Bath, Avon

Printed and bound in Great Britain by
Butler & Tanner Ltd, Frome and London

Weidenfeld & Nicolson Ltd
The Orion Publishing Group
Orion House
5 Upper St Martin's Lane
London WC2H 9EA

ISBN: 0 297 814931

CONTENTS

Contents

Contents

ILLUSTRATIONS

ACKNOWLEDGEMENTS

The author and publishers wish to thank the following who have kindly given permission for the use of copyright material:

Aitken, Stone & Wylie Ltd for an extract from Osbert Burdett, *The Art of Living*, Eyre & Spottiswoode, 1933; Cambridge University Press for extracts from Cecil Torr, *Small Talk at Wreyland*, 1918; Carcanet Press Ltd for David Wright, 'The Musician' from *Selected Poems*, 1988; Austin Coates for an extract from Eric Coates, *Suite in Four Movements*, Heinemann, 1953; David & Charles Publishers for an extract from Henry Livings, *That the Medals and the Baton be Put on View*, 1975; J. M. Dent & Sons Ltd for an extract from George Melly, *Owning Up*, 1965; Faber & Faber Ltd for an extract from George Ewart Evans, *The Strength of the Hills*, 1983; The Financial Times Ltd for David Lascelles, 'Around the horn under full scale', *Financial Times*, 2 August 1986; Victor Gollancz and Doubleday, a division of Bantam Doubleday Dell Publishing Group Inc., for extracts from Kingsley Amis, *Lucky Jim* (copyright © 1954 by Kingsley Amis); Harcourt Brace & Company for extracts from *History of my Life, Giacomo Casanova*, vols. 3–4, trans. William R. Trask (copyright © 1966 by Harcourt Brace & Company); HarperCollins Publishers for extracts from Boris Pasternak, *Essay in Autobiography*, trans. Manya Harari, Harvill, 1959, and Samuel Pepys, ed. Robert Latham and William Matthews, *Diary*, Master and Fellows of Magdalene College, Cambridge and Bell & Hyman; A.M. Heath & Company Ltd on behalf of the author for an extract from Eudora Welty, *Delta Wedding*, Bodley Head, 1947; William Heinemann Ltd and McGraw-Hill Inc., for extracts from Arthur Hedley, trans. and ed., *Selected Correspondence of Fryderyk Chopin*, 1963. (copyright © 1963 Arthur Hedley); David Higham Associates Ltd on behalf of the author for John Heath-Stubbs, 'The watchman's flute' from *Selected Poems*, Carcanet Press, 1990; Knight Publishing Corporation for Tristram Cary, 'Trudy Cary as a musician', *Adam Magazine*, 23 December 1988 (copyright © 1988 Adam Magazine); Oxford University Press for extracts from Anne Fremantle, ed., *The Wynne Diaries 1789–1820*, 1952, Jerrold Northrop Moore, ed., *Edward Elgar: Letters of a Lifetime*, 1990, E. S. Beer, ed., *The Diary of John Evelyn*, 1955, and Charles Burney, *An Eighteenth-Century Musical Tour in France and Italy, Vol. 1*, ed. Percy A. Scholes, 1959; Oxford University Press, Inc., for Conrad Aiken, 'Music' from *Collected Poems*, 2nd edn. (copyright © 1970 by Conrad Aiken); Harold Ober Associates, Inc. for extract from Catherine Drinker Bowen, *Friends and Fiddlers* (copyright © 1935, 1962 by Catherine Drinker Bowen); The Observer Ltd for Jonathan Steinberg, 'Practice makes sort-of-perfect', *New Society*, 13 September 1979, and Allister Sparks, 'Soweto Quartet, Johannesburg', *The Observer*, 14 June 1992; Penguin Books USA Inc. for an extract from James Joyce, 'The Dead' in *Dubliners*, Viking Penguin (copyright 1916 by B.W. Heubsch, definitive text copyright © 1967 by the Estate of James Joyce), and D.H. Lawrence, 'Piano' from *The Complete Poems of D.H. Lawrence*, ed. V. de Sola Pinto and F.W. Roberts, Viking Penguin, (copyright © 1964, 1971 by Angelo Ravagli and C.M. Weekley, Executors of the Estate of Frieda Lawrence Ravagli); Peters Fraser & Dunlop Group Ltd on behalf of the author for extracts from Rebecca West, *The Fountain Overflows*, Macmillan, 1957;

Random Century Group for extracts from Laurie Lee, *Cider with Rosie*, Hogarth Press, 1959, Stanley Middleton, *Ends and Means*, Hutchinson, 1977, with the Reece Halsy agency on behalf of Mrs Laura Huxley for extracts from Aldous Huxley, *Beyond the Mexique Bay*, Chatto & Windus, 1934, and with Jonathan Clowes on behalf of the author for Kingsley Amis, 'A chromatic passing-note' from *Collected Poems*, Hutchinson, 1979 (copyright © 1967 by Kingsley Amis); Random House, Inc. for extracts from Gustave Flaubert, *Madame Bovary*, trans. Francis Steegmuller (copyright © 1957 by Francis Steegmuller); Routledge for an extract from Mabel Dolmetsch, *Personal Reflections of Arnold Dolmetsch*, Routledge & Kegan Paul, 1957; Rogers, Coleridge & White Ltd on behalf of the author for extracts from Frances Partridge, *Everything to Lose*, Gollancz, 1985 and *A Pacifist's War*, Hogarth Press, 1978; The Society of Authors on behalf of the Bernard Shaw Estate for G.B. Shaw, 'Amateur concert at Richmond', 26 April 1893 from *Music in London*, Constable, 1932, and an extract from G.B. Shaw, *Major Barbara*, Constable, 1905, and on behalf of the E.M. Forster Estate and King's College, Cambridge, with Alfred A. Knopf, Inc., for an extract from E.M. Forster, *Room With A View*, Edward Arnold, 1908; The Tantivy Press Ltd for an extract from Freddy Buache, *The Cinema of Luis Buñuel*, trans. Peter Graham, 1973; A.P. Watt Ltd and Melanie Jackson Agency on behalf of the author, for an extract from Alison Lurie, *Love and Friendship* (copyright © 1990 by Alison Lurie; Yale University Press for extracts from Gordon S. Haight, ed., *The Yale Edition of the Letters of George Eliot*, 1954–78.

Every effort has been made to trace all the copyright holders but if any have been inadvertently overlooked the publishers will be pleased to make the necessary arrangements at the first opportunity.

INTRODUCTION

Any book is a minority taste. So is live music. An anthology that appeals to both pleasures has to take its chance from the uncommon customer. But just as fishermen and mountaineers pay good money for their patient or perilous pastimes, most spare-time musicians are not wholly sane. That is, they are fit to survive 'in the community', as the euphemism puts it, but they become restive if they are deprived of regular access to remedial tuition, day centres and custodial care at special schools, equipped with soundproof cells. (I once saw a Londoner parked on a meter in his Mini. He was practising the trumpet.) If these requisites are met, they give no trouble and my publisher is in favour. After all, she too has been seen in her office with a fiddle case, trying to pretend that it belongs to someone else.

She and I and uncounted people in the British Isles are what Ruth Finnegan calls *The Hidden Musicians**. A social anthropologist at the Open University, the author studied the entire spectrum of live music-making in her own neighbourhood, Milton Keynes, a loosely knit new city, based on old towns and villages. The population is weighted towards youngish, white-collar, two-income families. She names many of the players and groups whom she met or observed: classical, brass band, jazz, folk, rock and the rest. The scene is extraordinarily rich. She shows that piped music in supermarket and station concourse, on one hand, and full-dress professional concerts on the South Bank or on television, are peripheral to what actually happens musically in after-hours Britain: the nightly tootling and warbling and stroking behind closed doors,

* *The Hidden Musicians* (Cambridge, 1989).

13

rehearsing an operetta or playing a pub gig or taking turns at piano practice at home: 'Mum, do I have to?' This cultural diversity has long roots in spite of the supposed 'Land without Music', the pre-1914 German polemic which gave great offence at the time – though, as we shall see, there was also a kernel of truth about nineteenth-century English musical diffidence, hardening into philistinism, from the point of view of a Berliner or Viennese.

As Finnegan writes, all this music-making is taken for granted to the point of invisibility. 'Are these activities still robust or by now fading away? – and who are their patrons today? What is the significance of local music-making for the people who manage and make sense of modern life or, more widely, for our experience as active and creative human beings? There has been little work on the "micro-sociology" of amateur music; and, incredibly, questions on active music-making as such seldom or never appear in official surveys – almost as if local music-making did not exist at all.'

Her book constitutes a freeze-frame of musical events as they *are*. The present book reminds us of musical events as they *were*. Some of the writers represented evoke memories too deep for tears (Thomas Hardy, James Joyce, Eudora Welty); others flower into merriment or vituperation ('Hell is amateur musicians').

My own preferences both in literature and music are obvious enough for the reader to scorn or enjoy. Even Ruth Finnegan's scholarly objectivity surely betrays her own enthusiasms in one passage about people committed to the classical music world: 'The rewards ... are hard to capture in precise words, but they certainly included a sense of beauty and fundamental value, of intense and profoundly felt artistic experience which could reach to the depths of one's nature.' However, one characteristic of twentieth-century music is our own composers' greedy borrowing from cultures hitherto thought alien by the concert-going classes. My own ignorance precludes more than token literary representation of such music-making.

The title of this book is studiously vague. But implicit in almost all inclusions and exclusions is the thread of 'music for love' in at least two senses: descriptions of music for pleasure, played by off-duty people who may or may not be adequately trained. But even that begs numerous questions, especially when scrupulous social scientists or historians start to unpick the labels for 'amateurs' and 'professionals'. By tradition, a trained musician who earns his or her living is called 'professional', while the 'amateur' does it 'for love'. A singular example of the latter was W. W. Cobbett (1847–1937) who was lucky enough to strike rich in the City out of patent royalties. He devoted himself not only to playing his Stradivari violin and leading numerous amateur ensembles but also established a much-coveted composition prize and published his own *Cyclopaedia of Chamber Music* (1929, enlarged and revised by Colin Mason in 1963). It was once said of him that he devoted to commerce the little time he could spare from music.

Greater complications arise today as soon as one tries to apply strict categories to actual cases. As Ruth Finnegan reports: 'There was the classically trained vocalist who decided not to pursue her full-time career after the birth of her daughter but picked up the odd local engagement for a moderate fee, often accompanied by a local guitar teacher: professional or amateur? ... One of the interesting characteristics of local music organisation is precisely the absence of an absolute distinction between "the amateur" and "the professional".'

Many passages in novels, letters and diaries of the past centuries use this distinction. But the history of Western music since the Renaissance has been and still is changing in front of our eyes, while the word 'amateur' itself has remained constant for about 200 years. For instance, Rees's *Cyclopaedia* (1803) offers: 'Amateur, in the Arts, is a foreign term introduced and now passing current amongst us, to denote a person understanding, and loving, or practising the polite arts of painting, sculpture, or architecture, without any regard to pecuniary advantage.' That was all right as long as gentlemen avoided public performance; while women painting, playing the harp and acting charades could be praised for their accomplishment and congratulated for their marriageability.

But the social climb of the cultural professions – often accompanied by modest 'pecuniary advantage' – gradually degraded the status of amateur watercolourists and ballad-singers in thousands of Victorian parlours. Both social and educational changes were involved in different notions of what was expected of ladies and gentlemen from one century to another, and indeed one continental country to another. At the extremes in this book, compare Henry Peacham (p. 117) with Lord Chesterfield (p. 260) on the propriety of a gentleman's instrumental accomplishment. At another historical watershed, contemplate the relative social status of two great composers (friends and contemporaries): the treatment of young

Mozart below stairs in provincial Salzburg during the 1770s, and the fees commanded by Herr Haydn on his visits to commercial London during the 1790s. In the same context, when we read Jane Austen's comments to her sister Cassandra about a London concert party in 1811 (p. 77), we realize that the gentlemanly diffidence of the English amateur musician is already a world away from the royal confidence displayed by King Frederick of Prussia, who could order from Mozart a set of string quartets emphasizing the role of his own cello as though he were ordering a suit from his tailor to flatter his figure.

It is hardly surprising that our own present complex set of musical and social relationships is straining the ancient categories. One most significant change in British musical life arrived during the 1930s: the influence of German-speaking refugees. Not only did particular Jewish musicians – the late Max Rostal comes to mind – transform a whole generation's string playing and teaching in London, with a knock-on effect thereafter. Thousands of displaced European scholars, scientists, doctors and artists migrated from a culture where the aged Esther Simpson, scholar and violinist, has lately recalled Vienna across sixty years: 'Playing music was part of life, like brushing your teeth.'

In our own time, even after a brutish decade of resurgent hostility to state patronage and humane education, postwar access to good music, live or recorded, has enabled instrumentalists of all kinds (and ages) to move in and out of 'the profession' and its periphery. While standards of technique and style edge ever upwards in conservatoires and specialized ensembles, other musically educated and trained young people may choose different professions – for *Apollon Musagète* is a hard taskmaster – but remain able to please appreciative audiences and even turn a few honest pennies. Truth to tell, more dubious pennies are often earned by jaded, under-rehearsed professionals, obliged to churn out routine performances of hackneyed classics for mediocre conductors and uncritical audiences. But that is the prejudice of an amateur, in the original sense of the word.

It remains true, however, that outside a few privileged localities – university towns, for instance – music-makers often have the sense of belonging to a secret discipline, like early Christians. No official body enumerates or evaluates our skills, acquired in youth, with luck refreshed in maturity and retained as a principal solace even while some faculties are blunted or mobility is curtailed. Illiteracy is a scandal in a developed country like ours but at least someone can tell the public what proportion of our compatriots can read *The Times* or are baffled by *The Sun*. By contrast, musical literacy is unquantified: should we not know how many of us can identify the intervals and durations of the notes in a simple tune and sing it or play it on some instrument?

One per cent musical literacy may be a generous guess, judging by the unexpected delights of the secret discipline. From time to time I pick up for the London Underground not a book or magazine but a score. Twice this year complete strangers have glanced at the page and broken the British tabu by actually *speaking*. The first traveller asked, 'Is that Haydn?' (It was.) The second encounter was uncanny. For a particular purpose on a single journey, I was looking through the parts of Shostakovich's Viola Sonata (his last work), which may be a masterpiece but is certainly unfamiliar. A young man got in at Euston, sat down beside me and noticed the clefs. 'You're reading a viola sonata?' 'Yes, Shostakovich.' 'I know that piano part. I used to play it with a friend in Munich.'

Perhaps the infinitely remote chances of that London Transport encounter with two willing players should be run through the Open University's computer in Milton Keynes.

Christopher Driver

1
LADIES, LADIES, LADIES

KINGSLEY AMIS

A Chromatic Passing-Note

'That slimy tune' I said, and got a laugh,
In the middle of old Franck's D minor thing:
The dotted-rhythm clarinet motif.

Not always slimy. I thought, at fifteen,
It went to show that real love was found
At the far end of the right country lane.

I thought that, like Keats and the rest of them,
Old Franck was giving me a preview of
The world, action in art, a paradigm.

Yes, I know better now, or different.
Not image: buffer only, syrup, crutch.
'Slimy' was a snarl of disappointment.

JANE AUSTEN

For Jane Austen, playing an instrument had a double significance, first in life, then in fiction. Her modest voice and pianism could almost be taken for granted in her milieu and in her role in the family circle. Her critical ear or 'taste' enriched her novels no more and no less than her pleasure in dancing, shopping or planning a strawberry picnic: in such familiar settings her characters, observed or imagined, betray themselves with a clarity devastating as Mozart's.

Most of Jane Austen's surviving letters were written unselfconsciously to her beloved sister Cassandra. Both there and in her novels it is evident that she could take or leave the generally mediocre music of her time and place. Compare the more cosmopolitan upbringing and musical perception of Betsey Wynne (pp. 194–7) in a similar generation. While Betsey in the 1790s could play a Pleyel concerto or a Mozart sonata 'with accompaniment of violin', in *Emma* (1816) Jane Fairfax would hardly have been capable of late Haydn, let alone the young Beethoven, on that Frank Churchill's mysterious Broadwood pianoforte (no mean gift, the Bechstein of its day). By contrast, Mary Crawford in *Mansfield Park* (1814) predictably chose the fashionable harp rather than the keyboard to bewitch stolid Edward Bertram: she knew how to make a lady's arms appear to advantage.

But there is no doubt about which fictional Austen character's musical activity expressed the novelist's own inner self. No one who has entered into the long-cherished, seemingly hopeless love of Anne Elliot in *Persuasion* will forget similarly therapeutic evenings 'while her fingers were mechanically at work, proceeding for half an hour together, equally without error, and without consciousness'.

Mary Crawford's seductive harp

'Mr Bertram,' said Miss Crawford, 'I have tidings of my harp at last. I am assured that it is safe at Northampton; and there it has probably been these ten days, in spite of the solemn assurances we have so often received to the contrary.' Edmund expressed his pleasure and surprise. 'The truth is, that our inquiries were too direct; we sent a servant, we went ourselves: this will not do seventy miles from London – but this morning we heard of it in the right way. It was seen by some farmer, and he told the miller, and the miller told the butcher, and the butcher's son-in-law left word at the shop.'

'I am very glad that you have heard of it, by whatever means; and hope there will be no farther delay.'

'I am to have it to-morrow; but how do you think it is to be conveyed? Not by a waggon or cart; – Oh! no, nothing of that kind could be hired in the village. I might as well have asked for porters and a hand-barrow.'

'You would find it difficult, I dare say, just now, in the middle of a very late hay harvest, to hire a horse and cart?'

'I was astonished to find what a piece of work was made of it! To want a horse and cart in the country seemed impossible, so I told my maid to speak for one directly; and as I cannot look out of my dressing-closet without seeing one farm yard, nor walk in the shrubbery without passing another, I thought it would be only ask and have, and was rather grieved that I could not give the advantage to all. Guess my surprise, when I found that I had been asking the most unreasonable, most impossible thing in the world, had offended all the farmers, all the labourers, all the hay in the parish. As for Dr Grant's bailiff, I believe I had better keep out of *his* way; and my brother-in-law himself, who is all kindness in general, looked rather black upon me, when he found what I had been at.'

'You could not be expected to have thought on the subject before, but when you *do* think of it, you must see the importance of getting in the grass. The hire of a cart at any time, might not be so easy as you suppose; our farmers are not in the habit of letting them out; but in harvest, it must be quite out of their power to spare a horse.'

'I shall understand all your ways in time; but coming down with the true London maxim, that every thing is to be got with money, I was a little embarrassed at first by the sturdy independence of your country customs. However, I am to have my harp fetched to-morrow. Henry, who is good-nature itself, has offered to fetch it in his barouche. Will it not be honourably conveyed?'

Edmund spoke of the harp as his favourite instrument, and hoped to be soon allowed to hear her. Fanny had never heard the harp at all, and wished for it very much.

'I shall be most happy to play to you both,' said Miss Crawford; 'at least, as long as you can like to listen; probably much longer, for I dearly love music myself, and where the natural taste is equal, the player must always be best off, for she is gratified in more ways than one. Now, Mr Bertram, if you write to your brother, I entreat you to tell him that my harp *is* come, he heard so much of my misery about it. And you may say, if you please, that I shall prepare my most plaintive airs against his return, in compassion to his feelings, as I know his horse will lose.'

... Miss Crawford's attractions did not lessen. The harp arrived, and rather added to her beauty, wit, and good humour, for she played with the greatest obligingness, with an expression and taste which were peculiarly becoming, and there was something clever to be said at the close of every air. Edmund was at the parsonage every day to be indulged with his favourite instrument; one morning secured an invitation for the next, for the lady could not be unwilling to have a listener, and every thing was soon in a fair train.

A young woman, pretty, lively, with a harp as elegant as herself; and both placed near a window, cut down to the ground, and opening on a little lawn, surrounded by shrubs in the rich foliage of summer, was enough to catch any man's heart. The season, the scene, the air, were all favourable to tenderness and sentiment. Mrs Grant and her tambour frame were not without their use; it was all in harmony; and as every thing will turn to account when love is once set going, even the sandwich tray, and Dr Grant doing the honours of it, were worth looking at. Without studying the business, however, or knowing what he was about, Edmund was beginning at the end of a week of such intercourse, to be a good deal in love; and to the credit of the lady it may be added, that without his being a man of the world or an elder brother, without any of the arts of flattery or the gaieties of small talk, he began to be agreeable to her.

(*Mansfield Park*)

CATHERINE DRINKER BOWEN

On viola wives, keeping up

The viola is an excellent instrument for wives. It is not a solo instrument, it is the alto voice – an excellent thing in women. Placed midway between solid bass and brilliant soprano fiddle, the viola is your perfect instrument of ensemble, its spirit that of sturdy, self-respecting subordination.

I have known three very satisfactory violists who were also extremely satisfactory as wives. You may, if it suits better your sense of values, turn the sentence round the other way; for myself, not being a husband, I prefer the statement as it stands. The viola is not, on the face of it, a woman's instrument. It is large and bulky; to produce a real viola tone requires strong fingers; to sustain such a tone, no inconsiderable muscular endurance. The three wives I speak of are all amateurs; two of them are married to professional musicians. The first of these was encountered in student days in Baltimore; the charming household Van Bart gave me that revelation of delight which was my first string quartet, my first glimpse, indeed, of real *Haus-musik*.

Van Bart directed the quartet; we played in his room in the Conservatory, a bare, bright room with skylight and ancient, dusty grand piano – a room that came alive when the four of us were seated at the stands and Van Bart had struck the air with his right forefinger. I, whose acquaintance with wine had been limited to a taste of my father's claret at dinner, a gulp of whiskey in the bathroom tumbler when I was catching cold, breathed wine in that dusty room. And I breathed a headier wine when Van Bart, selecting three of us from the string pupils, invited us to his house in the country. Every Sunday we played there, Mrs Van Bart at – as the phrase goes – the viola. Perhaps the phrase does not properly go that way unless applied to the piano or the bat, but it fits Mrs Van Bart. She went, indeed, *at* the viola. She tore it to pieces; not before or since have I heard a viola emit such crucifying sounds. Mrs Van Bart suffered from these sounds as much as any of us, for she was truly musical, but she never apologized. She made faces, she drew in her breath through her teeth, but she never apologized.

Our cellist was excellent; I have forgotten her name, but I recall with pleasure her smooth dark hair and bright cheek at the cello's neck, the round resonance of her tone. My place as first fiddle was easy because Van Bart always stood by and conducted. Once when he had a cold he conducted from his bed in the next room; when he called me in to unravel some repeated stupidity, I was paralyzed with shyness. This was, I believe, the first time my careful Philadelphia existence had ever included a man in bed. But I knew instantly that no male of my clan could wear successfully those wild, delightful striped silk pajamas, that no room in our house could achieve at the same time so crazy a disorder and so indubitable, so exhilarating a style. I stood in the doorway, violin in hand, and a voice from the bed, stopped with cold, a little irritated, said to me:

'Come in, Miss Dr-rinkair! Why do you stand there dumb like a fish? Do not take the sixteenth notes so fast and do not, for the love of God, slur the last one in the measure. How many timces –' he pronounced the word with a *c* in it – 'how many timces must I remind you? Such an effect! Vulgar – A-ah! Give me your fiddle – here – play the notes evenly, all alike. Not to hurry, not to be gasping for breath like a hooked trout.... So!'

It mattered not if I were called fish twice in the same breath; halibut or God-forsaken amateur – let them name me what names they chose, if only they would let my fiddle in their door. As to the Van Barts, well or sick, they were always jolly. Van Bart's interest in our very uncertain playing never flagged; when his wife committed some too flagrant atrocity, he would whack her on the shoulder and she would give vent to some loud foreign ejaculation and recover herself.... The old stone house was furnished in oak and pewter, things Mrs Van Bart had brought from Holland; the three round-cheeked Van Bart sons tumbled and shrieked about the room, but nobody rebuked them. The place was full of animals, shaggy dogs, cats, birds in cages – and I loved it. At some indeterminate time during the evening we would have supper before the fire – cold meat, bread, cheese, and beer. When the Van Barts began to eat and drink they became even jollier. They roared with laughter, they pounded on the table, they fed the dogs with huge chunks of meat. Van Bart at such times lost his dapperness, his man-of-the-world veneer; he would seize Marya, the dark-eyed little second violinist, and kiss her heartily. I know that I became very silent, a little awed. Not so was Sunday evening conducted in Philadelphia. The Van Bart boys were never put to bed; they fell asleep anywhere, on the floor, on the wooden settles before the fire.... Van Bart would tease me. 'She sits there, so white and still with her face of a Madonna. To whom do you pray, Madonna? What god watches over musicians in your Philadelphia? What *patron*?'

... Such was the household Van Bart, and the first viola wife my life encountered. The other two viola wives, while as effective in their way as Mrs Van Bart, are effective more by design than by instinct or that easy, contagious appetite for music that ruled the establishment Van Bart.... Mrs Whitelaw, married to that indefatigable lawyer-cellist whom we have met before, was invited by John 'on spec,' as it were, to come to Philadelphia with her husband and play. The day of their arrival was Sunday, and it rained. It began early, a cold November mist that drove against the long windows of the music room. At breakfast John looked at the weather with glee in his eye. 'Ha!' he said. 'We can play all day. We won't have to go for a walk and we won't have to ask anybody if they'd like a little golf – '

We did play all day; with time out for dinner and tea and supper, we were at it for eight hours. The Whitelaws performed well, excellently well. I know nothing of Mr Whitelaw in the law courts save what John has told me, but for all those hours I sat across the music stand from him and saw no sign of weakening other than a slight, repeated sniffle toward the eighth hour. John was right; an adult who is indefatigable at one exercise is likely to be indefatigable at another. The following month I went to New York and spent a night with the Whitelaws to play quartets; Mrs Whitelaw – a powerful woman – confessed that her shoulder had been lame for a week after her visit to us. 'But I didn't want to stop playing,' she added hastily.

... That is Mrs Whitelaw ... The third viola wife is perhaps more wife than violist, but then – she has a testy husband. Not unattractively testy, – he is a professional musician, – but a husband that requires delicate handling, and delicate handling takes time and energy. Mrs Sereno's viola playing, done, perhaps, with what is left over, is a little feeble, but she is there on time, musically speaking; she never loses the place, nor does she tire and want to stop. She is as round and soft as her husband is lean and hungry, and her viola's voice is like her own, hushed and pleasant and a bit deprecatory. She is always ready to play what the rest of us want to play. 'Yes, yes,' she will assent eagerly, 'let us, by all means, begin with Mozart. You are right, it is good to begin the evening with Mozart and, as you say, work up to Brahms.' In a family where the five playing members are wont to shout, all at once, the names of their five favourite composers, this soft assenting voice comes as nothing short of a miracle. The lady has become a byword with us. 'Why can't you say yes, like Mrs Sereno?'

But I am not sure, in my heart, about saying yes. By saying yes, Mrs Sereno achieved security, peace, and Mr Sereno – but is Mr Sereno worth all those yeses? Is anybody?

... Of all the long-distance players I have known, Dr Richard Cabot of Boston is champion. He is insatiable. Like Joe Knoedler, Dr Cabot does not say, 'I am having a good time.' Simply, it does not occur to him to stop. And like John, like every academically sincere music player, Dr Cabot takes all the repeats. He believes in repeats; not only does he take them in minuet and trio, but in the slowest *largo*, in the most interminably numerous variations. When one plays with Dr Cabot there is never the customary shouted query at the end of the first *allegro*, – the middle repeat has of course been accepted, – '*Repeat?*' The three of us plunge on and take it, without question.... A lawyer-violinist with whom I play in Buffalo – like the sailor and his girl, we fiddlers have a quartet in every port – told me he played with Dr Cabot one night last summer. After the other three players were completely exhausted, Dr Cabot sighed, shook his head, and remarked, 'I have been playing quartets for forty years, and never yet have I found people who would play as long as I wanted.'

... Looking back, I see I have written a chapter on compromise, on how to be a musician though married, on the joys of wifely self-sacrifice – and it makes me faintly uneasy. How smoothly, with what sugar of virtue, it dripped from the pen ... Wives? Husbands? I would hang fifty wives, sixty husbands on a tree as against two lines of Beethoven Opus 132. Mothers of children, said Katherine Mansfield, grow on every bush.

No one ever said that about good fiddle players.

(*Friends and Fiddlers*)

JACQUES CASANOVA

Casanova, known to the world as the eighteenth-century erotic adventurer who helped da Ponte's libretto for Mozart's *Don Giovanni*, was no myth. Indeed, he is an invaluable source for the European society in which he moved, both high and low. Recent scholarship has identified several of his *inamorate*, just as Graham Greene's real-life mistresses are now tagged like birds to particular novels.

In 1749 Casanova met 'Henriette' at Cesena, easily detached her from a Hungarian officer and accompanied her to Parma. Her real name was almost certainly Jeanne Marie d'Albert de St Hippolyte. A beautiful and accomplished Frenchwoman from Aix-en-Provence, she had escaped from her husband and father-in-law ('monsters') and the pair embarked on what Edmund Wilson has called 'one of the most attractive love affairs in literature' – but in near-seclusion, for well-founded fear of discovery. By Casanova's own self-examination in the *Memoirs*, no other woman so captivated and plumbed his susceptible, predatory yet never mechanical affections. When eventually they had to part (in Geneva) she took a diamond and traced a farewell on a pane of their hotel room for him to find: 'Tu oublieras aussi Henriette.' (She was wrong – but that is another story.)

As for his mistress's impromptu virtuosity on the cello (learnt in the convent), Casanova's love of making the best of a story and his pride at showing off his prize in company inevitably leave the reader taking a pinch of salt. Yet he knew what he was talking about. Elsewhere in the *Memoirs* (vol. 2, ch. 7, p.185 in the Trask edition) he wrote about his dissolute youth:

'Playing the violin, I earned enough to keep myself without turning to anyone. Happy are they who can boast that they are self-sufficient. My profession was not a noble one, but I did not care. Calling everything prejudice, I soon acquired all the habits of my degraded fellow musicians.'

His mistress Henriette, the cellist

Madame de France, the Infante's wife, having arrived, I told Henriette that I would engage a box for every day. She had said several times that her ruling passion was music. As she had never seen an Italian opera I was surprised to hear her answer me coldly:

'*You mean you want us to go to the opera every day?*'

'I even think we should get ourselves talked about if we did not go; but if you will not enjoy going, my dear, you know that you are under no obligation to put yourself out. I prefer our conversations in this room to all the music in the universe.'

'I am mad about music, my dear; but I cannot help trembling at the very thought of going out.'

'If you tremble, I shudder; but we must go to the opera, or leave for London or somewhere else. You have only to command.'

'Take a box that is not too conspicuous.'

I took a box in the second tier; but as the theater was small a pretty woman could not fail to be noticed in it. I told her so, and she replied that she did not think she was in danger of being recognized, since none of the names in the list of foreigners then in Parma which I had given her to read was known to her.

So Henriette came to the opera; but in the second tier, without rouge and without a candle. It was an *opera buffa*, the music to which, by Buranello, was as excellent as the actors. She used her opera glass only for them, never turning it either on the boxes or the parterre. No one seemed to be curious about us; so we went home well satisfied, in the bosom of peace and love. As the finale of the second act had pleased her greatly, I promised it to her. It was to Monsieur Dubois that I went to obtain it; and thinking that she might play the harpsichord, I offered her one. She answered that she had never learned to play the instrument.

. . . I was very happy with Henriette, and she was no less happy with me: never a moment of ill-humor, never a yawn, never did a folded rose petal come to trouble our content.

The day after the closing of the opera, Dubois, after dining with us, told us that he was having the two leading singers, male and female, to dinner the next day, and that we had only to wish it and we could hear the finest pieces they had sung at the theater in the vaulted drawing room of his country house, where music lost nothing. Henriette, first thanking him heartily, answered that her health was so poor that she could make no engagements from one day to the next; and she at once turned the conversation to other subjects.

As soon as we were alone I asked her why she did not wish to allow herself the diversion of going to Dubois's house.

'I would go, my dear, and with great pleasure; but I am afraid that I may find someone at his dinner who would recognize me and so put an end to our happiness.'

'If you have some new reason for being afraid, you are right; but if it is only a groundless fear, my angel, why do you take it upon yourself to give up a real pleasure? If you knew what joy I feel when I see you ravished and as if in ecstasy when you hear some beautiful piece of music!'

'Very well. I do not want you to think I have less courage than you. We will go to Dubois's directly after dinner. The singers will not sing before then. Besides, it is likely that, since he will not be counting on us, he will not have invited anyone who is curious to speak with me. We will go without telling him and without his expecting us. He said that he is at his country house, and Caudagna knows where it is.'

In accordance with her reasoning, to which she had been inspired by prudence and love, which so seldom agree, the next day at four in the afternoon we went to his house. We were surprised to find him alone with a pretty girl, whom he introduced to us, saying that she was his niece, whom private reasons prevented him from letting everyone see.

Professing to be delighted to see us, he said that as he did not expect us he had changed his dinner to a small supper party, which he hoped we would honor him by attending, and that the *virtuosi* would soon arrive. So it was that we were obliged to stay for supper. I ask him if he has invited many people, and he answers triumphantly that we shall be in company worthy of us, and that he only regretted that he had not invited any ladies. Henriette made him a little curtsy and smiled. I saw her looking carefree and content; but she was forcing herself. Her noble soul refused to show uneasiness; but in any case I did not believe she had any real cause for fear. I would have believed it if she had told me her whole story; and I would certainly have taken her to England, and she would have been very glad to go.

A quarter of an hour later the two singers arrived: they were Laschi and La Baglioni, who in those days was very pretty. Then all the people whom Dubois had invited arrived. They were all Spaniards or Frenchmen, and all at least middle-aged. There was no question of introductions, in which I admired the hunchback's tact; but since all the guests were seasoned courtiers, the breach of etiquette did not prevent them from paying Henriette all the honors of the gathering, which she received with an ease unknown anywhere but in France, and indeed only in the most exalted circles, except for certain provinces where haughtiness is too often displayed.

The concert began with a magnificent symphony; then the singers performed a duet, then a pupil of Vandini's played a concerto for violoncello, which was much applauded. But now for what caused me the greatest surprise. Henriette rises and, praising the young man who had played the *à solo*, she takes his violoncello from him, telling him modestly and calmly that she would do it even better justice. She sits down in his place, takes the instrument between her knees, and asks the orchestra to begin the concerto over again. Most profound silence descends on the company, and deathly fear on me; but – thank God! – no one was looking at me. For her part, she did not dare. If she had raised her beautiful eyes to mine she would have lost courage. But seeing her merely strike the pose of being ready to play, I thought it was only a joke which would end with this really charming tableau; but when I saw her make the first strike of the bow, I thought the excessive palpitation of my heart would strike me dead. Knowing me well, Henriette had no resource but never to look at me.

But what was not my state when I heard her play the *à solo*, and when after the first movement the applause almost deafened the orchestra? The transition from fear to a satisfaction as excessive as it was unexpected produced such a paroxysm in me as the most violent fever could not do at its height. The applause had not the slightest effect on Henriette, at least visibly. Without raising her eyes from the notes, which she knew only from having followed the entire concerto while the professor was playing, she did not rise until after she had played alone six times. She did not thank the company for having applauded her; but turning to the professor she told him, with an air of gracious and noble courtesy, that she had never played a better instrument. After thus complimenting him, she smilingly told the audience that they must forgive the vanity which had induced her to increase the length of the concert by half an hour.

This compliment having put the finishing touch to my astonishment, I vanished to go and weep in the garden, where no one could see me. Who

*Jacques
Casanova*

can this Henriette be? What is this treasure whose master I have become? I
thought it impossible that I should be the fortunate mortal who possessed
her.

Lost in these reflections, which increased the pleasure of my tears, I
should have stayed there for a long time if Dubois himself had not come to
look for me and had not found me despite the darkness of the night. He
summoned me to supper. I relieved his anxiety by telling him that a
momentary dizziness had obliged me to come out to cure it by taking the
air.

On the way I had time to dry my tears, but not to restore their normal
color to the whites of my eyes. However, no one noticed me. Only
Henriette, seeing me reappear, told me by a sweet smile that she knew
what I had gone to do in the garden. At table my place was opposite her.

... The talk turned to music. A Spaniard asked Henriette if, besides the
violoncello, she played any other instrument, and she answered that it was
the only one for which she had ever felt any inclination.

'I learned in the convent,' she said, 'in the hope of pleasing my mother,
who plays it quite well; however, without a downright order from my

father, supported by the Bishop, the Mother Abbess would never have allowed me to study.'

'And what reasons could the Abbess allege for refusing?'

'Pious bride of Our Lord that she was, she insisted that I could not hold the instrument except by assuming an indecent posture.'

At this dictum of the Abbess I saw the Spaniards bite their lips, but the Frenchmen roared with laughter. After a silence of a few minutes, Henriette having made a gesture which seemed to ask permission to rise, everyone rose, and a quarter of an hour later we left. Dubois attended her to the step of our carriage, thanking her endlessly.

I could not wait to clasp the idol of my soul in my arms. I did not give her time to answer all the questions I asked her.

'You were right,' I said, 'not to want to go, for you were certain to make me enemies. At this moment I must be mortally hated; but you are my universe. Cruel Henriette! You very nearly killed me with your violoncello! As I could not believe that you would have kept it a secret, I thought you had gone mad, and as soon as I heard you I had to go out to dry the tears which you forced from my heart. Tell me now, I beg you, what other accomplishments you have which you are hiding from me and in which you excel, so that when they are manifested to me for the first time they will not make me die of terror or surprise.'

'No, my dear love, I have no others, I have emptied my sack, and now you know your Henriette completely. If you had not told me a month ago that you had no liking for music, I would have told you that I can play the instrument. If I had told you so, you could have got me one, and I do not wish to amuse myself with something which may bore you.'

No later than the next day I went and found her a violoncello; and she was very far from boring me with it. It is impossible for a man who has no marked passion for music not to become a passionate devotee of it when the person who performs it to perfection is the object of his love. The human voice of the violoncello, which is superior to that of any other instrument, went to my heart when Henriette played it, and she was convinced of it. She offered me the pleasure every day, and I suggested to her that she should give concerts; but she was prudent enough never to consent. Despite that, the course of destiny was not to be halted. *Fata viam inveniunt.*

(*History of my Life*)

GEOFFREY CHAUCER

For syngyng moost she gaf hir to

... From hennes forth hou that I wroughte,
I shal you tellen, as me thoughte.
First, wherof Myrthe served there,
And eke what folk there with hym were,
Withoute fable I wol discryve.
And of that gardyn eke as blyve
I wole you tellen aftir this
The faire fasoun all, ywys,
That wel wrought was for the nones.
I may not telle you all at ones;
But, as I may and can, I shall
By ordre tellen you it all.
Ful fair servise and eke ful swete
These briddis maden as they sete.
Layes of love, ful wel sownyng,
They songen in hir jargonyng;
Summe high and summe eke lowe songe
Upon the braunches grene ysprenge.
The swetnesse of her melodye
Made al myn herte in reverdye.
And whan that I hadde herd, I trowe,
These briddis syngyng on a rowe,
Than myght I not withholde me
That I ne wente inne for to see

Sir Myrthe; for my desiryng
Was hym to seen, over alle thyng,
His countenaunce and his manere;
That sighte was to me ful dere.
  Tho wente I forth on my right hond
Doun by a lytel path I fond
Of mentes full, and fenell grene;
And faste by, without wene,
Sir Myrthe I fond, and right anoon
Unto Sir Myrthe gan I goon,
There as he was, hym to solace.
And with hym in that lusty place
So fair folk and so fresh had he
That whan I saw, I wondred me
Fro whennes siche folk myght come,
So faire they weren, alle and some;
For they were lyk, as to my sighte,
To angels that ben fethered brighte.
This folk, of which I telle you soo,
Upon a karole wenten thoo.
A lady karolede hem that hyghte
Gladnesse, [the] blisfull and the lighte;
Wel coude she synge and lustyly, –
Noon half so wel and semely, –
And make in song sich refreynynge,
It sat hir wondir wel to synge.
Hir vois ful clere was and ful swete.
She was nought rude ne unmete
But couthe ynow of sich doyng
As longeth unto karolyng;
For she was wont in every place
To syngen first, folk to solace.
For syngyng moost she gaf hir to;
No craft had she so leef to do.
  Tho myghtist thou karoles sen,
And folk daunce and mery ben,
And made many a fair tournyng
Upon the grene gras springyng.

There myghtist thou see these flowtours,
Mynstrales, and eke jogelours,
That wel to synge dide her peyne.
Somme songe songes of Loreyne;
For in Loreyn her notes bee
Full swetter than in this contre.
There was many a tymbestere,
And saillouris, that I dar wel swere
Couthe her craft ful parfitly.
The tymbres up ful sotilly
They caste and hente full ofte
Upon a fynger fair and softe,
That they failide never mo.
Ful fetys damyseles two,
Ryght yonge, and full of semelyhede,
In kirtles, and noon other wede,
And faire tressed every tresse,
Hadde Myrthe doon, for his noblesse,
Amydde the karole for to daunce;
But herof lieth no remembraunce,
Hou that they daunced queyntely.
That oon wolde come all pryvyly
Agayn that other, and whan they were
Togidre almost, they threwe yfere
Her mouthis so, that thorough her play
It semed as they kiste alway.
To dauncen well koude they the gise;
What shulde I more to you devyse?
Ne bede I never thennes go,
Whiles that I saw hem daunce so....

(*The Romaunt of the Rose*)

KATE CHOPIN

Kate Chopin, in spite of the surname and the name she bestowed on her daughter (Lelia, after the novel by 'George Sand'), had nothing to do with the composer and his mistress. Born to an Irish immigrant and a French Creole in St Louis, Missouri, Kate married a planter, Oscar Chopin, and lived in the literary and musical society of New Orleans or the bayous of Louisiana. Left by her husband's death and debts, at the age of 32 she took her six children home to St Louis and started to write.

The Awakening (1899), a novel about a married woman's psycho-sexual liberation, set in the summer resort Grand Isle, damned Kate Chopin even in that relatively liberal milieu and she was forgotten for fifty years, other than by a few critics such as Edmund Wilson, until the feminists rediscovered her in the 1970s. Even in that welcome rediscovery (most recently issued in Random Century's Everyman Library) she is easily belittled as 'one of us'. Rather, her autobiographical heroine, Edna Pontellier, is a free-born solitary who touches masculine and feminine sensibility alike. She vibrates as a living *Lied ohne Wörte*. Like Flaubert's *Madame Bovary* (a comparison sometimes made), and like certain classic films that owe their erotic charge to external censorship or implicit restraint, *The Awakening* conveys far more than licence could.

In this chapter, 'Robert' is Mme Pontellier's lover, 'Mme Ratignolle' is her friend Adèle, desirable and cultivated but content with her husband and children. 'Mademoiselle Reisz' – a pupil of Clara Schumann, perhaps? – is self-explanatory.

Edna Pontellier and Mlle Reisz

Every light in the hall was ablaze, every lamp turned as high as it could be without smoking the chimney or threatening explosion. The lamps were fixed at intervals against the wall, encircling the whole room. Some one had gathered orange and lemon branches, and with these fashioned graceful festoons between. The dark green of the branches stood out and glistened against the white muslin curtains which draped the windows, and which puffed, floated, and flapped at the capricious will of a stiff breeze that swept up from the Gulf.

It was Saturday night a few weeks after the intimate conversation held between Robert and Madame Ratignolle on their way from the beach. An unusual number of husbands, fathers, and friends had come down to stay over Sunday, and they were being suitably entertained by their families, with the material help of Madame Lebrun. The dining tables had all been removed to one end of the hall, and the chairs ranged about in rows and in clusters. Each little family group had had its say and exchanged its domestic gossip earlier in the evening. There was now an apparent disposition to relax, to widen the circle of confidences and give a more general tone to the conversation.

Many of the children had been permitted to sit up beyond their usual bedtime. A small band of them were lying on their stomachs on the floor looking at the colored sheets of the comic papers which Mr Pontellier had brought down. The little Pontellier boys were permitting them to do so, and making their authority felt.

Music, dancing, and a recitation or two were the entertainments furnished, or rather, offered. But there was nothing systematic about the programme, no appearance of prearrangement nor even pre-meditation.

At an early hour in the evening the Farival twins were prevailed upon to play the piano. They were girls of fourteen, always clad in the Virgin's colors, blue and white, having been dedicated to the Blessed Virgin at their baptism. They played a duet from 'Zampa,' and at the earnest solicitation of everyone present followed it with the overture to 'The Poet and the Peasant.'

'*Allez vous-en! Sapristi!*' shrieked the parrot outside the door. He was the only being present who possessed sufficient candor to admit that he was not listening to these gracious performances for the first time that summer. Old Monsieur Farival, grandfather of the twins, grew indignant over the interruption, and insisted upon having the bird removed and consigned to regions of darkness. Victor Lebrun objected, and his decrees were as immutable as those of Fate. The parrot fortunately offered no further interruption to the entertainment, the whole venom of his nature apparently having been cherished up and hurled against the twins in that one impetuous outburst.

Later a young brother and sister gave recitations, which everyone present had heard many times at winter evening entertainments in the city.

A little girl performed a skirt dance in the center of the floor. The mother played her accompaniments and at the same time watched her daughter with greedy admiration and nervous apprehension. She need have had no apprehension. The child was mistress of the situation. She had been properly dressed for the occasion in black tulle and black silk tights. Her little neck and arms were bare, and her hair, artificially crimped, stood out like fluffy black plumes over her head. Her poses were full of grace, and her little black-shod toes twinkled as they shot out and upward with a rapidity and suddenness which were bewildering.

But there was no reason why everyone should not dance. Madame Ratignolle could not, so it was she who gaily consented to play for the others. She played very well, keeping excellent waltz time and infusing an expression into the strains which was indeed inspiring. She was keeping up her music on account of the children, she said, because she and her husband both considered it a means of brightening the home and making it attractive.

Almost everyone danced but the twins, who could not be induced to separate during the brief period when one or the other should be whirling around the room in the arms of a man. They might have danced together, but they did not think of it.

The children were sent to bed. Some went submissively; others with shrieks and protests as they were dragged away. They had been permitted to sit up till after the ice cream, which naturally marked the limit of human indulgence.

The ice cream was passed around with cake – gold and silver cake arranged on platters in alternate slices; it had been made and frozen during the afternoon back of the kitchen by two black women, under the supervision of Victor. It was pronounced a great success – excellent if it had only contained a little less vanilla or a little more sugar, if it had been frozen a degree harder, and if the salt might have been kept out of portions of it. Victor was proud of his achievement, and went about recommending it and urging everyone to partake of it to excess.

After Mrs Pontellier had danced twice with her husband, once with Robert, and once with Monsieur Ratignolle, who was thin and tall and swayed like a reed in the wind when he danced, she went out on the gallery and seated herself on the low window sill, where she commanded a view of all that went on in the hall and could look out toward the Gulf. There was a soft effulgence in the east. The moon was coming up, and its mystic shimmer was casting a million lights across the distant, restless water.

'Would you like to hear Mademoiselle Reisz play?' asked Robert, coming out on the porch where she was. Of course Edna would like to hear Mademoiselle Reisz play; but she feared it would be useless to entreat her.

'I'll ask her,' he said. 'I'll tell her that you want to hear her. She likes you. She will come.' He turned and hurried away to one of the far cottages, where Mademoiselle Reisz was shuffling away. She was dragging a chair in and out of her room, and at intervals objecting to the crying of a baby, which a nurse in the adjoining cottage was endeavoring to put to sleep. She was a disagreeable little woman, no longer young, who had quarreled with almost everyone, owing to a temper which was self-assertive and a disposition to trample upon the rights of others. Robert prevailed upon her without any too great difficulty.

She entered the hall with him during a lull in the dance. She made an awkward, imperious little bow as she went in. She was a homely woman, with a small weazened face and body and eyes that glowed. She had absolutely no taste in dress, and wore a batch of rusty black lace with a bunch of artificial violets pinned to the side of her hair.

'Ask Mrs Pontellier what she would like to hear me play,' she requested of Robert. She sat perfectly still before the piano, not touching the keys, while Robert carried her message to Edna at the window. A general air of surprise and genuine satisfaction fell upon everyone as they saw the pianist enter. There was a settling down, and a prevailing air of expectancy everywhere. Edna was a trifle embarrassed at being thus signaled out for the imperious little woman's favor. She would not dare to choose, and begged that Mademoiselle Reisz would please herself in her selections.

Edna was what she herself called very fond of music. Musical strains, well rendered, had a way of evoking pictures in her mind. She sometimes liked to sit in the room of mornings when Madame Ratignolle played or practiced. One piece which that lady played Edna had entitled 'Solitude.' It was a short, plaintive, minor strain. The name of the piece was something else, but she called it 'Solitude.' When she heard it there came before her imagination the figure of a man standing beside a desolate rock on the seashore. He was naked. His attitude was one of hopeless resignation as he looked toward a distant bird winging its flight away from him.

Another piece called to her mind a dainty young woman clad in an Empire gown, taking mincing dancing steps as she came down a long avenue between tall hedges. Again, another reminded her of children at play, and still another of nothing on earth but a demure lady stroking a cat.

The very first chords which Mademoiselle Reisz struck upon the piano sent a keen tremor down Mrs Pontellier's spinal column. It was not the first time she had heard an artist at the piano. Perhaps it was the first time she was ready, perhaps the first time her being was tempered to take an impress of the abiding truth.

She waited for the material pictures which she thought would gather and blaze before her imagination. She waited in vain. She saw no pictures of solitude, of hope, of longing, or of despair. But the very passions themselves were aroused within her soul, swaying it, lashing it, as the waves daily beat upon her splendid body. She trembled, she was choking, and the tears blinded her.

Mademoiselle had finished. She arose, and bowing her stiff, lofty bow, she went away, stopping for neither thanks nor applause. As she passed along the gallery she patted Edna upon the shoulder.

'Well, how did you like my music?' she asked. The young woman was unable to answer; she pressed the hand of the pianist convulsively. Mademoiselle Reisz perceived her agitation and even her tears. She patted her again upon the shoulder as she said:

'You are the only one worth playing for. Those others? Bah!' and she went shuffling and sliding on down the gallery toward her room.

But she was mistaken about 'those others.' Her playing had aroused a fever of enthusiasm. 'What passion!' 'What an artist!' 'I have always said no one could play Chopin like Mademoiselle Reisz!' 'That last prelude! Bon Dieu! It shakes a man!'

It was growing late, and there was a general disposition to disband. But some one, perhaps it was Robert, thought of a bath at that mystic hour and under that mystic moon.

(*The Awakening*)

JOHN CLARE

From 'Summer Images'

... Me not the noise of brawling pleasures cheer
In nightly revels or in city streets
But joys which sooth and not distract mine ear
   That one at leisure meets
In the green woods and meadows summer shorn
   Or fields where bee flye greets
   Ones ear with mellow horn

Where green swathed grass hoppers on treble pipe
Singeth and danceth in mad hearted pranks
And bees go courting every flower thats ripe
   On baulks and sunny banks
And droning dragon flye on rude bassoon
   Striveth to god thanks
   In no discordant tune ...

CHRISTOPHER DRIVER

Round the clock with 80 quartets

Throughout a whole weekend one December two violins, a viola and a cello read through the entire output of the most succinct yet prolific composer of Western music who invented a form and exploited it until his pen fell from his octogenarian hand. The cycle stretched the resources of string-playing London and the patience of the Barbican: 84 quartets, 38 ensembles, and about 30 hours of music. By Haydn, of course.

H. C. Robbins Landon, the Great Cham of Haydn musicology, told *Music Weekly* that Music Aid's *grand bouffe* for Save for the Children would be enough to put even a classicist off for life, like a surfeit of scampi. But quite apart from the sociable droppers-in in their hundreds during the three days, and with the side shows and auctions (a decorated baroque violin starting at £8,000) and craft demonstrations, the event turned out much more musical than could be expected.

At least one man, Peter Ledgerwood, heard the whole oeuvre through, pointing out that live performances of at least half the quartets are rare, not only the early, divertimento-like quartets from the recently warranted op. 0 and onwards, but middle-period masterpieces like the Ornati Quartet's op. 55/2 yesterday (which Haydn gave his English publisher for a pair of good razors: hence the nickname). Stylistic differences too were opened out: the formidable Lindsay Quartet's pair of late, big op. 76 quartets preceded in the programme the recently reconstituted Fitzwilliam, playing op. 2/6 of the 1760s on classical instruments with appropriate delicacy.

Outside the recorded cycles, most of the big professional quartets

The Panic Quartet (Jean Rowath, John Cumming, Peter Holden, Jessica Mycroft): contributors to the Haydn Marathon

concentrate on the most popular sets (ops. 33, 64, 76, 77) or the nick-named quartets (the Bird, the Lark, the Rider and others). Jim Haworth, an amateur viola-player who did all the crucial timings for the Barbican schedule, learned more silly names he knew from the Evening Prayer to the Railwayman: 'the rushing contrapuntal finale anachronistically called the Railwayman'. (Late on Saturday night, the cellist went through a red signal, to his colleagues' mirth.)

However, that last ad hoc group of good professionals sent-up their own programme note: 'This "instant" quartet has pledged itself to mini-mal rehearsal in the interests of spontaneity in performance' – sight-reading, as we coarse chamber music players know it. Even the Lindsays were forced by the second-fiddle's flu to borrow the viola's father, the all-purpose and far-from-emeritus Patrick Ireland ('I suppose you do remember where to find the E string?').

Lesser players no doubt certainly practised harder than that, as in the Panic Quartet – no, not a name reminiscent of virtuoso Serbs, but an understandably 'Pan'-stricken amateur group of 'accountant, general manager, researcher, and architect.' Not a bad set of qualifications for playing quartets, if they could be translated into musical projection: one to manage, one to count, one to research the style and the architect to keep the compositional structure up from the bass foundations.

But nobody was counting winners or losers, unless you count Jocelyn Selson who got the event off the ground and made the money for Save the Children; the students and instrumental teachers whose skill demonstrated again the huge leap of string-playing in London in the past (ILEA) generation; and Haydn himself, whose last unfinished quartet was played last night as the finale. The composer's parting musical 'visiting card' to his publisher is transcribed in *The Great Haydn Quartets* (Dent) by the late Hans Keller, whose widow Milein Cosman drew this and other sketches during the weekend. By the end of the musical marathon, long-stayers too could say 'Hin ist alle meine Kraft, alt und schwach bin ich.' (Gone is every ounce of strength; old and weak am I.)

(*The Guardian*)

GUSTAVE FLAUBERT

Emma Bovary's musical alibi

Before long, Léon began to give himself superior airs around the office. He kept aloof from his colleagues and totally neglected his work. He waited for Emma's letters, and read them over and over. He wrote to her. He evoked her image with all the strength of his passion and his memories. Far from being lessened by absence, his longing to see her again increased, until finally one Saturday morning he took the road to Yonville.

When he looked down on the valley from the top of the hill and saw the church steeple with its tin flag turning in the wind, he was filled with an exquisite pleasure: smug satisfaction and selfish sentimentality were mingled in it – it was the feeling that a millionaire must experience on revisiting his boyhood village.

He prowled around her house. A light was burning in the kitchen. He watched for her shadow behind the curtains. Not a soul was to be seen.

Madame Lefrançois uttered loud cries at the sight of him, and said that he was 'taller and thinner.' Artémise, on the other hand, found that he had grown 'heavier and darker.'

He took his dinner in the small dining room, just as in the old days, but alone, without the tax collector: for Binet, sick of waiting for the Hirondelle, had permanently changed his mealtime to an hour earlier, and now dined on the stroke of five. Even so he never missed a chance to grumble that 'the rusty old clock was slow.'

Finally Léon got up his courage and knocked on the doctor's door. Madame was in her room: it was a quarter of an hour before she came down. Monsieur seemed delighted to see him again, but didn't stir from the house all evening or all the next day.

Only late Sunday evening did he see her alone, in the lane behind the garden – in the lane, just like Rodolphe. It was during a thunderstorm, and they talked under an umbrella, with lightning flashing around them.

The thought of parting was unbearable.

'I'd rather die!' said Emma.

She clung convulsively to his arm and wept:

'Adieu! Adieu! When will I see you again?'

They separated, then turned back for a last embrace; and it was at that moment that she promised him to find, soon, no matter how, some way in which they would be able to see each other alone and regularly, at least once a week. Emma had no doubt about succeeding. She looked forward to the future with confidence: the inheritance money would shortly be coming in.

... It was about this time – the beginning of winter – that she became intensely musical.

One evening while Charles was listening she started the same piece over again four times, each time expressing annoyance with herself. Charles was unaware of anything wrong. 'Bravo!' he cried. 'Very good! Why stop? Keep going.'

'No, I'm playing abominably. My fingers are rusty.'

The next day he asked her to 'play him something else.'

'Very well, if you like.'

Charles had to admit that she seemed a little out of practice. She fumbled, struck wrong notes, and finally broke off abruptly:

'That's enough of that! I should take some lessons, but ...'

She bit her lips and added: 'Twenty francs an hour – it's too expensive.'

'Yes, it certainly is ... a little ...' said Charles, with a silly giggle. 'But it seems to me you ought to be able to find somebody for less. There are plenty of musicians without big names who are better than the celebrities.'

'Try and find some,' said Emma.

When he came in the next day he gave her a sly look, and finally came out with: 'You certainly have a way sometimes of thinking you know better than anybody else. I was at Barfeuchères today and Madame Liégeard told me that her three girls – the three at school at the Miséricorde – take lessons at two and a half francs an hour, and from a marvelous teacher!'

She shrugged, and from then on left her instrument unopened.

But whenever she walked by it she would sigh (if Bovary happened to be there): 'Ah, my poor piano!'

And she always made a point of telling visitors that she had given up her music and now couldn't possibly go on with it again, for imperative reasons. Everybody pitied her. What a shame! She had so much talent! People even spoke to Bovary about it. They made him feel ashamed, especially the pharmacist.

'You're making a mistake! Natural faculties must never be let lie fallow! Besides, my friend, look at it this way: by encouraging Madame to take lessons now, you'll save money later on your daughter's lessons. In my opinion, mothers should teach their children themselves. It's an idea of Rousseau's – maybe a little new, still, but bound to prevail eventually, I'm sure, like mother's breast feeding and vaccination.'

So Charles brought up the question of the piano again. Emma answered tartly that they'd better sell it. Poor old piano! It had so often been a source of pride for him, that to see it go would be like watching Emma commit partial suicide.

'If you really want to go ahead with it,' he said, 'I suppose a lesson now and then wouldn't ruin us.'

'But lessons aren't worth taking,' she said, 'unless they're taken regularly.'

That was how she obtained her husband's permission to go to the city once a week to meet her lover. By the end of the first month everyone found that her playing had improved considerably.

(*Madame Bovary*)

ALISON LURIE

The philanderer at the piano

... Will began on a piece by Schoenberg.

'Oh, don't practise that dreadful stuff now! Play some real music.'

Will broke off and gave Miranda the first smile of his visit. 'All right. To please you.' He began Haydn's Andante and Variations.

As the notes met and echoed each other, Will's face took on what was for him a rare expression: one of ordinary concentration. Usually he was like an actor, a man before a mirror, moving his handsome features around into conscious images of interest, disinterest, pleasure, displeasure, irony, surprise, or resignation. Miranda most often saw this real face when Will played the piano, and even then only when he played for her alone, or for her and the children.

He trusts me, she thought. It's because he knows that I care for him quite disinterestedly. I like him, love him, whatever one wants to say, but I'm not asking for anything, not trying to use him the way the rest of them are, to give concerts or entertain at parties or teach harmony or make love to me.

A faint frown went with this last denial: the truth was that Miranda did use Will to make love to her. In the tales she made up when she could not sleep he alternated the role of romantic lover with a boy she had known in college and a red-haired man who had once talked to her about ghosts on the train between Boston and New York. But Will, like the others, would never know of the part he played, which physically in truth was a very innocent one. Nor would he, probably, have recognized himself in the exotic settings and costumes in which Miranda placed him. Miranda's

50

fantasies seldom took place in the contemporary world. At the moment she was reading Balzac, and they were laid in nineteenth-century Paris; earlier she had favoured, among backgrounds, the Trojan Wars and a witches' Sabbath in Scotland during the reign of James I.

But that was a game. The real life of romantic love, after its early flights, is nasty, brutish, and short, or so Miranda had found it; it deals in false images and false expectations. Marriage is kinder, but it also lives on lies, little tame ones – one makes the best of the bargain. Only friendship is completely real. Because he dropped all his disguises in front of her she (and nobody else) really knew Will Thomas. And knowledge was power, the only form of power worth having. The other kinds were gross, material – and because material, ephemeral: sooner or later, like all matter, they would rot and decay. Will would belong to her for ever, never to Emmy and the other girls he lay next to between dirty sheets, giving them what they wanted, pretending to be some imaginary lover they had invented. She didn't blame him, she didn't blame them; not even that.

Between the third and fourth variations, Will looked up. 'By the way, you won't tell Emily I told you about Avis and all that?' he said.

'Of course not.'

He began to play again. Leaning her head on her arm, Miranda looked past him now, out of the window. The sodden sky was splitting apart from the sodden earth, and through the trees a long bright streak of light widened. How happy I am, she thought. Drops of left-over rain shone light and dark on the grass.

'I love Haydn,' she said when Will had finished. 'He always makes me feel so much better.'

(*Love and Friendship*)

COMPTON MACKENZIE

Mackenzie, the author of *Sinister Street*, *Whisky Galore* and much else, lived a long time and lapsed into bufferdom, with too many autobiographies. But that is no reason to overlook the friskiness of his youth and middle age. *Extraordinary Women* (1928), dedicated to his friend Norman Douglas, narrowly escaped prosecution, possibly because the novel's relish for lesbians pursuing each other on Capri from grotto to *thé dansant* dips discreetly into French, which Sir Joynson Hicks was doubtless unable to follow.

The heroine, Rosalba, is wonderfully promiscuous (Cléo had been thinking for some time that she used her accomplished kisses as 'skeleton keys that would open any lock') and the narrator is charming in another sense:

'... What a woman really means by friendship with a man is being able to depend on him to look out trains for her in Bradshaw, which is not what a man understands by it. What a man understands by friendship with a woman with whom he has been in love is a complete relief from all responsibility either for her emotions or her trains. It is doubly hard for two women to pass from a highly emotional relationship to a humdrum talking-about-clothes friendship, because though a woman may forgive a man for a failure of emotion at last, since that is what she has been perpetually expecting, she is not going to forgive another woman...'

Devotees of the Sapphic mode

'Have you ever heard Busoni play?' Cléo asked.

Rosalba shook her head, tossing the sunbeams from her bronze hair.

'That is how I would like to play,' Cléo muttered to herself, for she was worrying about her concert now. 'And if you loved me as I dream of love, that is the way I could play.'

'I shall be in the front row, *mon cher*, so I am sure you will play *à merveille*.'

And Rosalba was in the front row with disastrous results, for throughout Schumann's Toccata she talked to Principessa Flavia Buonagrazia until Olga Linati who was sitting on her other side dragged herself out of a thicket of financial calculations and nudged her to observe how she was affecting the player by her behaviour. Rosalba looked at Cléo's face and did manage to remain silent during some Preludes of Chopin, in spite of turning with relief as each one finished to speak to the Princess and turning away again with growing disgust each time another one began. She watched contemptuously the expression on Olga's face. What frauds people made of themselves at concerts! She knew that Olga was not listening to the music any more profoundly than herself. Those blue eyes that seemed to be melting with emotion were really melting with addition and subtraction. Oh, why did Cléo choose such long pieces and why had she herself chosen to sit in the front row? The Preludes came to an end, and Rosalba had hardly time to turn to reply to the Princess's last question before Cléo was off on Brahms' Variations on a Theme by Paganini. Five minutes. Ten minutes. '*Buon Dio, la ragazza non finirà mai!*' A quarter of an hour. '*Basta! basta!*' Rosalba muttered viciously inside herself, looking at the clock as big as the moon which hung on the white wall above Cléo, a great silent clock that was enough to drive the audience mad with its slowness. The composer's ingenuity was exhausted at last. The Variations came to an end, and the player leaping up from her stool lit a cigarette and prowled like a tiger up and down the end of the room while the applause of the audience died away into chatter.

The hands of the clock retarded by the music seemed to leap wantonly forward during the interval, and before Rosalba had nearly finished what she wanted to say to the Princess, Cléo was seated at the piano again and beginning one of the later sonatas of Beethoven. Now, Rosalba had heard it said that Cléo did not play Beethoven well, and in her resentment against the briefness of the interval she could not help whispering to the Princess what a pity she thought it was that Cléo should have chosen to play Beethoven this afternoon. A smashing chord made her jump. She thought for an instant it was addressed to herself. But no, Cléo, although her eyebrows were meeting over a chasmy frown, was still presumably playing what the composer had written. Yet something was wrong, and hearing a low 'tut-tut' behind her Rosalba looked round to see a man with long black hair clicking his tongue in pained surprise at the performance. Suddenly Cléo brought both hands down on the notes in a couple of crashing discords that would have restored Beethoven's reputation in the most advanced côteries. The Sonata was apparently finished, and the player was rubbing her forehead in a dazed way; but the applause which followed was the compassionate applause for an amateur reciter who has forgotten her words, when the throats of the audience tighten in sympathy. Cléo hunched her shoulders and broke into some dance of Albeniz or Granados from an instinct to help her patrons out of their embarrassment. At the end of it she jumped up from her stool and called fiercely to Rosalba and Olga, whom she drew aside with her to the farthest corner of the room.

'If you stay here,' she said to Rosalba, 'I will play not one more note this afternoon. You are not what you pretend to be. I am sure of that now. I regret that I have made myself a fool for you. *Tu es une cocotte manquée, ma petite Rosalba. Donc, cherche quelque gigolo. Tu n'as aucun besoin de moi.*'

'A lie! A lie!' Rosalba exclaimed. 'I find you insufferably arrogant, *ma chère chère Cléo*. I do not admit that a complete lack of *chic* gives you the right to criticize my sincerity. I am quite as abnormal as you are.'

'You are not. You are not. You are as normal as a *petite bourgeoise*,' Cléo declared. 'You would be much happier to find a man to protect you.'

'I hate men. How dare you say that I don't!' Rosalba cried wrathfully.

The interval at a concert in the *salone* of a Roman palace before a fashionable and artistic audience hardly makes the most suitable time and place to discuss one of the major problems of psychopathy. Olga begged the antagonists to be silent. She who was unfortunately so much more normal than either of them was able to see the point of view of both a little more clearly perhaps than they could. If they talked so loudly about their temperaments it must cause a scandal. Could not the discussion be postponed? They knew how busy she was, but she was so fond of them both that somehow she would find the time to reconcile them. But Cléo waved aside her intervention. *Cette femme* – and the contempt was more for the noun than the demonstrative pronoun in front of it – *cette femme* must leave the *salle* before she could ever bring herself to offer the fashionable part of the audience the piece of musical sugar with which she intended to bring her concert to a close.

'It is better that you go, my dear,' Olga took Rosalba aside to whisper. 'Cléo is in a state of mind when one cannot argue with her. But as soon as the concert is over and she is at home I am quite sure she will send you a word how sorry she is.'

'*Elle est tellement femme soi-même,*' Rosalba declared bitterly, 'that to call me *femme* I find altogether ridiculous. I am quite disgusted by her behaviour. *Dis, Olga, n'est-ce pas vrai qu'elle est beaucoup plus femme que moi? Moi, je n'ai jamais fait l'amour avec un homme, je te jure; mais Cléo l'a fait deux fois. Elle m'a dit. Une fois, oui, on peut dire peut-être une curieuse; mais deux fois, non, ça veut dire une devergondée.*'

'*No, ma senti, Rosalba,*' the intermediary begged. '*Parla più piano, ti prego. La gente ti ascolterà.*'

'*Che la gente mi ascolti! Non mi importa.*'

With this declaration Rosalba went back and took her seat by the Princess, defying Cléo not to go on with the concert. Apparently Olga's entreaties to avoid a public scene had been successful, for Cléo came back to the piano and began the familiar Chopin waltzes that were intended to give her less musical listeners an opportunity of tapping their well-shod feet in time and rocking their lustrous eyes on the bosom of the lilting melody.

(*Extraordinary Women*)

FRIDTJOF NANSEN

Passing the long Arctic evenings

Nansen's 'Fram' and its crew explored the Arctic for three years (1893–6), attaining 86° 14′ N, the highest latitude then reached by man. The list of musical instruments on board was as follows: an accordion, on which Hjalmar Johansen, who accompanied his leader on the famous sledging expedition, was a skilled performer; a flute, violin, and several Jew's harps belonging to one of the ship's company. It was commonly alleged that there was a grand pianoforte on board, but Dr Nansen candidly dispels this illusion. It was not a pianoforte, but an organ turned by a handle. Describing an average evening, he says: 'About half-past seven or eight, cards or other games were brought out, and we played well on into the night, seated in groups round the saloon table. One or other of us might go to the organ, and, with the assistance of the crank handle, perform some of our beautiful pieces, or Johansen would bring out the accordion and play many a fine tune. His crowning efforts were 'O Susanna' and 'Napoleon's March across the Alps in an open boat.'

(*The Mirror of Music*)

FRANCES PARTRIDGE

O brave new world, my violin

July 28, 1941. To tea at the Padels. Their sons, both schoolmasters, were home on leave. One plays the 'cello and one the violin, and they played us a Beethoven trio after tea. I was much moved by the sight of this admirable family setting to with such a will and producing music of so high a standard.

September 26. The Padels have been trying to persuade me to take up the violin again, and though I could never have dreamed of the possibility without their instigation, I feel very tempted – but sheepish. (I had started learning at nine and dropped it at thirteen.) Mr Padel swears I could play chamber music in six months. What a thought!

That a mother should teach her own child is one of Mrs Padel's blind beliefs; she is against schools, meat-eating, Mrs Molesworth and water-closets.

October 3. Off on my bicycle to the Padels to consider the question of re-starting the violin, for the seeds they sowed have taken root. Mr Padel was waiting for me, and handed me a violin with a sweet and mellow tone. His manner could not have been better designed to cure me of my sheepishness. I took it up and struck a few strange wobbling notes. Before I left we were playing exercises together.

April 2, 1942. To a concert in Newbury, with Mr Padel in his floppy tweed hat. Handel Concerto Grosso, Mozart Divertimento, Brandenburg No 3. How long it is since I was at a concert. I had forgotten the visual (apart from the audible) pleasures; the intent expressions of the players as they filed in and settled round their instruments, the satin brown of violins and 'cellos, hands quivering on their necks like humming-bird moths tirelessly extracting honey.

June 18. The Padels have got a 'cellist and we are to try quartets next Tuesday. I have been playing a Haydn and a Mozart on records. The gates of paradise seem to be opening – only to shut with a bang no doubt, leaving me mangled and discomfited.

January 20, 1944. Music is my great solace: quartets every week, and the other day our company was swollen to an octet – an occasion I looked forward to and thought about afterwards much as I used in my youth to think of a ball or party. I found it very exciting to be in a small room with so many instruments at once, and in danger of stumbling over 'cellos and violas if one moved.

February 2. We have had Angelica [Garnett] for a week, with her baby, Amaryllis.... The cold was appalling throughout her visit, and we went about rubbing blue hands together, and with chattering teeth. Cold and music were the chief features of her stay. She played the violin to my piano and vice versa; we played the Bach Double Concerto, and she sang to my accompaniment. We even had a session at the Padels, Angelica playing the piano in the Schumann quintet. Mr Padel was instantly bowled over by Angelica, and although it was snowing and Mrs Padel ill in bed, he insisted on bicycling over next day in his tweed deer-stalker to hear her sing.

October 2, 1944. Unexpectedly summoned to the Padels, who had a clarinettist staying with them. We played both the Brahms and the Mozart quintets. I have seldom got such pleasure from a sound I was helping to make. What exhilaration!

February 14, 1945. This afternoon to play quartets. I asked Mr Padel if he thought the war would soon be over. 'Oh yes, and then the real war will begin.' (He is a dedicated Communist.) I dared no more, but good God, if this war isn't real I should like to know what is.

While we were playing I thought how chamber music could be a model for the conduct of personal relations – which, as is easy to forget – need constant attention of each part to all the others.

(*A Pacifist's Diary*)

Mr Punch's Fair Sextett

November 14th 1945.... After a delicious lunch off a brace of pheasants shot by Clive [Bell] and beautifully roasted (I must say) by me, we drove to Marlborough for the concert at the school – a French string quartet playing Mozart, César Franck and Debussy. I realized I hadn't watched a string quartet since I tried to play in one myself, and I found it mesmerically fascinating – the sudden concentration of four individuals into a single unit; the first violin's raised bow, and they are off! The weaving of four threads of different sounds to ravish the ear was expressed in very different movements: the first violin, a mild little fellow, raised his bottom on short pin-striped legs in moments of crisis and sank again into his chair. The grey-haired second, looking like a distinguished surgeon, bent and becked as if the music were some invisible royalty, the viola rode it like a conscientious jockey; but best of all to watch was the sultry-eyed cellist, who rolled and swayed in orgiastic ecstasy, while his dark eyes in his pale face swam from one to another of his fellow-players and shudders of unutterable feeling floated across his features.

May 13th 1954. Not long ago I got a letter inviting me to join the Newbury Orchestra, and I accepted with joy, since there seemed little chance of any more quartet playing. Yesterday I went to my third rehearsal – the last before the long summer break. I had found them absorbingly interesting and exciting, but alarming also, because although I can read fairly well, the Brahms symphony we are playing is much too difficult for me, so I am tempted to sit by myself and make as little noise as possible. This time, however, I shared a desk with a prim young schoolmistress from Downe House School who was about my level. I had been practising quite arduously and all at once began to feel I was getting a grasp on the music, certainly I love it. The sensation that one is minutely contributing to this massed sound, this combined tweedling, fluting, thrumming and hooting, is intoxicating. I am determined to go on with it if I possibly can.

(*Everything to Lose*)

March 1st 1963. Musically speaking, I have been hovering between two stools. Vaguely discontented with my Hampstead orchestra, I eagerly hurried off yesterday to try another, a Medical one heard of from the Penroses. The first two sessions were alarming, a *much* higher standard, a conductor with a difficult beat, a programme they had already been practising for some weeks. Then, at the third go last night, the authentic magic caught on. What had seemed almost out of reach was suddenly attainable with an effort, and the excitement of becoming integrated into this huge mass of combined sound set a match to the sticks that had been waiting unlit, or at most giving out a little greasy smoke. It is a much bigger, more professional affair, very much alive, and composed of intelligent interesting faces, old and young, white and black, including a lot of German and Austrian Jews. Our concert has Hephzibah Menuhin for a soloist. The excitement, the lift and intoxication with which I flew home down the Edgware Road last night has proved to me this is what I want, and though it's difficult for me, I now *think* (with hard work) I can perhaps make the grade.

(*Hanging On*)

CONCHITA [BUÑUEL] PORTOLÈS

Luis Buñuel's musical offering

When he was about thirteen, Luis [Buñuel] began to learn the violin. He was very keen on the instrument, partly because he seemed to be gifted for it. He waited until we were in bed, then, violin in hand, he would walk into the bedroom where I and two sisters of mine used to sleep; he used to begin by playing the 'subject', which I realise now, as I look back, must have been very Wagnerian even though at the time he wasn't any more aware of this than we were. At that period, we used to spend each summer at our house in Calanda. Luis managed to form an orchestra, and during solemn religious ceremonies he would play phrases from Perosi's Mass or Schubert's Ave Maria to the great delight of the congregation.

(*Mon Frère Luis*)

WILLIAM SHAKESPEARE

How oft, when thou, my music, music play'st,
Upon that blessed wood whose motion sounds
With thy sweet fingers, when thou gently sway'st
The wiry concord that mine ear confounds,
Do I envy those jacks that nimble leap
To kiss the tender inward of thy hand,
Whilst my poor lips, which should that harvest reap,
At the wood's boldness by thee blushing stand!
To be so tickled, they would change their state
And situation with those dancing chips,
O'er whom they fingers walk with gentle gait,
Making dead wood more blest than living lips.
Since saucy jacks so happy are in this,
Give them thy fingers, me thy lips to kiss.

(*Sonnet 128*)

GEORGE BERNARD SHAW

Undershaft's trombone in Major Barbara

MRS BAINES. Mr Undershaft: have you ever seen a thousand people fall on their knees with one impulse and pray? Come with us to the meeting. Barbara shall tell them that the Army is saved, and saved through you.

CUSINS [*returning impetuously from the shelter with a flag and a trombone, and coming between Mrs Baines and Undershaft*] You shall carry the flag down the first street, Mrs Baines [*he gives her the flag*]. Mr Undershaft is a gifted trombonist: he shall intone an Olympian diapason to the West Ham Salvation March. [*Aside to Undershaft, as he forces the trombone on him*] Blow, Machiavelli, blow.

UNDERSHAFT [*aside to him, as he takes the trombone*] The trumpet in Zion! [*Cusins rushes to the drum, which he takes up and puts on. Undershaft continues, aloud*] I will do my best. I could vamp a bass if I knew the tune.

CUSINS. It is a wedding chorus from one of Donizetti's operas; but we have converted it. We convert everything to good here, including Bodger. You remember the chorus. 'For thee immense rejoicing – immenso giubilo – immenso giubilo.' [*With drum obbligato*] Rum tum ti tum tum, tum tum ti ta –

BARBARA. Dolly: you are breaking my heart.

CUSINS. What is a broken heart more or less here? Dionysos Undershaft has descended. I am possessed.

MRS BAINES. Come, Barbara: I must have my dear Major to carry the flag with me.

JENNY. Yes, yes, Major darling.

CUSINS [*snatches the tambourine out of Jenny's hand and mutely offers it to Barbara*].

BARBARA [*coming forward a little as she puts the offer behind her with a shudder, whilst Cusins recklessly tosses the tambourine back to Jenny and goes to the gate*] I cant come.

JENNY. Not come!

MRS BAINES [*with tears in her eyes*] Barbara: do you think I am wrong to take the money?

BARBARA [*impulsively going to her and kissing her*] No, no: God help you, dear, you must: you are saving the Army. Go; and may you have a great meeting!

JENNY. But arnt you coming?

BARBARA. NO. [*She begins taking off the silver S brooch from her collar*].

MRS BAINES. Barbara: what are you doing?

JENNY. Why are you taking your badge off? You cant be going to leave us, Major.

BARBARA [*quietly*] Father: come here.

UNDERSHAFT [*coming to her*] My dear! [*Seeing that she is going to pin the badge on his collar, he retreats to the penthouse in some alarm*].

BARBARA [*following him*] Dont be frightened. [*She pins the badge on and steps back towards the table, shewing him to the others*] There! It's not much for £5000, is it?

MRS BAINES. Barbara: if you wont come and pray with us, promise me you will pray for us.

BARBARA. I cant pray now. Perhaps I shall never pray again.

MRS BAINES. Barbara!

JENNY. Major!

BARBARA [*almost delirious*] I cant bear any more. Quick march!

CUSINS [*calling to the procession in the street outside*] Off we go. Play up, there! Immenso giubilo. [*He gives the time with his drum; and the band strikes up the march, which rapidly becomes more distant as the procession moves briskly away*].

(*Major Barbara*)

PERCY BYSSHE SHELLEY

'The Keen Stars Were Twinkling', and the dedicatory verses, 'With a guitar, to Jane', are among the most touching lines that Shelley wrote, even without the poignant circumstances. On 8 July 1822, he and his friend Edward Williams drowned when the boat *Don Juan* went down off Lerici. Williams's common-law wife, Jane, was Shelley's last 'muse'. On 5 March Mary Shelley had written to Marianne Hunt that Jane 'has a very pretty voice, and a taste and ear for music which is almost miraculous. The harp is her favourite instrument; but we have none and a very bad piano.' By 11 April Shelley ('Ariel') had found a guitar by a Pisan maker and given it to Jane ('Miranda') by the supposed permission of her 'Prince Ferdinando' (that is, her husband), as: '. . . this silent token/Of more than ever can be spoken.' One can imagine the poet's delight at finding the label and apposite name inside the sound-box of the guitar: 'Ferdinando Bottari/*Fece in Pisa nel 1816.*'

His friend Trelawny found Shelley at work on the 90 lines of 'With a guitar' beside a river in the pine-forest outside Pisa, one brilliant day. The apostrophe to the Spirit that inhabits the instrument ends:

> But, sweetly as it[']s answers will
> Flatter hands of perfect skill,
> It keeps it[']s highest holiest tone
> For our belovèd Jane alone.

After the disaster, Jane took the guitar home with her to London and cherished it for the rest of her long life (she died in 1884). It lies in the Bodleian Library (see the 1992 bicentenary exhibition, *Shelley's Guitar*, with manuscripts, first editions and relics, catalogued by B. C. Barker-Benfield).

Two poems to Jane and her guitar

Ariel to Miranda: – Take
This slave of Music, for the sake
Of him who is the slave of thee,
And teach it all the harmony
In which thou canst, and only thou,
Make the delighted spirit glow,
Till joy denies itself again,
And, too intense, is turned to pain;
For by permission and command
Of thine own Prince Ferdinand,
Poor Ariel sends this silent token
Of more than ever can be spoken;
Your guardian spirit, Ariel, who,
From life to life, must still pursue
Your happiness; – for thus alone
Can Ariel ever find his own.
From Prospero's enchanted cell,
As the mighty verses tell,
To the throne of Naples, he
Lit you o'er the trackless sea,
Flitting on, your prow before,
Like a living meteor.
When you die, the silent Moon,
In her interlunar swoon,
Is not sadder in her cell
Than deserted Ariel.
When you live again on earth,
Like an unseen star of birth,
Ariel guides you o'er the sea
Of life from your nativity.
Many changes have been run
Since Ferdinand and you begun
Your course of love, and Ariel still
Has tracked your steps, and served your will;
Now, in humbler, happier lot,
This is all remembered not;

And now, alas! the poor sprite is
Imprisoned, for some fault of his,
In a body like a grave; –
From you he only dares to crave,
For his service and his sorrow,
A smile to-day, a song to-morrow.
The artist who this idol wrought,
To echo all harmonious thought,
Felled a tree, while on the steep
The woods were in their winter sleep,
Rocked in that repose divine
On the wind-swept Apennine;
And dreaming, some of Autumn past,
And some of Spring approaching fast,
And some of April buds and showers,
And some of songs in July bowers,
And all of love; and so this tree, –
O that such our death may be! –
Died in sleep, and felt no pain,
To live in happier form again:
From which, beneath Heaven's fairest star,
The artist wrought this loved Guitar,
And taught it justly to reply,
To all who question skilfully,
In language gentle as thine own;
Whispering in enamoured tone
Sweet oracles of woods and dells,
And summer winds in sylvan cells;
For it had learned all harmonies
Of the plains and of the skies,
Of the forests and the mountains,
And the many-voicèd fountains;
The clearest echoes of the hills,
The softest notes of falling rills,
The melodies of birds and bees,
The murmuring of summer seas,
And pattering rain, and breathing dew,
And airs of evening; and it knew

That seldom-heard mysterious sound,
Which, driven on its diurnal round,
As it floats through boundless day,
Our world enkindles on its way. –
All this it knows, but will not tell
To those who cannot question well
The Spirit that inhabits it;
It talks according to the wit
Of its companions; and no more
Is heard than has been felt before,
By those who tempt it to betray
These secrets of an elder day:
But, sweetly as its answers will
Flatter hands of perfect skill,
It keeps its highest, holiest tone
For our belovèd Jane alone.

(*'With a Guitar, to Jane'*)

I

The keen stars were twinkling,
And the fair moon was rising among them,
Dear Jane!
The guitar was tinkling,
But the notes were not sweet till you sung them
Again.

II

As the moon's soft splendour
O'er the faint cold starlight of Heaven
Is thrown,
So your voice most tender
To the strings without soul had then given
Its own.

III

The stars will awaken,
Though the moon sleep a full hour later,
To-night;
No leaf will be shaken
Whilst the dews of your melody scatter
Delight.

IV

Though the sound overpowers,
Sing again, with your dear voice revealing
A tone
Of some world far from ours,
Where music and moonlight and feeling
Are one.

('*The Keen Stars Were Twinkling*')

GEORGINA SIME

George Meredith's treble and bass dogs

... Mr Meredith sat down, and I stood by his side, eagerly awaiting whatever was to come. The dachshunds had, I think, an inkling of what this was; they had that pleasant look, typical of dachshunds, of being delighted to do whatever may be asked of them. They were, like most dogs, gratified at being noticed at all, and at the first look and call of their master they came into line with one accord, ranged themselves before him, erected themselves on their hind legs, and, with perfectly straight backs (their 'posture', as we say now, was superb) and eyes intently fixed on him waited, as the men of the orchestra wait with their eyes on the conductor's baton, *all* ready, every single inch of them alert to do what Nelson expected of every Englishman.

After a pause, just as at the beginning of an orchestral concert, the master gave the sign to the right-hand dog, who immediately produced from somewhere down in the depths of his being the deepest growling note that ever I heard emitted from a canine frame. His left-hand compan-ion meanwhile kept erect, his eyes glued to his master's face; you felt that his dog's heart would break if he were to miss or falter over his entry-cue. In due time the moment came; Mr Meredith turned to him and addressed him with the words, 'And now let us hear Jacobus sing his sweet flute note.'

Forthwith Jacobus emitted as high a note as can ever, I think, have issued from a dog's throat; and the two musicians continued their duet until the master raised his hand, and then they stopped. They evidently felt that they had deserved well of God and man, and when the rewarding

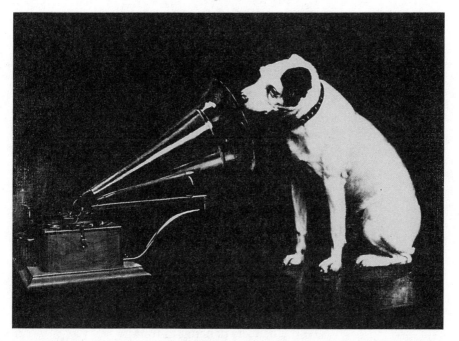

His Master's Voice: a rival to George Meredith's musical dogs? (By kind permission of Thorn EMI)

biscuit was divided between them enjoyed it in the happy assurance that they were getting no more than they were entitled to.

'Now,' Mr Meredith said, as he turned to me and took my hands in his, 'you have heard Brutus's loud bassoon' (I am a little doubtful now if the name was Brutus, but I am pretty sure that it began with a B) 'and Jacobus's sweet flute note. How do you think they sing?'

(*Brave Spirits*)

ALFRED TENNYSON

From 'Maud: A Monodrama'

All night have the roses heard
The flute, violin, bassoon;
All night has the casement jessamine stirr'd
To the dancers dancing in tune;
Till a silence fell with the waking bird,
And a hush with the setting moon.

NED WARD

Paradise at The Mitre, Wapping

'Remembering we had heard of a famous Amphibious House of Entertainment, compounded of one half *Tavern* and t'other *Musick-House*,
made us willing to Dedicate half an hour to what Diversion we might there
meet with. . . . As soon as we came to the Sign of the *Spiritual Helmet* [The
Mitre, Wapping], such as the *High-Priests* us'd to wear when they bid
Defiance to the Devil, we no sooner enter'd the House, but we heard
Fidlers and *Hoitboys*, together with a Humdrum *Organ*, make such incomparable Musick, that had the Harmonious Grunting of a *Hog* been added
as a *Bass* to a Ravishing Concert of Caterwauling Performers, in the Height
of their Extasie, the unusualness of the sound could not have render'd it,
to a Nice Ear, more engaging. Having heard of the Beauty and Contrivance of the Publick *Musick-Room*, as well as other parts of the House, very
highly Commended, we agreed, first to take a view of that which was likely
to be most remarkable. In order to which we *Ascended* the *Grades*, and
were Usher'd into a most Stately Apartment, Dedicated purely to the
Lovers of *Musick, Painting, Dancing*, and t'other thing too. No *Gilding,
Carving, Colouring*, or good *Contrivance*, was here wanting to Illustrate
the Beauty of this most noble Academy; where a good Genius may Learn
with safety to abominate Vice; and a bad Genius as (with as much danger)
to Practice it. The Room by its compact Order and costly Improvements,
looks so far above the use its now converted to, that the Seats are more like
Pews than Boxes; and the upper-end, being divided by a Rail, looks more
like a *Chancel* than a *Musick-Box*; that I could not but imagine it was Built
for a *Fanatick Meeting-House*, but that they have for ever destroy'd the

Sanctity of the place by putting an *Organ* in it; round which hung a great many pretty *Whimsical Pictures*.... There were but few Companies in the Room; the most Remarkable Person was a Drunken Commander, who plucking out a Handful of Money, to give the *Musick* Six-pence, dropt a Shilling, and was so very generous, that he gave an Officious Drawer, standing by, half a Crown for stooping to take it up again.... ' [After inspecting the rest of the premises] 'we return'd up Stairs, where we Drank a Quart of good *Red*, thank'd the Master for his Civility, and so departed the House, which may very justly be Stiled, by such who Love Good Wine, and a *Pleasant Room* to sit in, *The Paradice* of Wapping.'

(*The London Spy*)

2
PRACTICE, PRACTICE, PRACTICE

JANE AUSTEN

A musical evening in Sloane Street

To her sister Cassandra, Sloane Street, 25 April 1811

... Our party went off extremely well. There were many solicitudes; alarms
& vexations beforehand of course, but at last everything was quite right.
The rooms were dressed up with flowers &c, & looked very pretty. – A
glass for the Mantlepiece was lent, by the Man who is making their own. –
Mr Egerton & Mr Walter came at 1/2 past 5, & the festivities began with a
p^r of very fine Soals. Yes, Mr Walter – for he postponed his leaving London
on Purpose – which did not give much pleasure at the time, any more than
the circumstance from which it rose, his calling on Sunday & being asked
by Henry to take the family dinner on that day, which he did – but it is all
smooth'd over now; – & she likes him very well. – At 1/2 past 7 arrived the
Musicians in two Hackney coaches, & by 8 the lordly company began to
appear. Among the earliest were George & Mary Cooke, & I spent the
greatest part of the even^g very pleasantly with them. – The Draw^g room
being soon hotter than we liked, we placed ourselves in the connecting
Passage, which was comparatively cool, & gave us all the advantage of the
Music at a pleasant distance, as well as that of the first view of every new
comer. – I was quite surrounded by acquaintance, especially Gentlemen ... – Including everybody we were 66 – which was considerably more
than Eliza had expected, & quite enough to fill the Back Draw^g room, &
leave a few to be scattered about in the other, & in the passage. The Music
was extremely good. It opened (tell Fanny, with 'Poike pe Parp pin praise
pof Prapela' – & of the other Glees I remember, 'In Peace Love tunes,'

'Rosabelle,' 'The red cross Knight,' & 'Poor Insect.' Between the Songs were Lessons on the Harp, or Harp & Piano Forte together – & the Harp Player was Wiepart, whose name seems famous, tho' new to me. – There was one female singer, a short Miss Davis all in blue, bringing up for the Public Line, whose voice was said to be very fine indeed; & all the Performers gave great satisfaction by doing what they were paid for, & giving themselves no airs. – No amateur could be persuaded to do anything. – The House was not clear till after 12. –

To the same, Hans Place, 2 December 1815

[Mr Haden] is no Apothecary, he has never been an Apothecary, there is not an Apothecary in this Neighbourhood – the only inconvenience of the situation perhaps, but so it is – we have not a medical Man within reach – he is a Haden, nothing but a Haden, a sort of wonderful nondescript Creature on two legs, something between a Man & an Angel – but without the least spice of an Apothecary. – He is perhaps the only Person *not* an Apothecary hereabouts. – He has never sung to us. He will not sing without a P. Forté accompaniment. Mr Meyers gives his three Lessons a week – altering his days & his hours however just as he chuses, never very punctual, & never giving good Measure. – I have not Fanny's fondness for Masters, & Mr Meyers does not give me any Longing after them. The truth is I think, that they are all, at least Music Masters, made of too much consequence & allowed to take too many Liberties with their Scholar's time.

(*The Letters of Jane Austen*)

OSBERT BURDETT

The delights of the pianola

With a perverted precocity, I could spell before I could hear or speak. Thus desultorily, and almost insensible to sound, the years of childhood and of school-life drifted away.

Then at college I met a brilliant young musician, to whose criticisms London now delights to listen as he used to delight me when listening to his touch upon the keys. On many evenings I would sit in his rooms, until suddenly one night, after many repetitions, another composer revealed himself. This was Beethoven, who penetrated my occluded ears with the onset of the *Waldstein Sonata*. What an evening that was! For, as the music began to be felt, the themes and the phrases defined themselves clearly, and the ear began to wait expectantly for each restatement or suggestion of them, in this and in a few other pieces. From that evening I resolved to enlarge the discovery which H. E. Wortham's playing of the *Waldstein*, the rarest of the many gifts bestowed by his friendship, had revealed.

Something like this, I take it, must be the experience of many unmusical people: of those, I mean, who have that vice in the ears of which Cloten complained when he told the musicians that, if their rendering of

> Hark, hark! the lark at heaven's gate sings

did not penetrate the heart of Imogen, it would be because of 'a vice in her ears' which neither horse-hairs nor the voice of a eunuch itself could ever amend. The present example should encourage any, unhappily aware of their own deafness, not to despair.

After the first step, the hardest and most mysterious, the following proceeded orderly enough with the prompt hiring of a pianola. For this I began by choosing only the music with which I had begun to be familiar upon Wortham's piano. The *Waldstein*, the *Kreutzer Sonata*, the *Funeral Marches* of Handel and of Chopin, the dance of the trolls from Grieg's *Peer Gynt*, the *Moonlight Sonata*, the *Overture to Tannhauser*, Chopin's *Nocturnes* and *Polonaises*: these, and the like, I practised from morning till night, sometimes to the neglect of reading or lectures; so often indeed that, in the innocence of my enthusiasm and on his first visit to my rooms, I greeted my father, rather to his irritation, with the *Dead March in Saul*, before we lunched. Also I made a point of hearing one or two different pianists play these pieces, and thus compared Leonard Borwick's rendering of the *Waldstein* with Wortham's exquisite interpretation (and my own).

It was the pianola that taught one most; and I soon ceased to be troubled by its mechanical whistling and creaking, or even to notice them; and, at the moment when I ceased to notice them, I began to grow aware of the mechanical noises associated with the production of sound by an orchestra, by a violin or a pianoforte, and by the human voice; for the voice is also a mechanism, and your singer, pianist or orchestra can add as much noise to the music that they produce as any machine. This elementary discovery made one indifferent to most of the superior criticisms levelled at the pianola because, in the universe of space and time, pure music hardly anywhere, or for more than a few moments, exists. The piano-player had taught me to hear by teaching me in some sort to play: I learned to hear in the only way in which it is possible to learn anything – by doing. I did not attend 'a course of lectures,' frequent evening-classes, seek tuition by correspondence, or buy 'a set of inexpensive books.' But, in the doing, one began to detect the faults of execution that one could not remedy; to discover that there was more than one way of playing a familiar piece, and even to teach oneself how to play unfamiliar music, for all the world as if one were no more stupid than other people.

Now all this would have been impossible without the aid of a mechanical instrument. The case for the piano-player was complete. It can make the deaf to hear, and the fingers of the dumb to utter music, even though it may be a superfluity to those who were born with a pianola inside them.

(*The Art of Living*)

WILLIAM BYRD

To perswade every one to sing

Reasons briefly set downe by th' auctor, to perswade every one to learne to sing:

First, it is a knowledge easely taught, and quickly learned, where there is a good Master, and an apt Scoller

(2) The exercise of singing is delightfull to Nature, and good to preserve the health of Man

(3) It doth strengthen all parts of the brest, and doth open the pipes

(4) It is a singuler good remedie for a stutting [*sic*] and stammering in the speech

(5) It is the best meanes to procure a perfect pronunciation and to make a good Orator

(6) It is the onley way to know where Nature hath bestowed the benefit of a good voyce: which gift is so rare, as there is not one among a thousand that hath it; and in many, that excellent gift is lost, because they want Art to expresse Nature

(7) There is not any Musicke of Instruments whatsoever, comparable to that which is made of the voyces of Men, where the voyces are good, and the same well sorted and ordered

(8) The better the voyce is, the meeter it is to honour and serve God therewith as the voyce of man is chiefely to be imployed to that ende. *Omnis spiritus laudet Deo.*

> Since singing is so good a thing
> I wish all men would learne to sing.

(Psalmes, Sonets & Songs of sadness and pietie)

81

CHRISTOPHER DRIVER

How to survive summer schools

Richard Crashaw's Musick's Duell

The Proms and the Edinburgh Festival are not the only August musical activities that keep a cast of thousands in rehearsal. It is an odds-on bet that at this very moment – unless you read THE LISTENER during radically unsocial hours – four people in a charmless classroom in one of our schools, colleges or universities have struggled to the first double bar of a Haydn quartet (probably 'The Lark') and collapsed at the tape because two of them have taken the repeat and the other two have carried on to the development.

In other words, the music summer school season is in full swing. A moment from now, one of the short-of-sleep professionals presiding over the course will put his or her head round the door and start sorting out the cat's-cradle of accidentals and cross-rhythms that are making normally equable middle-income citizens so cross with each other that in another 24 hours or so one of them is going to throw a terminal temper tantrum and seek another partner, for the week if not for life.

Summer music courses have become a highly competitive business. Once there was Dartington and Bernard Robinson's Music Camp and precious little else. This year, *Classical Music* fortnightly tots them up at well over 200. The prices of most fall closely in line with each other for a week's board and lodging, tuition and evening concerts. By festival town standards this is a bargain for a July-August holiday week, even if the ensemble coaching is perfunctory (which is unusual) and the beds lumpy (which is common).

It is also a bargain which only Britain offers in such abundance. Marketing of the service to potential foreign clients is as yet primitive, but the opportunity is there, and most such courses can show at least a couple of Dutch, Germans, Swedes or Norwegians who have lugged their trumpets, bassoons and violas on to the Euro ferries. (French applicants are rarer birds, and not only for dietary or linguistic reasons: not many French people over the age of 30 combine to play musical instruments together unless they are doing it professionally.)

No one has life, let alone holiday allowance, enough to experience more than a tithe of these courses as a participant, which is the only way to discover where the seams leak. Few musicians, professional or amateur, perform on more than two or three different instruments in as many centuries' styles. On the larger courses (100 people or more) the same setting can feel very different according to your orientation: prearranged amateur string quartet; music student performing in public master classes; professional musician seeking a chance to conduct or try the crumhorn; and so on. The sketch that follows has been composed by an amateur string player who prefers the chamber music repertoire to other forms of music making and listening, and whose summer school notches include Dartington, ERMA, Giggleswick, Keele, Stowe, and two specialised quartet courses, the Gabrieli's at the University of Essex and the Alberni's at Madingley, near Cambridge. The details are documentary, not fiction. But the definitive consumer's guide – a document badly needed – requires a *Good Food Guide*-style co-operative: see the conclusion.

Preludio: moderato con speranza

Back in February/March, you sent off for the brochures advertised in the music magazines. Hope was the key signature. The cooking at Stowe couldn't be worse than it was at Roedean, could it? The cellist they hitch us to at Giggleswick couldn't be as grumpy and garrulous as last year's, surely? This preliminary stage includes that most delicate task, the completion of an ominously amateurish questionnaire designed to elicit for the organiser's information what you can do as a player and what you can't.

Self-evaluation, it's called in other contexts. Completing the form correctly has little to do with string playing and everything to do with gamesmanship. It's like computer dating without the computer, and with no guarantee that there'll be a date. This is because there are two ineluctable laws of playing an instrument: everyone else is either better or worse at it than you, and, failing friendship or other emotional ties, everyone wants to play with their betters, not their inferiors.

For the organisers of a music course, with the exception of the lucky few whose strength in the marketplace enables them to turn away all but previously formed ensembles, the effect of these laws is compounded by a third, more general law of human behaviour: when asked to state their capabilities on paper, talented people understate, and ignoramuses exaggerate.

Allemanda: andante laborioso

The typical summer school brochure suggests that players should 'have a look at' a few listed works before the course opens. Old hands sniff these lists cautiously. Not only are they aware that Bartok 1 or Brahms 2 are well beyond their own powers and those of any foreseeable partners, they are also old enough to expect any curriculum to suit the teacher, not the pupil. In other words, the resident professionals on the course have recently recorded the quartet in question, or are about to do so, and know exactly what the second violin ought to be doing in bar 167, which every sensible player of coarse chamber music tries to fudge as unobtrusively as possible.

Of course, there are at least a few movements – seldom whole works – in the standard chamber music repertoire that can be made to sound like music even by players of very modest accomplishments: in Beethoven, for instance, the Andante scherzoso of the Quartet Op. 18 No. 4, and the Andante of the String Trio Op. 3. But when these possibilities have been exhausted, the tables can occasionally be turned on coaches by playing them a piece that even they have never heard. The pro walks in for a coaching session, sees a string quartet with a second cello attached, and braces himself for yet another unspeakable Schubert C major Quintet. Say nothing, and open fire with the Glazunov.

It is nevertheless a good idea to do some regular practice before a summer school. Otherwise an eight-hour playing day will raise blisters on your chin.

Sarabanda: studioso

Some people take whole libraries of music with them to summer schools. Others travel light, and only notice what the music stand is laden with when the baton comes down or the quartet leader says pointedly: 'I see this is written in 2 but we'd better do it in 8.'

Two points – at least – can be made about the chamber music repertoire. The first is that most professionals are ignorant of it. The second is that it wasn't written for people like you.

The first point may sound odd. Suppose a professional violinist – solo or orchestral – who has never played Mozart's string quartets, or Beethoven's Op. 70 piano trios, or the late quartets of Dvorak: is he not like a Shakespearian actor who cannot quote a line of the sonnets, or a writer whose knowledge of Keats and Milton is confined to the verse?

Of course he is. Still, that's how music-college pedagogy and the career structure work, or did until very recently. It's more important to learn by heart a virtuoso concerto you'll never be asked to play in public than to learn how to accompany a line and phrase the passagework in far greater music which you might meet tomorrow in a neighbour's house. This cultural quirk often narrows the otherwise yawning divide between professional training and the lack of it.

Unfortunately, the second point also applies. The most sublime or witty music ever written by the Viennese masters assumes an instrumental technique equal to the solo works of the same period. If you can play the top part of Haydn's 'Emperor' Quartet or Beethoven's C sharp minor or Mendelssohn's Octet – and have time over for listening and thinking as you go – you can cope with the fiddle concertos of the same composers. If you don't want to find yourself on a summer course in the role of a natural No. 9 batsman sent out to face the fast bowlers at first wicket down, make a special study of Mozart second viola parts and you might find yourself playing in better company than you deserve.

Corrente: strepitoso

You've arrived at your course's rundown stately home, registered, eaten, slept. You're now meeting the group you've been put in, either for the week or on appro for the first day. This is the very stuff of politics. You have room for manoeuvre, but not much. It doesn't help you to be marked down on the first day as one of the awkward squad. For the first hour you smile, even if it's clear to you from the first bar that the second violin can't count and that the leader plays sharp when he's playing the notes at all. It can only get better. Well, it surely can't get worse? Yes it can, by tomorrow, when the smiles wear thin and the cellist realises that if he dashes round the campus fixing players he can achieve a Schubert Octet and the second fiddle realises she faces relegation to the baroque group, whose notes have fewer tails to them.

Yet there are saints on these courses, too. Self-interested saints, sometimes, if that's not a contradiction in terms. It's not every dirndl-skirted cellist of uncertain age whose bedroom I would consent to clear of spiders before she retired for the night, had I not realised that a fit of the vapours then would deprive us of her company or her co-operation in the morning – and she could play, more or less.

I can also think of at least three middle-aged women – piano teachers playing their second instrument for the pleasure of quartet playing – who spent most of a previous week's holiday counting some idiot student or middle-aged male prima donna through the syncopated *fioriture* of a first violin part, when they deserved a fellow musician to play with. Even 20-year-old saints are not unknown. Organiser to music student: 'Mary, you wouldn't mind leading the Gentlecacketts for a morning, would you?

No one else will play with them, and they should have had the sense not to come, but we'll go into the red if they ask for a refund.' And Mary does.

Gavotta: con umiltà

Coaching is the eschatological goal of summer schools and the coarse musicians who attend them. After all, they know they would pay £25 an hour in London for instrumental and musical advice which here is coming to them free, in a manner of speaking:

'That spiccato stroke in the inner parts: it needs to be more saucer-shaped. Start nearer the string and use more arm movement.' 'I'd go up on the D in fourth position and avoid the open string.' 'You need a really full Brahms sound: try turning the bow so that you're using the flat of the hair, and give it all the vibrato you can.' 'The first violin has two unaccompanied semibreves on his own before the quavers start: to get the speed Beethoven wants, think of a bar of quavers before you start the long note.'

That was just a few snatches of the violinist Richard Deakin. But it could just as well have been dozens of gifted coaches. Not many instrumentalists succeed in articulating for lesser mortals what they themselves do by instinct, but blessed are those that can.

Giga: giocoso

Not many summer school organisers really know what sells their courses rather than someone else's: the names of the coaches, the programmes for the evening concerts, the massed Brahms Requiem from scratch on the last day, the sadistic pleasure of listening to Sandor Vegh at a master class squeeze a student till the pips squeak, the size of the swimming-pool, the dalliance in the shrubberies, the bar prices, or (in Dartington and Madingley and hardly anywhere else) the cooking.

As for the turn-offs, enough has been said to suggest that they are more often human than musical – though an exception should be made for a collector's piece in the student concert at Stowe this year: Barber's Adagio for Strings arranged for 12 clarinets, qualifying at the swiftly garrotted climax for noise-abatement relief under the Environmental Health Acts.

Till next year, then.

(*The Listener*)

GEORGE ELIOT

'Imaginary Conversations' (the title belongs to W. S. Landor in the 1820s) have often been imitated. One such might-have-been encounter is set in George Eliot's music room at the house she shared with G. H. Lewes in Regent's Park, one Saturday evening in 1865. Her *Felix Holt, the Radical* was nearly finished. She was preparing to play Mozart or Beethoven trios with friends on her new grand piano and broke off to greet a guest, a young architect in Blomfield's office, who learnt the violin at home in Dorchester and took it up again in London to play favourite tunes from the opera. They would have had other things in common. Both had abandoned or modified their religious belief. As writers a decade later, they were spoken of in the same breath: George Eliot's *Daniel Deronda* and Thomas Hardy's *Far from the Madding Crowd* belong to 1874, and several reviewers compared this new voice with the older novelist's social realism.

George Eliot's Midlands Evangelical background, which she soon escaped into freethinking journalism through her Coventry friends, Charles and Caroline Bray, never hindered her musical education. Later on, however, her astonishing application to languages and philosophy during her thirties, followed by her output of novels, overshadow her lifelong attachment to the piano and great music (from Haydn to Wagner). But her friends enjoyed her playing and helped her to find access to a good instrument. When she and Lewes went abroad in 1854 to damp down the London scandal of their common-law marriage, Liszt in Weimar invited them to lunch – and played. She wrote: 'I sat near him so that I could see both his hands and face. For the first time in my life I beheld inspiration – for the first time I heard the true tones of the piano.'

There is something of Liszt in Klesmer, Gwendolen's critic in *Daniel Deronda*. More to the point in George Eliot's personality, high seriousness extended to her music. Compare her dismissive phrase for young Dorothea's 'small tinkling' in *Middlemarch* with the letter she wrote to Mrs Richard Congreve (19 January 1864):

'I have been playing energetically on the piano lately and taking lessons in accompanying the violin from Herr Jansa, one of the old Beethoven Quartette players.'

Her duo partner's verdict (see below, p. 145) may sound like faint praise. But there are very few amateur pianists, even now, who could claim that they have played through the entire cycle of Mozart and Beethoven violin sonatas with a performer who clearly made no allowances.

Poor Gwendolen, poor Dorothea

'Ah, here comes Herr Klesmer,' said Mrs Arrowpoint, rising; and presently bringing him to Gwendolen, she left them to a dialogue which was agreeable on both sides, Herr Klesmer being a felicitous combination of the German, the Sclave, and the Semite, with grand features, brown hair floating in artistic fashion, and brown eyes in spectacles. His English had little foreignness except its fluency; and his alarming cleverness was made less formidable just then by a certain softening air of silliness which will sometimes befall even Genius in the desire of being agreeable to Beauty.

Music was soon begun. Miss Arrowpoint and Herr Klesmer played a four-handed piece on two pianos which convinced the company in general that it was long, and Gwendolen in particular that the neutral, placid-faced Miss Arrowpoint had a mastery of the instrument which put her own execution out of the question – though she was not discouraged as to her often-praised touch and style. After this every one became anxious to hear Gwendolen sing; especially Mr Arrowpoint; as was natural in a host and a perfect gentleman, of whom no one had anything to say but that he had married Miss Cuttler, and imported the best cigars; and he led her to the piano with easy politeness. Herr Klesmer closed the instrument in readiness for her, and smiled with pleasure at her approach; then placed himself at the distance of a few feet so that he could see her as she sang.

Gwendolen was not nervous: what she undertook to do she did without trembling, and singing was an enjoyment to her. Her voice was a moderately powerful soprano (some one had told her it was like Jenny Lind's), her ear good, and she was able to keep in tune, so that her singing gave

pleasure to ordinary hearers, and she had been used to unmingled applause. She had the rare advantage of looking almost prettier when she was
singing than at other times, and that Herr Klesmer was in front of her
seemed not disagreeable. Her song, determined on beforehand, was a
favourite aria of Bellini's, in which she felt quite sure of herself.

'Charming!' said Mr Arrowpoint, who had remained near, and the
word was echoed around without more insincerity than we recognise in a
brotherly way as human. But Herr Klesmer stood like a statue – if a statue
can be imagined in spectacles; at least, he was as mute as a statue.
Gwendolen was pressed to keep her seat and double the general pleasure,
and she did not wish to refuse; but before resolving to do so, she moved a
little towards Herr Klesmer, saying with a look of smiling appeal, 'It would
be too cruel to a great musician. You cannot like to hear poor amateur
singing.'

'No, truly; but that makes nothing,' said Herr Klesmer, suddenly
speaking in an odious German fashion with staccato endings, quite unob-
servable in him before, and apparently depending on a change of mood, as
Irishmen resume their strongest brogue when they are fervid or quarrelsome. 'That makes nothing. It is always acceptable to see you sing.'

Was there ever so unexpected an assertion of superiority? at least before
the late Teutonic conquest? Gwendolen coloured deeply, but, with her
usual presence of mind, did not show an ungraceful resentment by moving
away immediately; and Miss Arrowpoint, who had been near enough to
overhear (and also to observe that Herr Klesmer's mode of looking at
Gwendolen was more conspicuously admiring than was quite consistent
with good taste), now with the utmost tact and kindness came close to her
and said –

'Imagine what I have to go through with this professor! He can hardly
tolerate anything we English do in music. We can only put up with his
severity, and make use of it to find out the worst that can be said of us. It is a
little comfort to know that; and one can bear it when every one else is
admiring.'

'I should be very much obliged to him for telling me the worst,' said
Gwendolen, recovering herself. 'I daresay I have been extremely ill taught,
in addition to having no talent – only liking for music.' This was very well
expressed considering that it had never entered her mind before.

'Yes, it is true; you have not been well taught,' said Herr Klesmer,
quietly. Woman was dear to him, but music was dearer. 'Still, you are not

quite without gifts. You sing in tune, and you have a pretty fair organ. But you produce your notes badly; and that music which you sing is beneath you. It is a form of melody which expresses a puerile state of culture – a dandling, canting, see-saw kind of stuff – the passion and thought of people without any breadth of horizon. There is a sort of self-satisfied folly about every phrase of such melody; no cries of deep, mysterious passion – no conflict – no sense of the universal. It makes men small as they listen to it. Sing now something larger. And I shall see.'

'Oh, not now – by-and-by,' said Gwendolen, with a sinking of heart at the sudden width of horizon opened round her small musical performance. For a young lady desiring to lead, this first encounter in her campaign was startling. But she was bent on not behaving foolishly, and Miss Arrowpoint helped her by saying –

'Yes, by-and-by. I always require half an hour to get up my courage after being criticised by Herr Klesmer. We will ask him to play to us now: he is bound to show us what is good music.'

To be quite safe on this point Herr Klesmer played a composition of his own, a fantasia called *Freudvoll, Leidvoll, Gedankenvoll* – an extensive commentary on some melodic ideas not too grossly evident; and he certainly fetched as much variety and depth of passion out of the piano as that moderately responsive instrument lends itself to, having an imperious magic in his fingers that seemed to send a nerve-thrill through ivory key and wooden hammer, and compel the strings to make a quivering lingering speech for him. Gwendolen, in spite of her wounded egoism, had fulness of nature enough to feel the power of this playing, and it gradually turned her inward sob of mortification into an excitement which lifted her for the moment into a desperate indifference about her own doings, or at least a determination to get a superiority over them by laughing at them as if they belonged to somebody else. Her eyes had become brighter, her cheeks slightly flushed, and her tongue ready for any mischievous remarks.

'I wish you would sing to us again, Miss Harleth,' said young Clintock, the archdeacon's classical son, who had been so fortunate as to take her to dinner, and came up to renew conversation as soon as Herr Klesmer's performance was ended. 'That is the style of music for me. I never can make anything of this tip-top playing. It is like a jar of leeches, where you can never tell either beginnings or endings. I could listen to your singing all day.'

(Daniel Deronda)

Mr Brooke . . . expressed himself with his usual strength . . . one day that he came into the library while the reading was going forward.

'Well, but now, Casaubon, such deep studies, classics, mathematics, that kind of thing, are too taxing for a woman – too taxing, you know.'

'Dorothea is learning to read the characters simply,' said Mr Casaubon, evading the question. 'She had the very considerate thought of saving my eyes.'

Two Victorians trying over new music

'Ah, well, without understanding, you know – that may not be so bad. But there is a lightness about the feminine mind – a touch and go – music, the fine arts, that kind of thing – they should study those up to a certain point, women should; but in a light way, you know. A woman should be able to sit down and play you or sing you a good old English tune. That is what I like; though I have heard most things – been at the opera in Vienna: Gluck, Mozart, everything of that sort. But I'm a conservative in music – it's not like ideas, you know. I stick to the good old tunes.'

'Mr Casaubon is not fond of the piano, and I am very glad he is not,' said Dorothea, whose slight regard for domestic music and feminine fine art must be forgiven her, considering the small tinkling and smearing in which they chiefly consisted at that dark period. She smiled and looked up at her betrothed with grateful eyes. If he had always been asking her to play the 'Last Rose of Summer,' she would have required much resignation. 'He says there is only an old harpsichord at Lowick, and it is covered with books.'

'Ah, there you are behind Celia, my dear. Celia, now, plays very prettily, and is always ready to play. However, since Casaubon does not like it, you are all right. But it's a pity you should not have little recreations of that sort, Casaubon: the bow always strung – that kind of thing, you know – will not do.'

'I never could look on it in the light of a recreation to have my ears teased with measured noises,' said Mr Casaubon. 'A tune much iterated has the ridiculous effect of making the words in my mind perform a sort of minuet to keep time – an effect hardly tolerable, I imagine, after boyhood. As to the grander forms of music, worthy to accompany solemn celebrations, and even to serve as an educating influence according to the ancient conception, I say nothing, for with these we are not immediately concerned.'

'No; but music of that sort I should enjoy,' said Dorothea. 'When we were coming home from Lausanne my uncle took us to hear the great organ at Freiberg, and it made me sob.'

'That kind of thing is not healthy, my dear,' said Mr Brooke. 'Casaubon, she will be in your hands now: you must teach my niece to take things more quietly, eh, Dorothea?'

(*Middlemarch*)

JESSIE FOTHERGILL

An English heroine at a German audition

Miss Hallam fulfilled her promise with regard to my singing lessons. She had a conversation with Fräulein Sartorius, to whom, unpopular as she was, I noticed people constantly and almost instinctively went when in need of precise information or a slight dose of common sense and clear-headedness.

Miss Hallam inquired who was the best master.

'For singing, the Herr Direktor,' replied Anna very promptly. 'And then he directs the best of the musical *Vereine* – the clubs, societies, whatever you name them. At least he might try Miss Wedderburn's voice.'

'Who is he?'

'The head of anything belonging to music in the town – *königlicher Musikdirektor*. He conducts all the great concerts, and though he does not sing himself, yet he is one of the best teachers in the province. Lots of people come and stay here on purpose to learn from him.'

'And what are these *Vereine*?'

'Every season there are six great concerts given, and a seventh for the benefit of the Direktor. The orchestra and chorus together are called a *Verein – Musikverein*. The chorus is chiefly composed of ladies and gentlemen – amateurs, you know – *Dilettanten*. The Herr Direktor is very particular about voices. You pay so much for admission, and receive a card for the season. Then you have all the good teaching – the *Proben*.'

'What *is* a Probe?' I demanded hastily, remembering that Courvoisier had used the word.

'What you call a rehearsal.'

Ah! then he was musical. At last I had found it out. Perhaps *he* was one of the amateurs who sang at these concerts, and if so, I might see him again, and if so – But Anna went on:

'It is a very good thing for any one, particularly with such a teacher as von Francius.'

'You must join,' said Miss Hallam to me.

'There is Probe to-night to Rubinstein's "Paradise Lost,"' said Anna. 'I shall go, not to sing, but to listen. I can take Miss Wedderburn, if you like, and introduce her to Herr von Francius, whom I know.'

'Very nice! very much obliged to you. Certainly,' said Miss Hallam.

The Probe was fixed for seven, and shortly after that time we set off for the *Tonhalle*, or concert-hall, in which it was held.

'We shall be much too early,' said she. 'But the people are shamefully late. Most of them only come to *klatsch*, and flirt, or to try to flirt, with the Herr Direktor.'

This threw upon my mind a new light as to the Herr Direktor, and I walked by her side much impressed...

... Meanwhile, Anna took up her parable.

'May I introduce the young lady? Miss Wedderburn, Herr Musik-direktor von Francius. Miss Wedderburn wishes to join the *Verein*, if you think her voice will pass. Perhaps you will allow her to sing to-night?'

'Certainly, *mein Fräulein*,' said he to me, not to Anna. He had a long, rather Jewish-looking face, black hair, eyes, and moustache. The features were thin, fine, and pointed. The thing which most struck me then, at any rate, was a certain expression which, conquering all others, dominated them – at once a hardness and a hardihood which impressed me dis-agreeably then, though I afterwards learnt, in knowing the man, to know much more truly the real meaning of that unflinching gaze and iron look.

'Your voice is what, *mein Fräulein*?' he asked.

'Soprano.'

'Sopran? We will see. The Soprani sit over there, if you will have the goodness.'

He pointed to the left of the orchestra, and called out to the melan-choly-looking young man, 'Herr Schönfeld, a chair for the young lady!'

Herr von Francius then ascended the orchestra, himself went to the piano, and, after a few directions, gave us the signal to begin. Till that day – I confess it with shame – I had never heard of the *Verlorene Paradies*. It came upon me like a revelation. I sang my best, substituting *do, re, mi*, etc.,

95

for the German words. Once or twice, as Herr von Francius' forefinger beat time, I thought I saw his head turn a little in our direction, but I scarcely heeded it. When the first chorus was over, he turned to me:

'You have not sung in a chorus before?'

'No.'

'So! I should like to hear you sing something *sola*.' He pushed towards me a pile of music, and while the others stood looking on and whispering amongst themselves, he went on, 'Those are all sopran songs. Select one, if you please, and try it.'

Not at all aware that the incident was considered unprecedented, and was creating a sensation, I turned over the music, seeking something I knew, but could find nothing. All in German, and all strange. Suddenly I came upon one entitled *Blute nur, liebes Herz*, the sopran solo which I had heard as I sat with Courvoisier in the cathedral. It seemed almost like an old friend. I opened it, and found it had also English words. That decided me.

'I will try this,' said I, showing it to him.

He smiled. ''*S ist gut!*' Then he read the title of the song aloud, and there was a general titter, as if some very great joke were in agitation, and were much appreciated. Indeed I found that in general the jokes of the Herr Direktor, when he condescended to make any, were very keenly relished by at least the lady part of his pupils.

Not understanding the reason of the titter I took the music in my hand, and waiting for a moment until he gave me the signal, sang it after the best wise I could – not *very* brilliantly, I dare say, but with at least all my heart poured into it. I had one requisite at least of an artist nature – I could abstract myself upon occasion completely from my surroundings. I did so now. It was too beautiful, too grand. I remembered that afternoon at Köln – the golden sunshine streaming through the painted windows, the flood of melody poured forth by the invisible singer; above all, I remembered who had been by my side, and I felt as if again beside him – again influenced by the unusual beauty of his face and mien, and by his clear, strange, commanding eyes. It all came back to me – the strangest, happiest day of my life. I sang as I had never sung before – as I had not known I *could* sing.

When I stopped, the tittering had ceased: silence saluted me. The young ladies were all looking at me: some of them had put on their eye-glasses; others stared at me as if I were some strange animal from a menagerie. The young gentlemen were whispering amongst themselves and taking side-long glances at me. I scarcely heeded anything of it. I fixed my eyes upon the judge who had been listening to my performance – upon von Francius. He was pulling his moustache and at first made no remark.

'You have sung that song before, *mein Fräulein?*'

'No. I have heard it once. I have not seen the music before.'

'So!' He bowed slightly, and turning once more to the others, said:

'We will begin the next chorus. Chorus of the Damned. Now, *meine Herrschaften*, I would wish to impress upon you one thing, if I can, that is – Silence, *meine Herren!*' he called sharply towards the tenors, who were giggling inanely amongst themselves. 'A chorus of damned souls,' he proceeded composedly, 'would not sing in the same unruffled manner as a young lady who warbles, "Spring is come – tra la la! Spring is come – lira, lira!" in her mamma's drawing-room. Try to imagine yourself struggling in the tortures of hell – ' (a delighted giggle, and a sort of 'Oh, you dear, wicked man!' expression on the part of the young ladies; a nudging of each other on that of the young gentlemen), 'and *sing as if you were damned.*'

Scarcely any one seemed to take the matter the least earnestly. The young ladies continued to giggle, and the young gentlemen to nudge each other. Little enough of expression, if plenty of noise, was there in that magnificent and truly difficult passage, the changing choruses of the Condemned and the Blessed ones – with its crowning 'WEH!' thundering down from highest sopran to deepest bass.

'Lots of noise, and no meaning,' observed the conductor, leaning himself against the rail of the estrade, face to his audience, folding his arms and surveying them all one after the other with cold self-possession. It struck me that he despised them while he condescended to instruct them. The power of the man struck me again. I began to like him better. At least I venerated his thorough understanding of what was to me a splendid mystery. No softening appeared in the master's eyes in answer to the rows of pretty appealing faces turned to him; no smile upon his contemptuous lips responded to the eyes – black, brown, grey, blue, yellow – all turned with such affecting devotion to his own. Composing himself in an in-souciant attitude, he began in a cool, indifferent voice, which had, however, certain caustic tones in it which stung *me* at least to the quick:

'I never heard anything worse, even from you. My honoured *Fräulein*; my *jungen Herren*; just try *once* to imagine what you are singing about! It is not an exercise – it is not a love song, either of which you would no doubt perform excellently. Conceive what is happening! Put yourself back into those mythical times. Believe, for this evening, in the story of the forfeited Paradise. There is strife between the Blessed and the Damned; the obedient and the disobedient. There are thick clouds in the heavens – smoke, fire, and sulphur – a clashing of swords in the serried ranks of the angels: cannot you see Michael, Gabriel, Raphael, leading the heavenly host? Cannot some of you sympathise a little with *Satan* and his struggle?'

Looking at him, I thought they must indeed be an unimaginative set! in that dark face before them was Mephistopheles at least – *der Geist der stets verneint* – if nothing more violent. His cool, scornful features were lit up with some of the excitement which he could not drill into the assemblage before him. Had he been gifted with the requisite organ he would have acted and sung the chief character in *Faust con amore....*

For my own part, I was deeply moved. A vague excitement, a wild, and not altogether a holy one, had stolen over me. I understood now how the man might have influence. I bent to the power of his will, which reached me where I stood in the background, from his dark eyes, which turned for a moment to me now and then. It was that will of his which put me as it were suddenly into the spirit of the music, and revealed to me depths in my own heart, at which I had never even guessed. Excited, with cheeks burning and my heart hot within me, I followed his words and his gestures, and grew so impatient of the dull stupidity of the others, that tears came to my eyes. How *could* that young woman, in the midst of the chorus, deliberately pause, arrange the knot of her necktie, and then, after a smile and a side-glance at the conductor, go on again with a more self-satisfied simper than ever upon her lips? What might not the thing be with a whole chorus of sympathetic singers? The very dulness which in fact prevailed revealed to me great regions of possible splendour, almost too vast to think of.

At last it was over. I turned to the Director, who was still near the piano, and asked timidly:

'Do you think I may join? Will my voice do?'

An odd expression crossed his face; he answered dryly:

'You may join the *Verein, mein Fräulein* – yes. Please come this way with me. Pardon, Fräulein Stockhausen – another time. I am sorry to say I have business at present.'

(The First Violin)

THOMAS GAINSBOROUGH

A story about sight-reading

To David Garrick, Bath, 27 July 1768

Dear Sir,

... I will tell you a story about *first sight*. You must know, Sir, whilst I lived at Ipswich, there was a benefit concert in which a new song was to be interduced, and I being Steward, went to the honest cabinet-maker who was our singer instead of a better, and asked him if he could sing at sight, for that I had a new song with all the parts wrote out. 'Yes, Sir' said he 'I can'. Upon which I order Mr Giardini of Ipswich to begin the Symphony, & gave my signal for the attention of the company; but behold, a dead silence followed the Symphony instead of the song; upon which I jumped up to the fellow: 'D – n you, why dont you sing? did not you tell me you could sing at first *sight*?'. 'Yes, please your honour, I did say I could sing at sight, but not *first* sight.'

ANNETTA HOFFNUNG

Gerard Hoffnung learning the tuba

Soon after we met, Gerard had confessed to me his love for a particular musical instrument, the tuba. It attracted him both aurally and visually, and it seemed unlikely that he could live much longer without actually possessing one.

The momentous decision was taken. We met at our usual trysting place in Piccadilly. Whenever I reached there first, I would listen as well as watch out for Gerard. Our signature tune (more his than mine, since I was never able to whistle with such strength and verve) was the opening few bars of Bartok's Second Piano Concerto. Above the roar of the traffic I would hear the melody waft towards me before I saw him, and there he would be. On this particular afternoon I detected an air of expectancy and excitement, even of urgency as we greeted each other. 'I thought we might go and look at some tubas this afternoon,' he said.

Tilly, as she became known, was a B flat bombardon and was sitting in the window of Boosey and Hawkes music shop.

She was selected, after careful and lengthy deliberation, from all the other tubas inside the shop. The cheque was signed, and she was ours. Gerard carried her from the shop in his arms, and we walked across Piccadilly to a restaurant in Jermyn Street. The excitement had given Gerard an appetite. We must have appeared a curious trio as we sat at the table, the tuba occupying the third chair. We travelled home by taxi and laid the household's latest acquisition on the kitchen table. For the next three hours we cleaned and polished her, gingerly removing her valves, washing her mouthpiece and generally getting to know the intricacies of

*Gerard
Hoffnung's
happiest purchase*

her plumbing. If I felt a little put out at being confronted with such a mammoth and dirty job on my precious time off (cleaning a tuba is like painting the Forth Bridge – it goes on and on) this was made up for by Gerard's enthusiasm and delight, which knew no bounds. Finally, transformed by our endeavours, she lay there radiant, resplendent and magnificent, glowing shiny and silver, a veritable beauty of an instrument. Exhausted, we made ourselves a cup of tea and sat there for a long time admiring her.

Dear me! How different was the atmosphere next day when I received a telephone call from Gerard. The temperature of the previous day's euphoria had plummeted. Doubts and misgivings had replaced his confidence and optimism. Poor Gerard. A morning spent trying to play his new treasure had left him frustrated and unsettled. 'It sounds more like an elephant in pain,' he said, crestfallen and disgruntled. Marie's objections to the sounds coming from his room added insult to injury. Had he not acted frivolously without careful thought, he asked me? Spent too much money? Should he not take her back to Boosey and Hawkes and forget all about it? Would he ever be able to play the thing? There were very few superficial worries of Gerard's that could not be assuaged with a good meal. By the end of the repast he had reached the conclusion that it was all right on occasions to pander to a whim, that the £20 paid (much money in those days) could be thought of in terms of an investment, that Boosey and Hawkes would probably not be too happy to be asked to take Tilly back, and that he should have a few lessons before prejudging his performance on the instrument.

As Gerard became more ambitious, he was able to throw off longer and more complicated passages of music, and the thought that he might one day soon play in an orchestra became uppermost in his mind. To prepare for such an eventuality he borrowed a second instrument so that now there were two tubas lying on his sofa. The visitor, unlike Tilly, was an orchestral tuba pitched in 'F' and hard to come by in those days. (Later on, in 1955, Boosey and Hawkes made for Gerard the first 'F' tuba manufactured by their company in thirty years.)

Soon after this he journeyed forth to keep a very important appointment, an audition for the position of tuba player in the Ernest Read Junior Orchestra, where he met with a slight setback. 'Everyone in my orchestra has to read music,' said Ernie to Gerard who, having thrown off with admirable virtuosity several well-known themes, (albeit not all of them written for tuba since one of them was definitely the horn virtuoso melody from *Till Eulenspiegel*) was defeated by a request to do some sight reading. 'You'd better go away and learn and come back next week,' Ernie added with a twinkle in his eye.

(*Gerard Hoffnung*)

GERARD MANLEY HOPKINS

'Fallen Rain' and other melodies

Hopkins appears in this book not as the great, long misunderstood poet but as a would-be composer. His extant music and his comments about his preoccupation in his late thirties are reproduced and discussed by John Stevens in Hopkins's *Journals and Papers*, edited by Humphrey House and Graham Storey (OUP, 1959). Here is a taste of them (from two of his letters to Robert Bridges):

'I wish I could pursue music; for I have invented a new style, something standing to ordinary music as sprung rhythm to common rhythm: it employs quarter-tones' (1880).

'Every impulse and spring of art seems to have died in me except music, and that I pursue under almost an impossibility of getting on. Nevertheless I still put down my pieces for the airs seem worth it; they seem to me to have something in them which other modern music has not got' (1881).

I reproduce here 'Fallen Rain', Hopkins's melody for a poem by his Oxford friend R. W. Dixon. (Dixon belonged to a 'Set' which included William Morris, a more robust poet, already in print.) Hopkins literally fell in love with the poem. (He seldom attempted to set his own verse.) He was clearly a gifted melodist, wholly out of step with his prevailing culture, which was saturated in the plink-plonk rhythm and conventional harmony of drawing-room ballads: see the contemptuous 'Klesmer' in George Eliot's *Daniel Deronda* (pp. 89–91). His music in 'the secret catgut of the mind', as he once called it, was an extension of his own verbal lyricism. Consciously or unconsciously, Hopkins looked back to ancient Greek modes, Gregorian chant, the speech rhythms of seventeenth-century

FALLEN RAIN
(R. W. Dixon)

The symbol ° in bar 48 denotes a vocal quarter-tone (Hopkins autograph)

Words 1879
Melody 1881
Acct. 1993

105

'declamatory airs' (compare Pepys's similar trouble with harmonisation, pp. 119–23) – and English composers, unborn or unknown in 1880, who could have struck off Hopkins's musical fetters: Holst, Finzi, Britten, Tippett...

His melody for 'Fallen Rain', he wrote to Dixon in 1881, 'is so very peculiar that I cannot trust anyone to harmonise it.' (Note, by the way, his scrupulous notation.) To excuse my own strictly unprofessional attempt, Hopkins the frustrated composer deserves an admirer's tribute, making use of musical hindsight. For instance, both Gustav Holst and Frank Bridge set songs with violin or viola alone. Hopkins on a visit to the Victoria and Albert Museum was fascinated by the collection of early stringed instruments, and elsewhere he expressed a preference for string sonority (and spare harmonies) over piano 'infill'.

Stevens (op. cit., pp. 461–3) finds in Hopkins's melodies, as in his poetry, a paradoxical determination to use the 'native and natural', combined with the highest degree of 'heightening' and 'markedness'. I have tried to reflect these sudden changes in weather.

PAUL JENNINGS

The Philharmonia Chorus on tour

There can be few greater joys in life than being paid for what you enjoy doing (unless it's being paid for doing *nothing*, like a shareholder, but I've no experience of this); though doubtless it is mere naïve amateur's ideal-ism to imagine professional orchestral players going to every rehearsal with happy beams of anticipation. I daresay there are times when many of them feel towards their instrument the way I feel towards my typewriter – only happy when I've *done* it. All the same, in a funny, paradoxical kind of way, the choral singer, whether or not he is a spoiled pianist like me, does have a kind of legitimised short cut to musical joys. . . .

Of course one may find oneself singing (preferably in Russian) in Shostakovich 13, of a store where 'wordless, the women come, with the clanking of cans, the chinking of bottles. They smell of onions, cucumbers and Kabul sauce,' or bawling the strophic vulgarities of *Carmina Burana*. But on the whole the choral repertoire does aim, well, *cosmically* high. What does it matter if the *Missa Solemnis* was once thought not to be strictly Catholic? No saint ever pondered more deeply or expressed more universally the meaning of a word like *miserere* or *suscipe* or *dona*, those imploring, desperate imperatives, than Beethoven did. . . .

Of course, you don't need to smell of incense to be a choir freak (in fact I'm willing to bet that today the word *Sanctus*, for instance, is uttered by more agnostic singers than practising Catholics). Nor do you need to be attached to a large orchestral outfit (any four competent voices can enjoy the miracle of the *Dona nobis pacem* at the end of the Byrd four-part mass). But it is in the great works that you have the feeling of participating as much as the professionals and the soloists; as another writer once put it, 'today's composers in their isolated scratchy mathematical worlds don't seem to have the social confidence to assemble these vast expectant forces, the great rows of singers and the shining instruments under the towering organ.'

All of us who were lucky enough to be in the Klemperer *Missa* or the Frühbeck *Elijah* were as much part of it as Elizabeth Söderström or Fischer-Dieskau. And after all, who gets more to *sing* in *Messiah* – the tenor soloist or the tenor in the chorus? Of course one of the glories of the whole thing is that this amazing sense of communion, of being fused with other people in a supreme artistic effort, has to do with the special English ability to combine the amateur choir with the professional orchestra. If you are a writer or painter and are any good, people have only to read the first hundred words or see one picture to say 'I know who did *that*,' and theoretically the same is true of singers. You can't have a choir of individual artists. I've always thought that a large professional choir, apart from being a financial impossibility, is almost a contradiction in terms; so I was agog to hear what those uniquely gathered 125 professionals doing the *Choral* Symphony under Solti in the penultimate Prom would sound like. Well of course it was magnificent and very precise and very loud and very quick and with a look-it's-easy feeling that amateurs couldn't match. But it wasn't as much better than any good British chorus as any one of them singing, say, a Schubert *Lied* would be incomparably better than any one of us. I'd like to hear them make such a magic loving sound as the plagal-cadence *Amen* to the Bruckner *Ave Maria* on Pitz's old Philharmonia record.

I love rehearsals. Especially orchestra rehearsals. You get to the Festival Hall early enough some Sunday morning, often nobody there but the harp girls, who always seem to be first. Then maybe John McGaw, sending marvellous tootling roulades from his clarinet. A few strings. Flute. And all the time, chorus members, creeping quietly in (maybe some marvellous overture before it's us). Then, all of us. The raised baton. All of us, in *the* communal art.

(*Classical Music*)

DAVID LASCELLES

Making the grade on the horn

The french horn, I suspect, occupies a special place in most people's affections: that rich muffled sound, those glorious twirls of brass, that proneness to parody exploited by Flanders and Swann.

But I must assure anyone who holds to this loveable image that it could not be further from the truth. One year after taking it up, I can state with some authority that the french horn is the most devilish instrument ever devised by man: it is a femme fatale, a siren whose call should never be answered.

Not that I regret that fateful spring day when I walked into Paxman's in Covent Garden, the Foyle's of the french horn world. It is far too late for that. The deed is done, and I am now in its thrall; I labour daily to win its favour, I torture my lips to make it sound, I anoint its intricate moving parts with no fewer than three varieties of oil. I have even bought the score of Mozart's fourth horn concerto, and have made mastery of that famous Rondo my life's work.

Had I known what I know now, I might have stayed my hand as I pushed open Paxman's door (whose handle is even the shape of a french horn). But it seemed such a good idea. I had been a mediocre piano player for 20 years and needed a change. My children were both learning new instruments and deserved a good parental example. My doctor even told me it would be good for my health – a slight asthma problem. When my neighbour's daughter at the Royal Academy of Music offered to give me lessons, I needed no further urging.

The horn itself cost some 400 pounds sterling, which is not cheap. But I quickly found that horn players, endearingly stricken as they are with their own instruments, are incapable of agreeing on what 'a good horn' is, or of offering useful advice. So I was left to the mercy of the man in the shop who was under the impression for a few minutes that I wanted to borrow the horn to use it as a prop in a TV commercial. 'That's what most people want them for,' he said.

For the first month I managed only to produce sounds that might have summoned a cow seeking her distressed calf. The trick is to blow a raspberry into the horn's finely honed mouthpiece (the most delicate of the brass family) with air summoned from deep in the belly. (Try coughing and feel your diaphragm move – that's what it's all about. Most people just blow from their throats.)

The horn only respects air that has risen from your deepest innards. Offer it anything less, and it will mock you by making a hideous sound, or by blaring out a note quite different to the one you intended. There is also the constant embarrassment of having to dispose of large quantities of water that collects in the tubes. The advice from my teacher was just to tip it out on to the carpet. 'It's only condensed air,' she said. But that was hard to get used to.

After three months in which I spent as much time exercising my diaphragm in front of a mirror as I did with my lips to the mouthpiece, I could play a simple tune, Haydn's St Anthony Chorale, with each note requiring an enormous effort of concentration. But I was making good progress and I got the rash idea that I should go for a musical grade.

The syllabus for Grade Three (the lowest for the horn) consisted of two set pieces, one classical and one modern, a study, three scales and musical theory. I toiled at them all through the winter, half an hour in the morning and half an hour in the evening too if I had the strength. If you leave off the horn for a few days, your lips quickly go flabby, so I got into the habit of taking the mouthpiece with me on business trips, and tootled away quietly in hotel rooms.

Finally, on a bright, chilly afternoon in March I drove out to a house in Finchley for my exam, where I was due to perform after a violinist aged seven. It was, I realised, the first time I had submitted myself to a test of any kind for nearly two decades. Although my examiner – a nice chatty man with glasses – went out of his way to put me at my ease, I was stricken by a dreadful fit of nervousness and my lips went dry – fatal. The room also echoed strangely, and I found all my sounds coming straight back at me. I

Giovanni Punto, Mozart's horn virtuoso

performed poorly, and reckoned I had at best just scraped through (I was hoping that the examiner would pity a struggling adult).

I was right, as it turned out. Three weeks later a certificate arrived in the post informing me that I scored 110 out of a possible 150, with a 100 passmark. The comment said that my playing had weaknesses, (true, I admit) but that I had obviously worked hard on my pieces (oh so true). It filled me with an unexpected sense of pride. It also left me little choice but to go on and scale the towering peak of Grade Four.

Supercilious string players may say that the horn always sounds the same, that its repertoire is limited and there are really only three major composers for the solo instrument, Telemann, Mozart and Richard Strauss. It may also be true that most horn players end up playing rather dull background parts in orchestral pieces (though horn players in opera orchestras have more fun, especially with Wagner). But violinists, let's face it, are three a penny, and anyone can scrape horsehair on gut. To make music from eight intractable feet of brass piping – that takes something special.

(*Financial Times*)

WILLIAM HASLAM MILLS

People seldom know the names of great journalists in the first half of the century because at that time serious newspapers did not give staff writers bylines. To emerge in their own right, they had to become novelists or historians or critics: Howard Spring or J. L. Hammond or Neville Cardus, for example. But all of them they looked up, not down, at Haslam Mills, Chief Reporter of the *Manchester Guardian* in the first two decades of the century. He was born into 'Chapel' culture and his essays appear in an evocative – and elusive – book called *Grey Pastures* (1924).

Forty years later, when I joined that reporters' room in Cross Street, Manchester – a historic building now demolished – I sat opposite a fine photograph of Mills. It revealed something of the aesthete, even the dandy, but also the piercing eyes of a good commander. Arnold Bennett noticed this, on a day he spent observing the *Manchester Guardian* for his own purposes (*Journal*): 'Mills has a good manner, which he has conventionalised and hardened, of telling yarns.' David Ayerst, the *Guardian*'s own historian, caught another side of the Chief Reporter during the 1909 General Election. Winston Churchill (then a Liberal minister) was campaigning in Lancashire for what we now know as the first flickers of the Welfare State. The paper assigned five shorthand reporters for verbatim reports of the speeches next morning, for there was no radio, no television.... Mills sat apart to imbibe and convey the colour, the excitement – and the historical perspective. Quoting some of this, Ayerst wrote: 'A good sketch writer, like Mills, can be to the speaker something of what an accompanist is to the singer.'

Pitch pine and rosin dust

It had once been a chapel. So much was clear from its oblong configuration – a building in which it had been more important to hear than to see, with two shallow galleries and a deep one facing the stage. And as they were still using up quantities of maroon brocade with tassels, I judged it to have been a Dissenting chapel, belonging to one of the more recondite sects, small in number and very dainty of belief, for maroon hangings are the mark of the higher Nonconformity, just as white lawn is the mark of the Church of England and purple velvet that of Rome. When and at what conjecture in the rise and fall of faiths it became a music-hall I hardly know, but if one came early, when the audience was still arriving in ones and twos, it might still have been a chapel, and the tilting of the plush seats punctuated one's reverie very much like the desultory opening and shutting of pew doors – the same note of preparation for a quiet, customary event. But here the illusion ceased, for instead of the pulpit with its plush and morocco, the *carafe* of water with the down-turned glass, and the demure glimmer of light through an egg-shell globe, there was a drop-curtain, and on the drop-curtain a highly seductive view of life on the North Coast of Africa, with the god Pan playing some part.

For my part I never thought he had enough elbow-room for a mannered instrument like the violin. The brass rail which cut off the orchestra from the stalls irked him, and his hand used to beat softly against the curtain when he was hard at work on his top string. Once when I was on the front row of the stalls he even smote me on the knee with his knuckle. The assault occurred in the fluent passage of 'Raymond,' and he opened his pale-blue eyes and glanced at me along the slope of the instrument, hoping that I should understand. And then when he was on his low string he had to allow for the neck of the other 'first,' a pathetic figure so placed as to have no view whatever of the stage, though when the house was convulsed he would pop up and peer over the stage, still sawing.

And yet the First Violin was not without learning in the technique of his art, and particularly was he skilled in the reading of obscure and not infrequently corrupt musical text. Much journeying to and fro in the jungle of song and badinage and dance had given him fortitude for the doubling back of the path and a kind of instinct for the right way through. And this, though the finger-posts were laconic and far between! Several

113

sheets of blank music-paper and then in the middle of a page in a spiky hand the words 'Father Brings the Milk Home in the Morning' and two thumb-marks! The treble of the refrain pushes on with sudden volubility for several bars, and then a long passage has been scored out by someone who seems to have been in a temper, and the thread is resumed over the next page but one, and is pursued through a good deal of ambiguity and some sticking-plaster, until suddenly out of the mist there shoots an alarming rocket of semi-quavers. The chorus is repeated as often as it suffices Miss Wax Vesta to change for the next song. The First Violin has got to know it – he lets it go. And Miss Vesta having signalled that she is ready, the conductor taps twice and stops matters on a chord which is still unresolved. The First Violin makes no protest. He turns over his manu-script. 'I'm a Dashing Militaire,' remarks the spiky hand, and Miss Vesta herself appears – a very final corroboration of the announcement. She walks several times the breadth of the stage to induce that *rapport* between herself and the audience which is a condition of her art. Incidentally she hums the melody hard through her teeth, bringing the orchestra by the scruff of its neck into the rhythm. The First Violin glances from her to his music and back to her again, anxious to be taught. By and by he has it right. His violin is frosty with resin-dust for a considerable area around the bridge.

But I admire him most at those moments when the orchestra, having made a false start, gathers round and becomes a parliament of clashing and conflicting views; when the voice of an unseen presence at the wings is hissing 'No, no, the Spring Song'; when the dancer on whom the curtain has just risen is held up against a black-velvet background in an effective preliminary attitude of some constraint which in the anatomical nature of things she cannot preserve much longer. The conductor is receiving suggestions from right and left, from the cornet player who has removed his instrument an inch from his mouth to enforce a theory which he holds rather strongly – from everybody except the broad-backed man at the piano, who sits deep down and in some detachment, and to whom, however they settle it, it is sure to resolve itself into 'pom' with the left and 'pom-pom' with the right. I suspect the First Violin on such occasions of a tendency to giggle; certainly there is in his eye a cheerful recognition of the fact that in art as in life the ideal is always some way ahead. He glances to this effect at the derisive audience over his brass rail, and when eventually they find the right place and the voice at the wings is appeased and the lady on the stage released, he goes on as though nothing worth mentioning had occurred – a happy warrior!

Two ducks shouldered through the ornamental water, sitting deep – saying something fretful. They left four oblique curling rollers behind them as they swam. On this Sunday morning they were the only entertainment in the recreation ground, for a third duck in deep apathy on a stony island was not spectacular. The smoke from a row of new houses over the palings beat down over the geometrical flowerbeds, and on everything beneath a grey, racing sky there was an unevaporated ooze – on the metal battledores which warned one off the grass, on all the cast-iron in which the recreation ground is rich, on the swings which stood like the gallows in an asphalt annexe. Down the path, the centre of a fidgety family group, came the First Violin. His right hand was on the brass rail of a perambulator; in his other hand there was a newspaper with a slab of reading matter turned up. But the reading went slowly, for the youngest but one, who was coming to years of indiscretion, exhibited a stubborn preference for walking over the benches along the path, a mode of progression which involved a good deal of quarrelling with his kindred and some risk. The First Violin intervened in the dispute at regular intervals. Once he was busy for some time extracting damp gravel from the knees and palms of the youngest but one. And none of those who looked on but I, knew that he led a band, sat night by night in the draught which comes from the little door under the stage, the draught which is nectarously flavoured with an escape of gas; that he co-operated in public with the accepted wits – that ladies who were 'the rage' dragged him by the scruff of his neck into the rhythm of a song. Slowly the family group worked its way home – twice round the ornamental water and into the road, the perambulator agitated violently on the stones. Progress was hampered all the way home by the inability of the youngest but two to be satisfied until he had touched with his five fingers each separate garden railing they passed. More than once the First Violin turned and called him on, urging the nearness of dinner-time. And then he was gathered into the empty distances of rather a long street. It was off hours with the First Violin.

Hallelujah to obbligato tea-cups

... Christmas Day was no carnival with our choir. On Christmas morning they had their last rehearsal, drifting in twos and threes to the place of practice with Novello editions under their arms. There are pitfalls in the 'Messiah' of which the most nimble contrapuntalist is not sure till he is safely past them. There is that penultimate Hallelujah, the one before the clincher, the one that hangs poised on the abyss – that abyss which tingles with the possibility of a sensational and solitary disaster. On Christmas morning the choir could be heard achieving the ultimate polish – 'Wonderful! Counsellor! the Mighty God! the Everlasting Father! the Prince of Peace!' It broke sharp and sudden as artillery fire over the deserted street, where only a stray milk-cart crunched the quiet snow; and to this day I cannot hear the opening bars of 'Comfort ye' but there breaks in upon the suavity and certitude of the melody the tinkle through a distant door of tea-cups as the schoolkeeper's wife and two odd women began to get forward with the washing-up. I also see the steam on the school windows beginning to be profuse.

(*Grey Pastures*)

HENRY PEACHAM

Every gentleman must keep his part

The physicians will tell you that the exercise of music is a great lengthener of the life by stirring and reviving of the spirits, holding a secret sympathy with them. Besides, the exercise of singing openeth the breast and pipes. It is an enemy to melancholy and dejection of the mind, which St Chrysostom truly calleth 'the Devil's Bath.' Yea, a curer of some diseases: in Apulia, in Italy, and thereabouts it is most certain that those who are stung ith the tarantula are cured only by music. Besides the aforesaid benefit of singing, it is a most ready help for a bad pronunciation and distinct speaking, which I have heard confirmed by many great divines. Yea, I myself have known many children to have been holpen of their stammering in speech only by it. . . .

I might run into an infinite sea of the praise and use of so excellent an art, but I only show it you with the finger because I desire not that any noble or gentleman should, save at his private recreation and leisurable hours, prove a master in the same or neglect his more weighty employments, though I avouch it a skill worthy the knowledge and exercise of the greatest prince.

King Henry the Eighth could not only sing his part sure but of himself compose a service of four, five, and six parts, as Erasmus in a certain epistle testifieth of his own knowledge.

The Duke of Venosa, an Italian prince, in like manner of late years hath given excellent proof of his knowledge and love to music, having himself composed many rare songs, which I have seen.

But above others who carrieth away the palm for excellency, not only in music, but in whatsoever is to be wished in a brave prince, is the yet-living Maurice, Landgrave of Hesse, of whose own composition I have seen eight or ten several sets of motets and solemn music set purposely for his own chapel, where, for the great honor of some festival, and many times for his recreation only, he is his own organist. Besides, he readily speaketh ten or twelve several languages. He is so universal a scholar that, coming, as he doth often, to his University of Marburg, what questions soever he meeteth with set up, as the manner is in the German and our universities, he will extempore dispute an hour or two, even in boots and spurs, upon them with their best professors. I pass over his rare skill in chirurgery, he being generally accounted the best bonesetter in the country. Who have seen his estate, his hospitality, his rich-furnished armory, his brave stable of great horses, his courtesy to all strangers, being men of quality and good parts, let them speak the rest.

But since the natural inclination of some men driveth them, as it were, perforce to the top of excellency, examples of this kind are very rare; yea, great personages many times are more violently carried than might well stand with their honors and necessity of their affairs; yet were it to these honest and commendable exercises savoring of virtue, it were well. But many, neglecting their duties and places, will addict themselves wholly to trifles and the most ridiculous and childish practices: As Europus, King of Macedonia, took pleasure only in making of candles; Domitian his recreation was to catch and kill flies, and could not be spoken with many times in so serious employment; Ptolomaeus Philadelphus was an excellent smith and a basket-maker; Alphonse Atestino, Duke of Ferrara, delighted himself only in turning and playing the joiner; Rodolph, the late emperor, in setting of stones and making watches; which and the like much eclipse state and majesty, bringing familiarity and, by consequence, contempt with the meanest.

I desire no more in you than to sing your part sure and at the first sight withal to play the same upon your viol or the exercise of the lute, privately, to yourself.

(*The Complete Gentleman*)

SAMUEL PEPYS

If there is a single individual in any century who typifies the enthusiasms and skills celebrated in this book, it is Samuel Pepys, the diarist of the 1660s who spent his career putting British naval administration on to a professional footing. 'Everyone knows Pepys', people say, but everyone doesn't. Paradoxically, we are blinded by his dazzling readability and catholicity, cramming so many passions, pastimes and perceptions, often in a single day's entry. It is hard to focus.

However, for another specialist purpose* I combed the entire *Diary* in the magnificent Latham and Matthews edition (Bell & Hyman, 1970–83) with the help of the eleventh volume, the Index, for passages that illustrate Pepys's serious appetite for food and drink. In that Index there are a similar number of musical references – some 2000 – and most of them mention participant music-making, rather than listening to other people's. Yet at the outset of the first Restoration decade Pepys was aged 27, just appointed to the reconstituted Navy Board as Clerk of the Acts. The whole *Diary* reflects the ambitious, assiduous and omni-competent civil servant. Yet even in the middle of an anxious naval war with the Dutch, on a day (30 July 1666) much concerned with sea tactics and Admiralty victualling, he ended the evening with domestic singing, because 'music is the thing of the world that I love most, and all the pleasure almost that I can now take.' (That 'almost' perhaps covers the afternoon he took off with his favourite pretty widow, Mrs Burroughs, a fortnight previously.)

Pepys played at least six musical instruments: lute and theorbo; viols of different sizes; violin; flageolet; recorder. He could hold his part as a bass-baritone in semi-professional company in church services and private occasions

* *Pepys at Table* (Unwin Hyman, 1985).

and when he came to have his portrait painted, by Kneller, he is seen holding the 'declamatory air' of his own composition, called 'Beauty Retire'. His passion for musical sound and sense is best expressed in a classic passage (below), which was omitted by Anthony Storr's discussion of musical 'ecstasy' or 'transport' in his recent book, *Music and the Mind* (1992).

The only obvious gaps in Pepys's musical equipment were keyboard facility (though he could tune his virginals) and harmonic understanding. But in his time, as Richard Luckett explains in the *Companion* to the *Diary* (vol.10), musical theory and notation were in flux. The medieval system based on the 'hexachord' and the 'gamut' (for a brief explanation, see the *Oxford Companion to Music*) was gradually giving way to the 'figured bass' or continuo line which underpinned the interplay of melody and sufficed for a century from Purcell and Corelli, through Bach and Handel, to the First Viennese School. But in the mid-seventeenth century there were no intelligible text-books for the would-be amateur composer. Poor Pepys: he spent more time and energy than he could afford on 'conning the gamut' (as in *The Taming of the Shrew*, p. 124) and trying to create a bass line for his tunes. Gerard Manley Hopkins as a composer (pp. 103–6) had the same problem.

Instrumental style was in the middle of a revolution too. During the Puritan Commonwealth, domestic music-making was conservative: polyphony played by a 'chest of viols' at different pitches. The fretted lute family used Tudor tablature, not staff notation. But as soon as Charles II returned from his travels he insisted on dance music from France and Italy, played by incisive violins and woodwind. Hence Pepys's diversification into a fiddle and a recorder. He was that rarity in any period, a serious follower of fashion.

A 17th-century player of both flageolet and viol

23 February 1666.... I set them down at the Change, and I home to the office, and at noon dined at home, and to the office again. Anon comes Mrs Knipp to see my wife, who is gone out; so I fain to entertain her, and took her out by coach to look my wife at Mrs Pierces and Unthankes, but find her not; so back again, and then my wife comes home, having been buying of things. And at home I spent all the night talking with this baggage [Mrs Knipp] and teaching her my song of *Beauty retire*, which she sings and makes go most rarely, and a very fine song it seems to be. She also entertained me with repeating many of her own and others' parts of the play-house, which she doth most excellently; and tells me the whole practices of the play-house and players, and is in every respect most excellent company. So I supped, and was merry at home all the evening, and the rather it being my Birthday, 33 years – for which God be praised that I am in so good a condition of health and state and everything else as I am, beyond expectation in all. So she to Mrs Turner's to lie, and we to bed – mightily pleased to find myself in condition to have these people come about me, and to be able to entertain them and have the pleasure of their qualities, then which no man can have more in this world.

24. All the morning at the office, till past 3 a-clock. At that hour home and eat a bit alone, my wife being gone out. So abroad by coach with Mr Hill, who stayed for me to speak about business; and he and I to Hales's, where I find my wife and her woman, and Pierce and Knipp, and there sung and was mighty merry, and I joyed myself in it; but vexed at first, to find my wife's picture not so good as I expected; but it was only his having finished one part, and not another, of the face; but before I went, I was satisfied it will be an excellent picture. Here we had ale and cakes, and mighty merry and sung my song, which she now sings rarely, and makes me proud of myself.

Thence left my wife to go home with Mrs Pierce, while I home to the office; and there pretty late, and to bed – after fitting myself for tomorrow's journey.

1 March 1666.... Being returned home, I find Greeting the flagelette-master come and teaching my wife; and I do think my wife will take pleasure in it, and it will be easy for her and pleasant – so I, as I am well contented with the charge it will occasion me.

So to the office till dinner, busy; and then home to dinner, and before dinner making my wife to sing; poor wretch, her ear is so bad that it made me angry, till the poor wretch cried to see me so vexed at her, that I think I shall not discourage her so much again but will endeavour to make her understand sounds and do her good that way, for she hath a great mind to learn, only to please me; and therefore I am mighty unjust to her in discouraging her so much. But we were good friends, and to bed.

30 July 1666. . . . Thence home, and to sing with my wife and Mercer in the garden; and coming in, I find my wife plainly dissatisfied with me, that I can spend so much time with Mercer, teaching her to sing, and could never take that pains with her – which I acknowledge; but it is because that the girl doth take music mighty readily, and she doth not; and music is the thing of the world that I love most, and all the pleasure almost that I can now take. So to bed in some little discontent, but no words from me.

15 September 1667. . . . Mr Turner and his wife and their son the Captain dined with me, and I had a very good dinner for them – and very merry; and after dinner he was forced to go, though it rained, to Stepny to preach. We also to church, and then home, and there comes Mr Pelling with two men by promise, one Wallington and Piggott; the former whereof, being a very little fellow, did sing a most excellent bass, and yet a poor fellow, a working goldsmith, that goes without gloves to his hands. Here we sung several good things, but I am more and more confirmed that singing with many voices is not singing, but a sort of Instrumentall music, the sense of the words being lost by not being heard, and especially as they set them with Fuges of words, one after another; whereas singing properly, I think, should be but with one or two voices at most, and that counterpoint. They supped with me; and so broke up, and then my wife and I to my chamber, where through the badness of my eyes she was forced to read to me, which she doth very well; and was Mr Boyle's discourse upon the Style of the Scripture, which is a very fine piece. And so to bed.

27 February 1668. All the morning at the office, and at noon home to dinner; and thence with my wife and Deb to the King's House to see *Virgin Martyr*, the first time it hath been acted a great while, and it is mighty pleasant; not that the play is worth much, but it is finely Acted by Becke Marshall; but that which did please me beyond anything in the whole world was the wind-musique when the Angell comes down, which is so sweet that it ravished me; and endeed, in a word, did wrap up my soul so that it made me really sick, just as I have formerly been when in love with my wife; that neither then, nor all the evening going home and at home, I was able to think of anything, but remained all night transported, so as I could not believe that ever any music hath that real command over the soul of a man as this did upon me; and makes me resolve to practise wind-music and to make my wife do the like.

8 April 1668.... So home to my chamber, to be *fingering* of my Recorder and getting of the scale of Musique [the gamut: the contemporary method of naming the notes of the scale] without book, which I at last see is necessary, for a man that would understand music as it is now taught, to understand, though it be a ridiculous and troublesome way and I know I shall be able hereafter to show the world a simpler way. But like the old Hypotheses in philosophy, it must be learned, though a man knows a better.

(*Diary*)

WILLIAM SHAKESPEARE

Bianca's lute lesson on the gamut

ACT III

Scene I. *Padua.* BAPTISTA'S *house.*

Enter LUCENTIO, HORTENSIO, *and* BIANCA.

LUC. Fiddler, forbear; you grow too forward, sir:
  Have you so soon forgot the entertainment
  Her sister Katharine welcomed you withal?
HOR. But, wrangling pedant, this is
  The patroness of heavenly harmony:
  Then give me leave to have prerogative;
  And when in music we have spent an hour,
  Your lecture shall have leisure for as much.
LUC. Preposterous ass, that never read so far
  To know the cause why music was ordain'd!
  Was it not to refresh the mind of man
  After his studies or his usual pain?
  Then give me leave to read philosophy,
  And while I pause, serve in your harmony.
HOR. Sirrah, I will not bear these braves of thine.
BIAN. Why, gentlemen, you do me double wrong,
  To strive for that which resteth in my choice:
  I am no breeching scholar in the schools;
  I'll not be tied to hours nor 'pointed times,
  But learn my lessons as I please myself.

124

And, to cut off all strife, here sit we down:
Take you your instrument, play you the whiles;
His lecture will be done ere you have tuned.

HOR.   You'll leave his lecture when I am in tune?

LUC.   That will be never: tune your instrument.

BIAN.   Where left we last?

LUC.   Here, madam:
'Hic ibat Simois; hic est Sigeia tellus;
Hic steterat Priami regia celsa senis.'

BIAN.   Construe them.

LUC.   'Hic ibat,' as I told you before, 'Simois,'
I am Lucentio, 'hic est,' son unto Vincentio of Pisa, 'Sigeia tellus,'
disguised thus to get your love; 'Hic steterat,' and that Lucentio that
comes a-wooing, 'Priami,' is my man Tranio, 'regia,' bearing my
port, 'celsa senis,' that we might beguile the old pantaloon.

HOR.   Madam, my instrument's in tune.

BIAN.   Let's hear. O fie! the treble jars.

LUC.   Spit in the hole, man, and tune again.

BIAN.   Now let me see if I can construe it:
'Hic ibat Simois,' I know you not, 'hic est Sigeia tellus,' I trust you not;
'Hic steterat Priami,' take heed he hear us not, 'regia,' presume not,
'celsa senis,' despair not.

HOR. Madam, 'tis now in tune.

LUC.   All but the base.

HOR.   The base is right; 'tis the base knave that jars.
[*Aside*] How fiery and forward our pedant is!
Now, for my life, the knave doth court my love:
Pedascule, I'll watch you better yet.

BIAN.   In time I may believe, yet I mistrust.

LUC.   Mistrust it not; for, sure, Æacides
Was Ajax, call'd so from his grandfather.

BIAN.   I must believe my master; else, I promise you,
I should be arguing still upon that doubt:
But let it rest. Now, Licio, to you:
Good masters, take it not unkindly, pray,
That I have been thus pleasant with you both.

HOR.   You may go walk, and give me leave a while:
My lessons make no music in three parts.

125

LUC.   Are you so formal, sir? well, I must wait,
   [*Aside*] And watch withal; for, but I be deceived,
     Our fine musician groweth amorous.
HOR.   Madam, before you touch the instrument,
   To learn the order of my fingering,
   I must begin with rudiments of art;
   To teach you gamut in a briefer sort,
   More pleasant, pithy and effectual,
   Than hath been taught by any of my trade:
   And there it is in writing, fairly drawn.
BIAN.   Why, I am past my gamut long ago.
HOR.   Yet read the gamut of Hortensio.
BIAN. [*Reads*] '"Gamut" I am, the ground of all accord,
   'A re,' to plead Hortensio's passion;
   'B mi,' Bianca, take him for thy lord,
   'C fa ut,' that loves with all affection:
   'D sol re,' one clef, two notes have I:
   'E la mi,' show pity, or I die.'
   Call you this gamut? tut, I like it not:
   Old fashions please me best; I am not so nice,
   To change true rules for old inventions.

                        (*The Taming of the Shrew*)

ALLISTER SPARKS

∽∾

The Soweto Quartet

It is a long way from Mozart to Soweto. Jazz is Africa's métier: the thumping high life of the West Coast, the rock big bands of Zaire and the lively penny whistle tunes of South Africa's black townships. But a string quartet? Man, that's whitey's stuff. Not any more, it isn't.

In yet another reflection of the changes taking place in this transitional society, the Soweto String Quartet has emerged from its turbulent ghetto to enchant audiences, both white and black, with a polished repertoire of Mozart, Haydn, Bach and Elgar.

It has existed for several years, but was known only to a handful of *cognoscenti* and foreign embassies. Now it is in demand everywhere.

On Friday night it performed to a packed hall at the University of the Witwatersrand at a celebration of the magnificent African hymn 'Nkosi Sikelel i'Africa' (God Bless Africa), which is likely to be South Africa's new national anthem. In fact, that is what it is all about – a synthesis of cultures. Not only is a black group taking classical Western culture to the townships, it is bringing township culture to the classics as well.

Sandile Khemese, the 36-year-old leader of the group, has taken traditional African music and popular township jazz melodies and re-arranged them into classical forms. The result is a new genre of classical music. 'This must be our trademark,' says Sandile. He wants to try innovations to develop the African theme, such as adding a percussion player to the quartet.

The group's story is one of triumph over adversity. It began when Sandile first picked up a violin at the age of eight. His father ran a local church choir and his uncle, who owned the violin, had taken music lessons and learnt some classical pieces.

Every Saturday Sandile trudged four miles across Soweto to play with a small youth orchestra in a venue called Uncle Tom's Hall. Soon he was giving his two younger brothers, Malusi and Thamsanqa Khemese, lessons. Later, a friend, Makhosini Mnguni, who played the trumpet in a jazz band, switched to the violin and joined them. Makhosini now plays the viola and Malusi the cello, while Sandile and Thamsanqa are first and second violinists.

It was tough. 'We were a laughing stock among our friends,' Sandile recalls. 'They thought we were weird, playing white music.' The four carried their instruments in paper bags to avoid taunts. In 1980, Sandile won a scholarship to study music in Britain. He returned six years later and reassembled the quartet which last year played at South Africa's premier arts event, the Cape Arts Festival.

It is still not easy. They fit in their playing between factory jobs; none of them even has a record player to hear world-class performances. But they are undaunted. 'I live for and I live through my violin,' says Sandile. 'There are frustrating moments, but the violin has accepted me.'

(*The Observer*)

JONATHAN STEINBERG

On practising

Barnaby, who is six, was trying to play the note G on the descant recorder. He had already mastered the notes A and B, and if he could get G right, he could begin to play *Three Blind Mice*, an entirely worthy musical ambition.

The trouble was that every time he put his third finger on to the hole, he moved one of the fingers which were already covering holes higher up the bore of the instrument. Air leaked and produced that screeching noise only too familiar to parents of children in primary schools. The massed bands of recorder players at Christmas productions in the nation's junior schools – all blowing too hard into plastic recorders, none of which has been tuned or warmed before the event – probably produce as much suffering among parents and teachers as any other single cultural activity.

Barnaby was clearly suffering, too. I tried to hold his index and middle finger down while he played the note G. That worked beautifully and a nice round G sounded. As soon as I took my grip off, his fingers began to slip again. He just couldn't manage to move the third finger without affecting the other two. After about 15 minutes we pretended that it had been, really, quite a good practice, and that we would try again tomorrow. Barnaby smiled consolingly at me. He knew and I knew that we had both failed, and off he went with his little plastic descant drooping in his hand.

I knew Barnaby's despair only too well. I had just suffered the same humiliating defeat with the alternative E flat key on the oboe. Every time I reached for it with the little finger of my left hand, the third finger slipped and uncovered its hole. The sound produced, a kind of hoarse squawking, drove me to distraction. What is more, Barnaby had only suffered a

129

morning of frustration. I had been trying to master that unspeakable, alternative E flat for several weeks.

The next day Barnaby came over for his practice. We were both a little nervous. We began cautiously with the note B, which merely involves the thumb and first finger. Barnaby blew a mellow and satisfying B. We added the second finger, and out came an equally round A. Now the moment came to try the dreaded G again. Barnaby put his third finger down firmly. The first and second fingers stayed in place, and a lovely, clear G came out. What is more it came out every time. He played G and then A over and over again in strict, if slow, time, as if his fingers had always known where to go. The glow on his face as he went home would have lit up a darkened room.

I knew from experience that Barnaby's triumph was bound to happen, because I had been through that curious transformation too often myself. Weeks of frustration and awful noise followed by a sudden achievement, as if I had always been able to play it. I may say that now I can use the alternative E flat, but am having a lot of trouble with the B major scale instead.

But Barnaby did not know that his little drama would have a happy ending. How could he? If I had not been there to suffer with him and, more important, to make certain that he showed up the next day to try again, he could have been forgiven for hurling his descant out the window.

I know that temptation well myself. All over the country music teachers and parents are telling their children to go and practise. But THEY NEVER TELL THEM HOW. It's absolutely dotty. They assume that small children will be able to master what is, in fact, the most difficult single thing in music-making – efficient, economical practising.

The reason I think I know how to practise is because I started as a grown-up. Most of the music teachers, even the most brilliant of them, cannot remember what it was like not to be able to play the note G. They were Barnaby's age; I was 39. I saw in my frustration that practice did indeed make perfect, but at a great cost and over a long time.

Practice is, after all, a form of quality control. Like all such controls it needs to be strictly applied. Take an example. If a child plays a simple scale in strict time, no matter how slowly, or, like Barnaby, G and A over and over again, he will be able to tell when he can do it. If he speeds up when it's easy and slows down when it's hard, he will never know if he can play the thing. The quality control is lost.

There is nothing 'natural' about training one's fingers to move independently in peculiar patterns. Playing a musical instrument makes absurd demands on that miraculous computer we call our minds. No wonder complicated cross-fingerings produce jammed circuits in the brain. That's why one has to practise them so much.

But what applies to music applies, in my experience, to everything else. Take languages. I was lucky enough to escape being taught modern languages at school. The result was that I learned them by a much more sensible method: by practising every day, by reading bits aloud and trying to sound like the radio announcer, by talking in them to anyone who

would listen (and some who wouldn't) and by going over my vocabulary again and again and again.

Music and modern languages have, of course, the great advantage that they are objective. Either you can play fluently in A flat major or you can't. No amount of waffle will cover up the absence of practice. Either you find the right words coming to mind in a foreign language; or you don't. Here, too, practice makes the difference.

Is reading or writing or remembering things or even sitting still all that more natural than playing the note G? Gramsci says in the *Prison Notebooks* that the greatest and most civilising act of school is to teach seven year old animals to sit still. Mature students have told me the same thing. The hardest thing about study for those who are out of practice is simply sitting still in a library or at their desks. Remembering what they have read comes next. Why should remembering things be less dependent on daily practice than A flat major?

Reading (both speed and comprehension) and writing (both style and content) need practice, too. I reckon that you can transform your prose style by 15 minutes a day of intelligent practice. Take a good stylist, Orwell, Dame Rebecca West, C.S. Lewis, and choose a paragraph at random. Close the book and try to imitate what you have read.

In every case, you will find that where your text deviates from the original, the original is better. A fortnight of that, and you will have become incomparably more sensitive to the weight, surface and direction of words. Any scheme will do as long as it's regular and considered. Try writing everything without using the verb 'to be.' A week of that, and you will feel as I did with the alternative E flat key – frustrated and furious.

I am no educationist, nor do I know any physiology. Hence I am completely unqualified to pronounce on such matters; but I am as sure as I am of anything that the key to all human achievement is practice. If you do something over and over for long enough, you will get better at it, whatever it is. We are made that way, it would seem. Our brains need time and regularity to register the proper circuits for complex activities.

What we appear to be doing with our infants and junior school children is very different.

We send them to secondary schools where they have to learn French verbs by heart, never having learned anything by heart in their lives. Then we wonder why they cannot do it. In my terms, we are asking them to play fluently on the clarinet the first time they pick it up, or to hit good backhand shots in tennis the first time they go on court.

We have abolished memorisation because it's artificial and authoritarian and 'rote.' In my terms, we have denied our kids the chance to practise on the most amazing of all data retrieval systems: their memories.

Not everybody who practises his violin every day will be Menuhin; but not even Menuhin can be Menuhin unless he does practise every day. As he himself put it, 'If I don't practise every day, I know it; if I don't practise for two days, other violinists know it; if I don't practise for three days, everybody knows it.'

That seems to me to be a pretty sound educational maxim, which we ignore at great cost.

(*New Society*)

Jonathan Steinberg is a modern German historian and Vice-Master of Trinity Hall, Cambridge. His article 'Practice Makes Sort-of-Perfect' appeared in *New Society* in 1979 and I have preserved copies to distribute for fellow-musicians ever since. But for the present purpose, an update was called for and his reply follows:

'You ask what happened after September, 1979, and whether we all went on musically. The first character was one of the children at the Duxford Saturday Workshop, founded by my wife in 1972, for music, drama and poetry. Barnaby, then six, is now twenty. He went on to the trombone but dropped it and now repairs cars at a local garage. The Duxford Saturday Workshop turned into a charitable trust with £60,000 endowment, 300-plus members and a director paid to do what my wife did for nothing. (She now runs a bookshop in Sawston.) I went on practising and got to the stage where I could (and can – just) hold up my corner of a wind quintet and not make too many mistakes in the oboe section of the Workshop orchestra.

'I suppose the most significant musical outcome was my commitment to turning adult beginners into musicians (well, my kind anyway) and at 9.30 every Saturday morning my recorder big band meets to play Dowland or Peter Warlock, Handel or Delius. There are 45 players whose ages range from ten to over seventy, including several sets of parents and children. I practise my conducting and they practise being an orchestra. Every once in a while, in an ordinary classroom of an ordinary state primary school and on plastic recorders, we play something in tune, in time and in harmony. Then we have one of those luminous moments in the presence of great art that makes life and we know that something special has happened.'

3
THE PLEASURES OF ACCOMPLISHMENT

CONRAD AIKEN

Music

The calyx of the oboe breaks
silver and soft the flower it makes.
And next, beyond, the flute-notes seen
now are white and now are green.

What are these sounds, what daft device
mocking at flame, mimicking ice?
Musicians, will you never rest
from strange translation of the breast?

The heart, from which all horrors come,
grows like a vine, its gourd a drum;
the living pattern sprawls and climbs
eager to bear all worlds and times:

trilling leaf and tinkling grass
glide into darkness clear as glass;
then the musicians cease to play
and the world is waved away.

CHARLES BURNEY

A Milanese accademia

Frid. July 20, 1770. A private concert in Italy is called an *accademia*; the first I went to was composed entirely of *dilettanti*; *il padrone*, or the master of the house, played the first violin, and had a very powerful hand; there were twelve or fourteen performers, among whom were several good violins; there were likewise two German flutes, a violoncello, and small double base; they executed, reasonably well, several of our Bach's symphonies, different from those printed in England: all the music here is in MS. But what I liked most was the vocal part by *la Padrona della Casa*, or lady of the house; she had an agreeable well-toned voice, a good shake, the right sort of taste and expression, and sung sitting down, with the paper on the common instrumental desk, wholly without affectation, several pretty airs of Traetta.

Upon the whole, this concert was much upon a level with our own private concerts among gentlemen in England, the performers were sometimes in and sometimes out; in general, however, the music was rather better chosen, the execution more brilliant and full of fire, and the singing much nearer perfection than we can often boast on such occasions; not, indeed, in point of voice or execution, for in respect of these our females are, at least, equal to our neighbours, but in *portamento* or direction of the voice, in expression and in discretion.

(*An Eighteenth-century Musical Tour in France and Italy*)

GEOFFREY CHAUCER

Orpheus and his catalogue of instruments

. . . Ther herde I pleyen on an harpe
That sowned bothe wel and sharpe,
Orpheus ful craftely,
And on his syde, faste by,
Sat the harper Orion,
And Eacides Chiron,
And other harpers may oon,
And the Bret Glascurion;
And smale harpers with her gleës
Sate under hem in dyvers seës,
And gunne on hem upward to gape,
And countrefete hem as an ape,
Or as craft countrefeteth kynde.
   Tho saugh I stonden hem behynde,
Afer fro hem, al be hemselve,
Many thousand tymes twelve,
That maden lowde mynstralcies
In cornemuse and shalemyes,
And many other maner pipe,
That craftely begunne to pipe,
Bothe in doucet and in rede,
That ben at festes with the brede;
And many flowte and liltyng horn,
And pipes made of grene corn,

As han thise lytel herde-gromes,
That kepen bestes in the bromes.
Ther saugh I than Atiteris,
And of Athenes daun Pseustis,
And Marcia that loste her skyn,
Bothe in face, body, and chyn,
For that she wolde envien, loo!
To pipen bet than Appolloo.
Ther saugh I famous, olde and yonge,
Pipers of the Duche tonge,
To lerne love-daunces, sprynges,
Reyes, and these straunge thynges.
Tho saugh I in an other place
Stonden in a large space,
Of hem that maken blody soun
In trumpe, beme, and claryoun;
For in fight and blod-shedynge
Ys used gladly clarionynge.
Ther herde I trumpen Messenus,
Of whom that speketh Virgilius.
There herde I trumpe Joab also,
Theodomas, and other mo;
And alle that used clarion
In Cataloigne and Aragon,
That in her tyme famous were
To lerne, saugh I trumpe there.
There saugh I sitte in other seës,
Pleyinge upon sondry gleës,
Whiche that I kan not nevene,
Moo than sterres ben in hevene,
Of whiche I nyl as now not ryme,
For ese of yow, and los of tyme.
For tyme ylost, this knowen ye,
Be no way may recovered be....

(*The House of Fame*)

MABEL DOLMETSCH

Absorbed into the Dolmetsch ensemble

Inquiring from a musical friend (lately a pupil at Dulwich College) about a violin teacher of good standing, I was electrified by his reply: 'Why don't you learn from Dolmetsch?' 'What!' said I, 'do you mean that man I've been reading about, who has all those wonderful old instruments? Oh! *do* you think he'd let me see them?' The friend was encouraging; so thereupon I addressed a letter to Arnold Dolmetsch, Dowland, Dulwich, not knowing that he had recently moved to Keppel Street, Bloomsbury. The letter nevertheless reached him, and elicited a favourable reply. The handwriting, which struck me as most individual and interesting, added yet further zest to my devouring curiosity. In after years he told me (not recognizing the hand of Destiny) that he could never understand why he had accepted me! He had but recently dispersed his valuable teaching connection which had at one time included periodical visits to St James's Palace (where he had as a pupil a youthful relative of Queen Victoria), in order to free himself for his now entirely engrossing work. Yet, illogically, he gave way before the unknown applicant! At our first interview, it seemed as though there sprang up between us a spontaneous sympathy which was destined to last for ever.

Stray glimpses of the family, caught through half-opened doors, were most intriguing; and their very voluble French, interspersed with shrieks of laughter, was to my untrained ears mysterious and unintelligible.

During this initial period Arnold Dolmetsch was working against time to complete his first harpsichord, originally started in Dulwich at the suggestion of William Morris, who now and then visited the Dolmetsch workshop, in which he was keenly interested. The instrument was to be included in the Arts and Crafts Exhibition of 1896, the date of whose opening was drawing near. On my arrival one morning I heard him telling a departing visitor that he had been working himself to death, and had not had a meal for three days. Whereupon I concluded that he must be a stern ascetic, not having yet understood his tendency (characteristic of the southern races) to indulge in picturesque exaggeration, in the belief that this was the only way to impress truths upon the average mind.

Some little time elapsed before an opportunity of making acquaintance with the ancient instruments materialized, as the ground-floor room in which the lessons were given was furnished merely with a grand piano (a relic of the Dulwich days). But one day when I arrived at 6 Keppel Street the teacher failed to make his usual punctual appearance. As I sat waiting, suddenly the door opened and Elodie entered. Bowing low from the waist, she remarked: 'Eet-ees-*waarrm!*' I agreed, and from the ensuing conversation, learned that a concert, the first of a summer series, was to be held in the first-floor music-room that very evening. I was led upstairs to a large and pleasant room, actually composed of two, divided by folding doors. In the larger portion, rows of 'Art Workers' Guild' chairs had been set out, looking artistically suited to their surroundings, the inner room being reserved as a sanctum for the artists and their instruments. Here we found Arnold himself engaged in tuning a fine Kirkman harpsichord. Its reedy timbre was startling to an unaccustomed ear, and at first acquaintance I preferred the rounder and more sombre sonority of the old Italian virginals. Though unable to attend at such short notice, I straight away booked three seats for the second concert of the series. The extra two were intended for a musical sister and the indispensable chaperone! The person assuming this rôle was Lucy Carr Shaw, the sister of George Bernard Shaw. She had adopted the theatrical profession as a means of livelihood, and employed her fresh Irish voice in light opera. While touring in a popular production she had met and married a cousin of mine, who, having an agreeable tenor voice and a gift for comedy, had deserted the business career, which was to him loathsome, and gone on the stage (or, as his relatives put it, 'joined a troupe of actors!'). George Bernard Shaw, though he had by now transferred his activities from musical to dramatic criticism, still retained his vivid appreciation of the Dolmetsch concerts. When, therefore, I asked Lucy to accompany us to the concert she exclaimed: 'What! You mean Dolmetsch? Of *course* I will! George is crazy

A 16th-century woodcut of the viol family

about him!' The impression left on my mind by that entrancing evening remains undimmed, despite the lapse of many years.

The concert room, tinted a soft diaphanous green, was entirely illuminated by wax candles, set round the walls in hand-beaten brass sconces, and interspersed with rare lutes and viols, suspended from hooks. The inner half, with its varied assortment of instruments and players, all in a manner interesting, formed a picturesque *mise en scène* that focused the rapt attention of the audience.

Hélène and Elodie looked their best in dresses chosen for them with unerring taste by the master mind. As to himself, one's attention was drawn away from the neutral clothing to his brilliantly expressive eyes, which Lucy Shaw characterized as 'lamps of genius'.

The music itself more than lived up to the picture. From an entirely satisfying whole, there stood out certain gems. Notable among these were 'Sellenger's Round', set for the virginals by William Byrd (brought off with rhythmic aptness by Elodie) and a pavan whose mysterious solemnity produced its full effect as declaimed in the clear yet highly coloured tones of a chest of viols. A romantic suite by Marin Marais enabled one to appreciate the suave beauty of Hélène's bowing on the viola da gamba, the movements of her wrist calling to mind those of a swan's neck. The concert came to a triumphal close with Bach's Violin Concerto in A minor, on which Arnold Dolmetsch (in the solo part) brought to bear his fine sense of phrasing and interpretative genius, accompanied by a string quartet and the scintillating harpsichord, the whole combination forming an arrestingly beautiful ensemble.

There was a pleasantly informal atmosphere about these concerts; and the interlude, during which excellent coffee and *petits fours* were handed round, enabled one to appreciate the unusual nature of the audience. Prominent in their midst on this occasion was Violet Gordon Woodhouse, then a sparkling young bride. Other outstanding personalities were Margaret Mackail (fragile and fair like the etherealized pictorial creations of her father, Sir Edward Burne Jones) with her distinguished husband, Professor John Mackail. I also remarked a graceful golden-haired lady with a wondrous smile, accompanied by a thin, spare looking, dark man. She was the beautiful Miss Kingsley, and he the artist William Rothenstein, whom she married shortly afterwards. Naturally, I did not identify these people at sight, but came to know them later, together with many others of popular interest, such as Ellen Terry, kind, sweet and childlike; Lawrence Binyon, the poet and scholar in Oriental languages; Mrs Patrick Campbell, who inevitably drew all eyes to herself as she glided into her place; George Moore, the novelist, exchanging brisk badinage with Lucy, they having formerly been neighbours over in Ireland. Side by side with these were many members of the Art Workers' Guild, including Walter Crane and Cobden Sanderson, who in his latter years threw his printing-press into the sea so that it should never fall into the hands of some unworthy successor. Herbert Horne was, of course, a familiar figure, likewise Arthur Symons and, subsequently, Robert Steele, the consummate scholar and authority on Mediaeval French Literature and Early English Music Printing. He and Arnold developed an unshakeable friendship wherein they could say anything they pleased to each other with impunity. Each took the other on trust, and I have even seen Arnold, the epicure, consuming some distinctly high lobster from which I recoiled, because Steele had brought it and so it must be all right!

(*Personal Recollections of Arnold Dolmetsch*)

GEORGE ELIOT

A commitment to her craft

To Charles Lewes, 30 July, 1859:

Dear Charlie

I look forward to playing duets with you as one of my future pleasures, and if I am able to go on working I hope we shall afford to have a fine grand piano. I have none of Mozart's Symphonies, so that you can be guided in your choice of them entirely by your own tastes. I know Beethoven's Sonata in E flat well. It is a very charming one, and I shall like to hear you play it. That is one of my luxuries – to sit still and hear some one playing my favourite music; so that you may be sure you will find willing ears to listen to the fruits of your industrious practising.

There are ladies in the world, not a few, who play the violin [Charlie had remarked, 'I had never heard of a woman's playing the violin'], and I wish I were one of them, for then we could play together sonatas for the piano and violin which make a charming combination. The violin gives that keen edge of tone which the piano wants.

To the same, October 7, 1859:

... I was a very idle practiser, and I often regret now that when I had abundant time and opportunity for hours of piano-playing, I used them so little. I have about eighteen sonatas and symphonies of Beethoven, I think, but I shall be delighted to find that you can play them better than I can. ... I am sensitive to blunders and wrong notes, and instruments out of tune, but I have never played much from ear, though I used to play from memory a great deal.

To Sara Hennell and Mrs Charles Bray, October 6, 1861:

... We are enjoying a great, great pleasure – a new grand piano, and last evening we had a Beethoven night. [George Redford and Herbert Spencer were the guests. Redford had a fine baritone voice: GE wrote to Charlie two years earlier, 'He sings Adelaide, that exquisite song of Beethoven's, which I should like you to learn.'] We are looking out for a violinist: we have our violoncello, who is full of sensibility, but with no negative in him – i.e. no obstinate sense of time: a man who is all assent and perpetual rallentando. [Presumably 'Charley on the violoncello, which he now leaves with us, to be always ready when he comes.' He and E. F. S. Pigott, who sang tenor, came most Saturday evenings, 1861–2, according to Lewes's journal.]

(*The George Eliot Letters*)

The editor of *The George Eliot Letters*, Gordon S. Haight, also refers to Frederick Lehmann's *Memoirs of Half a Century*:

'In the winter of 1866 my wife and family were at Pau, while I was alone in London. George Eliot was a good pianist, not gifted, but enthusiastic, and extremely painstaking. During a great part of that winter I used to go to her every Monday evening at her house in North Bank, Regent's Park, always taking my violin with me. We played together every piano and violin sonata of Mozart and Beethoven.... Our audience consisted of George Lewes only, and he used to groan with delight whenever we were rather successful in playing some beautiful passage.'

JOHN EVELYN

The diarist's elegy for his daughter

I was solemnly invited to my L: Arundel of Wardour, (now newly releas'd
of his 6 yeares confinement in the Tower, upon suspicion of the plot, called
Oates's plot) where after dinner the same Mr *Pordage* entertained us with
his voice, that excellent & stupendious Artist Signor Jo: Baptist, playing to
it on the Harpsichord: My Daughter Mary being with us, she also sung to
the greate satisfaction of both Masters, & a world of people of quality
present: as she also did at my Lord Rochesters the Evening following,
when we had the *French boy* so fam'd for his singing: & indeede he had a
delicate voice, & had ben well taught:

. . . She had read & digested a considerable deale of History, & of Places,
the french Tongue being as familiar to her as English, she understood
Italian, and was able to render a laudable Account of what she read &
observed, to which assisted a most faithfull memory, & discernement, &
she did make very prudent & discreete reflections upon what she had
observe'd of the Conversations among which she had at any time ben
(which being continualy of persons of the best quality), she improved: She
had to all this an incomparable sweete Voice, to which she play'd a
through-base on the Harpsichord, in both which she ariv'd to that perfection, that of all the Schollars of those Two famous Masters, Signor *Pietro*
and *Bartolomeo*: she was esteem'd the best; [for] the sweetenesse of her
voice, and manegement of it, adding such an agreablenesse to her Coun-
tenance, without any constraint and concerne, that when she sung, it was
as charming to the Eye, as to the Eare; this I rather note, because it was a
universal remarke, & for which so many noble & judicious persons in

147

Musique, desir'd to heare her; the last, being at my Lord Arundels of Wardours, where was a solemn Meeting of about twenty persons of quality, some of them greate judges & Masters of Musique; where she sung with the famous Mr *Pordage*, Signor *Joh: Battist* touching the Harpsichord &c: with exceeding applause:...

Having some days after opened her Trunks, & looked into her Closset, amazed & even astonished we were to find that incredible number of papers and Collections she had made of severall material Authors, both Historians, Poets, Travells &c: but above all the Devotions, Contemplations, & resolutions upon those Contemplations, which we found under her hand in a booke most methodicaly disposed, & much exceeding the talent & usage of [so] young & beautifull women, who consume so much of their time in vaine things: with severall prayers, Meditations, & devotions on divers occasions; with a world of pretty letters to her confidents & others savoring of a greate witt, & breathing of piety & honor: There is one letter to some divine (who is not named) to whom she writes that he would be her Ghostly Father & guide, & that he would not despise her for the many errors & imperfections of her Youth, but beg of God, to give her courage, to acquaint him with all her faults, imploring his assistance, & spiritual direction: & well I remember, that she often desired me to recomend her to such a person, but (though I intended it) I did not think fit to do it as yet, seeing her apt to be scrupulous, & knowing the greate innocency & integrity of her life; but this (it seemes) she did of her selfe: There are many other books, offices & papers thus written by her selfe, so many indeede, as it is plainly astonishing how one that had acquired such substantiall & practical knowledge in other the ornamental parts of (Especialy) Music vocal & Instrumental, Dauncing; paying, & receiving visites, necessary Conversation, & other unavoidable impertinences of life could find, much more employ, her time to accomplish a quarter of what she has left: but as she never affected Play, Cards &c: (which consumes a world of precious time) so she was in continual exercise, which yet abated nothing of the most free & agreable Conversation in the world: But as she was a little miracle whilst she lived, so she died with out Example.

(*Kalendarium*)

E. M. FORSTER

Lucy Honeychurch's piano

It so happened that Lucy, who found daily life rather chaotic, entered a more solid world when she opened the piano. She was then no longer either deferential or patronizing; no longer either a rebel or a slave. The kingdom of music is not the kingdom of this world; it will accept those whom breeding and intellect and culture have alike rejected. The commonplace person begins to play, and shoots into the empyrean without effort, whilst we look up, marvelling how he has escaped us, and thinking how we could worship him and love him, would he but translate his visions into human words, and his experiences into human actions. Perhaps he cannot; certainly he does not, or does so very seldom. Lucy had done so never.

She was no dazzling *exécutante*; her runs were not at all like strings of pearls, and she struck no more right notes than was suitable for one of her age and situation. Nor was she the passionate young lady, who performs so tragically on a summer's evening with the window open. Passion was there, but it could not be easily labelled; it slipped between love and hatred and jealousy, and all the furniture of the pictorial style. And she was tragical only in the sense that she was great, for she loved to play on the side of Victory. Victory of what and over what – that is more than the words of daily life can tell us. But that some sonatas of Beethoven are written tragic no one can gainsay; yet they can triumph or despair as the player decides, and Lucy had decided that they should triumph.

A very wet afternoon at the Bertolini permitted her to do the thing she really liked, and after lunch she opened the little draped piano. A few people lingered round and praised her playing, but finding that she made no reply, dispersed to their rooms to write up their diaries or to sleep. She took no notice of Mr Emerson looking for his son, nor of Miss Bartlett looking for Miss Lavish, nor of Miss Lavish looking for her cigarette-case. Like every true performer, she was intoxicated by the mere feel of the notes: they were fingers caressing her own; and by touch, not by sound alone, did she come to her desire.

Mr Beebe, sitting unnoticed in the window, pondered over this illogical element in Miss Honeychurch, and recalled the occasion at Tunbridge Wells when he had discovered it. It was at one of those entertainments where the upper classes entertain the lower. The seats were filled with a respectful audience, and the ladies and gentlemen of the parish, under the auspices of their vicar, sang, or recited, or imitated the drawing of a champagne cork. Among the promised items was 'Miss Honeychurch. Piano. Beethoven,' and Mr Beebe was wondering whether it would be 'Adelaida,' or the march of 'The Ruins of Athens,' when his composure was disturbed by the opening bars of Opus 111. He was in suspense all through the introduction, for not until the pace quickens does one know what the performer intends. With the roar of the opening theme he knew that things were going extraordinarily; in the chords that herald the conclusion he heard the hammer strokes of victory. He was glad that she only played the first movement, for he could have paid no attention to the winding intricacies of the measure of nine-sixteen. The audience clapped, no less respectful. It was Mr Beebe who started the stamping; it was all that one could do.

'Who is she?' he asked the vicar afterwards.

'Cousin of one of my parishioners. I do not consider her choice of a piece happy. Beethoven is so usually simple and direct in his appeal that it is sheer perversity to choose a thing like that, which, if anything, disturbs.'

'Introduce me.'

'She will be delighted. She and Miss Bartlett are full of the praises of your sermon.'

'My sermon?' cried Mr Beebe. 'Why ever did she listen to it?'

When he was introduced he understood why, for Miss Honeychurch, disjoined from her music-stool, was only a young lady with a quantity of dark hair and a very pretty, pale, undeveloped face. She loved going to concerts, she loved stopping with her cousin, she loved iced coffee and meringues. He did not doubt that she loved his sermon also. But before he

Decorated Steinway upright piano, 1888

left Tunbridge Wells he made a remark to the vicar, which he now made to Lucy herself when she closed the little piano and moved dreamily towards him.

'If Miss Honeychurch ever takes to live as she plays, it will be very exciting – both for us and for her.'

Lucy at once re-entered daily life.

'Oh, what a funny thing! Someone said just the same to mother, and she said she trusted I should never live a duet.'

(A Room with a View)

JOHN FULLER

Trio

A gardener's triumph! But it was planted at an angle
And has to be supported on its frail root.
Her hands run up and down its trunk like squirrels
And she loves it like a child between her knees.

A feat of balance! But it all takes place
Between tight-rope fingers and clown-mouth
On a journey in a wooden boat with a single oar
Occurring in the guarded space belonging to kisses.

A banquet for one! But he toys with his food,
Eyes closed, head tilted back in rapture
At the enormous table, the black table,
The table with three legs and a lid.

THOMAS HARDY

Great novelists create their own worlds and inhabit or intuit their own characters, clothing them with whatever they need from real people's occupations and skills by observation, enquiry or memory. Unfortunately, the discipline of imaginative writing and the passion for music-making are often mutually exclusive. Good writers of fiction demand precise detail and atmosphere, understood from within. Musicians are quick to fasten scornfully on novels – and even more, films – that get musical scenes slightly out of focus.

Thomas Hardy was born and bred as a Wessex musician before he became by profession a London architect. Resin dust settled on three generations of spare-time string-players, and the young Hardy was equally familiar with jigs and psalm tunes, barn and church gallery. Other English novelists use music because they enjoy it (in these pages, see George Eliot or Kingsley Amis, for instance) but Hardy relives his own craft and culture in the narrative flow. In *Under the Greenwood Tree* his delight in local players and instruments bubbles out most obviously, but he also uses musical images or episodes to illuminate the great tragic novels. As for his verse, no poet in the entire language uses musical imagery and reminiscence more poignantly to shade human life, almost as Mozart does with the inner parts of a string quintet or Schubert with the accompaniment of a song.

The church choir and band practising

Shortly after ten o'clock the singing-boys arrived at the tranter's house, which was invariably the place of meeting, and preparations were made for the start. The older men and musicians wore thick coats, with stiff perpendicular collars, and coloured handkerchiefs wound round and round the neck till the end came to hand, over all which they just showed their ears and noses, like people looking over a wall. The remainder, stalwart ruddy men and boys, were dressed mainly in snow-white smock-frocks, embroidered upon the shoulders and breasts in ornamental forms of hearts, diamonds, and zigzags. The cider-mug was emptied for the ninth time, the music-books were arranged, and the pieces finally decided upon. The boys in the meantime put the old horn-lanterns in order, cut candles into short lengths to fit the lanterns; and, a thin fleece of snow having fallen since the early part of the evening, those who had no leggings went to the stable and wound wisps of hay round their ankles to keep the insidious flakes from the interior of their boots.

Mellstock was a parish of considerable acreage, the hamlets composing it lying at a much greater distance from each other than is ordinarily the case. Hence several hours were consumed in playing and singing within hearing of every family, even if but a single air were bestowed on each. There was Lower Mellstock, the main village; half a mile from this were the church and vicarage, and a few other houses, the spot being rather lonely now, though in past centuries it had been the most thickly-populated quarter of the parish. A mile north-east lay the hamlet of Upper Mellstock, where the tranter lived; and at other points knots of cottages, besides solitary farmsteads and dairies.

Old William Dewy, with the violoncello, played the bass; his grandson Dick the treble violin; and Reuben and Michael Mail the tenor and second violins respectively. The singers consisted of four men and seven boys, upon whom devolved the task of carrying and attending to the lanterns, and holding the books open for the players. Directly music was the theme old William ever and instinctively came to the front.

'Now mind, neighbours,' he said, as they all went out one by one at the door, he himself holding it ajar and regarding them with a critical face as they passed, like a shepherd counting out his sheep. 'You two counter-boys, keep your ears open to Michael's fingering, and don't ye go straying

into the treble part along o' Dick and his set, as ye did last year; and mind
this especially when we be in "Arise, and hail". Billy Chimlen, don't you
sing quite so raving mad as you fain would; and, all o' ye, whatever ye do,
keep from making a great scuffle on the ground when we go in at people's
gates; but go quietly, so as to strike up all of a sudden, like spirits.'

'Farmer Ledlow's first?'

'Farmer Ledlow's first, the rest as usual.'

'And, Voss,' said the tranter terminatively, 'you keep house here till
about half-past two; then heat the metheglin and cider in the warmer
you'll find turned up upon the copper; and bring it wi' the victuals to
church-hatch, as th'st know.'

Just before the clock struck twelve they lighted the lanterns and started.
The moon, in her third quarter, had risen since the snow-storm; but the
dense accumulation of snow-cloud weakened her power to a faint twilight
which was rather pervasive of the landscape than traceable to the sky. The
breeze had gone down, and the rustle of their feet and tones of their speech
echoed with an alert rebound from every post, boundary-stone, and
ancient wall they passed, even where the distance of the echo's origin was
less than a few yards. Beyond their own slight noises nothing was to be
heard save the occasional bark of foxes in the direction of Yalbury Wood,
or the brush of a rabbit among the grass now and then as it scampered out
of their way.

Most of the outlying homesteads and hamlets had been visited by about
two o'clock; they then passed across the outskirts of a wooded park toward
the main village, nobody being at home at the Manor. Pursuing no
recognized track, great care was necessary in walking lest their faces should
come in contact with the low-hanging boughs of the old lime-trees, which
in many spots formed dense overgrowths of interlaced branches.

'Times have changed from the times they used to be,' said Mail,
regarding nobody can tell what interesting old panoramas with an inward
eye, and letting his outward glance rest on the ground because it was as
convenient a position as any. 'People don't care much about us now! I've
been thinking we must be almost the last left in the country of the old
string players? Barrel-organs, and the things next door to 'em that you
blow wi' your foot, have come in terribly of late years.'

'Ay!' said Bowman shaking his head; and old William on seeing him did
the same thing.

'More's the pity,' replied another. 'Time was – long and merry ago now! – when not one of the varmints was to be heard of; but it served some of the quires right. They should have stuck to strings as we did, and kept out clarinets, and done away with serpents. If you'd thrive in musical religion, stick to strings, says I.'

'Strings be safe soul-lifters, as far as that do go,' said Mr Spinks.

'Yet there's worse things than serpents,' said Mr Penny. 'Old things pass away, 'tis true; but a serpent was a good old note: a deep rich note was the serpent.'

'Clar'nets, however, be bad at all times,' said Michael Mail. 'One Christmas – years agone now, years – I went the rounds wi' the Weatherbury quire. 'Twas a hard frosty night, and the keys of all the clar'nets froze – ah, they did freeze! – so that 'twas like drawing a cork every time a key was opened; and the players o' 'em had to go into a hedger-and-ditcher's chimley-corner, and thaw their clar'nets every now and then. An icicle o' spet hung down from the end of every man's clar'net a span long; and as to fingers – well, there, if ye'll believe me, we had no fingers at all, to our knowing.'

'I can well bring back to my mind,' said Mr Penny, 'what I said to poor Joseph Ryme (who took the treble part in Chalk-Newton Church for two-and-forty year) when they thought of having clar'nets there. 'Joseph,' I said says I, 'depend upon't, if so be you have them tooting clar'nets you'll spoil the whole set-out. Clar'nets were not made for the service of the Lard; you can see it by looking at 'em,' I said. And what came o't? Why, souls, the parson set up a barrel-organ on his own account within two years o' the time I spoke, and the old quire went to nothing.'

'As far as look is concerned,' said the tranter, 'I don't for my part see that a fiddle is much nearer heaven than a clar'net. 'Tis further off. There's always a rakish, scampish twist about a fiddle's looks that seems to say the Wicked One had a hand in making o'en; while angels be supposed to play clar'nets in heaven, or som'at like 'em if ye may believe picters.'

'Robert Penny, you was in the right,' broke in the eldest Dewy. 'They should ha' stuck to strings. Your brass-man is a rafting dog – well and good; your reed-man is a dab at stirring ye – well and good; your drumman is a rare bowel-shaker – good again. But I don't care who hears me say it, nothing will spak to your heart wi' the sweetness o' the man of strings!'

'Strings for ever!' said little Jimmy.

'Strings alone would have held their ground against all the newcomers in creation.' ('True, true!' said Bowman.) 'But clarinets was death.' ('Death they was!' said Mr Penny.) 'And harmonions,' William continued in a louder voice, and getting excited by these signs of approval, 'harmonions and barrel-organs' ('Ah!' and groans from Spinks) 'be miserable – what shall I call 'em? – miserable –'

'Sinners,' suggested Jimmy, who made large strides like the men and did not lag behind with the other little boys.

'Miserable dumbledores!'

'Right, William, and so they be – miserable dumbledores!' said the choir with unanimity.

By this time they were crossing to a gate in the direction of the school which, standing on a slight eminence at the junction of three ways, now rose in unvarying and dark flatness against the sky. The instruments were retuned, and all the band entered the school enclosure, enjoined by old William to keep upon the grass.

'Number seventy-eight,' he softly gave out as they formed round in a semicircle, the boys opening the lanterns to get a clearer light, and directing their rays on the books.

Then passed forth into the quiet night an ancient and time-worn hymn, embodying a quaint Christianity in words orally transmitted from father to son through several generations down to the present characters, who sang them out right earnestly:

> 'Remember Adam's fall,
> O thou Man...'

Having concluded the last note they listened for a minute or two, but found that no sound issued from the schoolhouse.

'Four breaths, and then, "Oh, what unbounded goodness!" number fifty-nine,' said William.

This was duly gone through, and no notice whatever seemed to be taken of the performance.

'Good guide us, surely 'tisn't a' empty house, as befell us in the year thirty-nine and forty-three!' said old Dewy.

'Perhaps she's just come from some musical city, and sneers at our doings?' the tranter whispered.

''Od rabbit her!' said Mr Penny, with an annihilating look at a corner of the school chimney, 'I don't quite stomach her, if this is it. Your plain

157

music well done is as worthy as your other sort done bad, a'b'lieve, souls; so say I.'

'Four breaths, and then the last,' said the leader authoritatively. '"Rejoice, ye Tenants of the Earth", number sixty-four.'

At the close, waiting yet another minute, he said in a clear loud voice, as he had said in the village at that hour and season for the previous forty years –

'A merry Christmas to ye!'

(*Under the Greenwood Tree*)

'At the Railway Station, Upway'

'There is not much that I can do,
    For I've no money that's quite my own!'
    Spoke up the pitying child –
A little boy with a violin
At the station before the train came in, –
'But I can play my fiddle to you,
And a nice one 'tis, and good in tone!'

    The man in the handcuffs smiled;
The constable looked, and he smiled, too,
    As the fiddle began to twang;
And the man in the handcuffs suddenly sang
        With grimful glee:
        'This life so free
        Is the thing for me!'
And the constable smiled, and said no word,
As if unconscious of what he heard;
And so they went on till the train came in –
The convict, and boy with the violin.

158

JOHN HEATH-STUBBS

The Watchman's Flute

Through the Nigerian night the Tuareg watchman,
Ferociously armed with sword, daggers and whip,
Intermittently blows his flute – a piece of piping
Bored with five holes : to pass the time –

To ward off tedium, and perhaps
Lurking malignant ghosts that always throng
This ambient, African darkness :

Infinite rhythmical variations
On a simple tetrachord, with a recurrent pedal point –
Libyan music, antique – as Orpheus
Cajoled the powers of Hell, made them disgorge
Eurydice – to him she was love
(Her jurisdiction be wide).

Those deliquescent forms shrink back
To hollow pits of non-entity :
Music implies an order – light,
Particles in regular motion,
The first articulate Word.

May my lips likewise
Mould such melodious mouthfuls still, amid
The European, the twentieth-century tediums:
We too are haunted, we are in the dark.

DOROTHEA HERBERT

High jinks and Handel's Messiah

Carrick on Suir, 1784. When the frost was over We resumed our Music – Mrs O Hara had a most enchanting Voice – loud, clear and Harmonious – She could pitch it to every Key and Modulate it as she pleased to the most difficult or most simple Music – for besides great taste and judgement she could thrill the Heart to tenderness and Rapture – We sang every Sunday at church joined by some of her Town Scholars and enchanted the Congregation with the Variety of our Hymns and Psalms – At home we hardly ever quitted the Harpsichord – Mrs O Hara had an unbounded Variety of the finest and most touching Airs – which she sang for me whenever I pleased, and we often sat whole Hours by Moonlight at the Harpsichord – She Singing and I listening 'In Rapture Wound' – I was then of a romantic Age – All around Me was Romance in a Retreat beautiful as the Garden of Eden, and in short every thing conspired to encrease that Sensibility, keen and Sharp as a Two Edged Sword which ever attended me from Youth to Age, and always prey'd on me whilst I nourish'd it with the blindest Vehemence, and fondly cherished the Viper that made succeeding Misfortunes intolerable – I often left the Harpsichord in hysterical fits of Crying without knowing Why or Wherefore, and Mrs O Hara pleased with an Auditress who felt her Music, indulged my foible Even to Madness – thus pass'd the first part of this Summer.

We Now received a Letter from My Aunt Blunden entreating us to pass a good Part of the Summer at Castle Blunden, which we promised to do after My Father return'd from the visitation of Cashel where there was a New ArchBishop, a New and Elegant Cathedral, and the first Choir in the

Kingdom, appointed by the ArchBishop (Doctor Agar), who was a great Amateur and Music Mad...

I had Never heard any powerful Music before – but the Oratorios no sooner began than I felt Myself quite overpower'd – I wept and laughd with secret Rapture – My Head Swam and I found Myself fainting Away and just on the wing to Heaven as it were – I knew not what passd till I found Mrs Hare holding a Smelling Bottle to my Nose which the Arch-Bishops Lady Mrs Agar had humanely handed over the Pew – I was quite Shocked at My Own behaviour, recollecting the Lecture Mrs Fleming gave me once before on an Occasion somewhat similar – The ArchBishops Throne was just over our Pew – He noticed all that passd and seemd delighted at the Effect his Music on a Novice – After Service Mrs Agar asked My Mother if I was her Daughter declaring herself much pleased with My Sensibility – 'Comfort Ye My people', 'Every Valley shall be Exalted', 'and the Trumpet shall sound' were the three principal Oratorios and I do believe there never was a more Capital Performance As the ArchBishop spared No cost or pains on it – Mr Hare rallied me a good deal on My feelings, the Effects of which were too obvious not to be seen by the Whole Congregation.

Castle Blunden, 1785, after Mrs Matthews Wedding. . . . In the Evening Sir John [Matthews] now disengaged from his armful of Rent Rolls drew me to the forte piano for the first time this last Excursion – He made me play push about the Jorum with my own Variations – a tune that obtained me much Celebrity at that time – He placed himself vis a vis – and swore in Raptures I surpassed Mrs Billington in Taste and engaged me to play and Sing for him the rest of the Evening – Accordingly we amused ourselves at the forte piano till Supper was Served – He made me sing for him Many old songs such as Molly Astore and how Sweet in the Woodlands declaring my soft plaintive Voice and Collections of plaintive old Tunes pleased him more than the finest Opera Performance And he Encored Me over and Over saying it was the last time perhaps he should ever ask me to sing for him – His Sisters sat round us and Made him Give a full Account of his Intended.

(*Retrospections of Dorothea Herbert*)

ALDOUS HUXLEY

A calypso tent in Trinidad

Our friends – and by the end of our single day in Trinidad we had the most charming friends – took us after dinner to a Calypso Tent. Now a Calypso Tent (as I think it almost goes without saying) is not a tent and has nothing to do with Calypso. It is a large shed without walls – a tin roof on posts – in which, during the weeks that precede Shrove Tuesday, the local talent assembles to rehearse certain songs specially composed against the coming of Carnival. The tune to which these songs are sung is always some variant of an old Spanish air called Calypso; the words are home-made and topical. (The singers, who are negroes and have the negro's more than Indian passion for grandiloquence, call themselves 'Calypsonians.' Calypsonians! – it is the sort of opulent word that Greene or Marlowe would have delighted in. Why is it that, to-day, only the vulgarest and most coarse-grained poetasters have the face to ride in triumph through Persepolis? Good poets would as soon publicly break wind as let fly at their readers with a purple passage. The *Zeitgeist* is a most tyrannous spirit; to evade its imperatives seems, for a sensitive artist, to be all but impossible. The Calypsonians of Trinidad live in another *Zeit*; so the *Geist* they obey is not the same as ours. In that, it may be, they are fortunate.)

The singing was introduced and accompanied by an orchestra consisting of flute, clarinet (the instrument mainly responsible for tracing the melodic line), violoncello and guitar. The performers played by ear and, as the spirit moved them, improvised elaborations on their parts. The resultant sounds were simply astonishing. These four negroes produced music like nothing else I have ever listened to. The orchestral colour was virulently aniline; in the end its very violence and intensity produced a kind of numb fatigue. But for the first minutes the ear was dazzled, as it were, and delightedly amazed.

There were four or five singers, all well known, it seemed, to the audience, and each possessing a stage name in the grandest negro-Elizabethan style.

'The Duke of Normandy!' announced the master of ceremonies. Up climbed a coal-black youth, and with an expression on his face of the most touching seriousness began to sing a song, of which the opening lines ran as follows:

> Oh, wouldn't it be-ee
> A good thing if we-ee
> Supported lo-cull industree!

At the end of every stanza came a refrain in the form of a question:

> Why shouldn' de products of dis island
> Support de popula-ashun?

This appeal for Trinidadian autarchy was warmly applauded. The idiocies of the greater world have penetrated even into the recesses of the Caribbean.

When he had finished, it was the turn of the 'Lord Executor.' A gnarled, little old man, white-skinned but entirely negro, you felt, in spirit, made his bow, and, pulling his hat down at a very sinister angle over his right eye, began to sing a long ballad about a female burglar, called Ruby, whose trial had recently made a great impression on the public of Port of Spain. Unhappily, I can recall little more than the refrain:

> But when Rub-ee
> Pleaded guilt-ee
> She got two years in custod-ee.

One other passage, from a long catalogue of the things that Ruby stole, remains in my memory:

> She took boots and she took shoes
> And bloomers such as ladies use.

But the rest, alas, is silence.

Silence, too, is all but the chorus of another song by the Duke of Normandy about the rail-versus-road controversy. The duke was a modernist and all for the road.

'So what I say,' he sang, while the orchestra improvised an extraordinary accompaniment that ran up and down the scale like the laughter of a giant woodpecker:

> So what I say
> Is, wouldn't it pay
> Much better for all of us
> To travel by de r-omnibus?

After that the Lord Adjudicator sang almost incomprehensibly (which was the more regrettable, as his song was evidently richly obscene) in that queer French patois which still lingers among the negroes of Trinidad. And when the laughter had died down, the Lord Executor went through a long Newgate Calendar of all the important crimes of the preceding year. Nothing of it remains with me, except the phrase 'lenient brutality' applied to a particularly savage murder.

The proceedings ended with a 'flyting.' Three of the singers got up on to the stage together and proceeded to improvise stanzas of derision at one another's expense, attack and counter-attack, to the unspeakable pleasure of all the listeners. The gigantic black matron sitting immediately in front of me heaved with such violent paroxysms of laughter, that I was afraid she would disintegrate. Happily I was wrong; goodly and great, like a black female Og, she sailed out of the Calypso Tent and in the tropical darkness outside was lost, as though in her native element.

(*Beyond the Mexique Bay*)

BISHOP JOHN JEWEL

Songs of praise 400 years ago

To Peter Martyr, 5 March 1560:

... Religion is now somewhat more established than it was. The people are everywhere exceedingly inclined to the better part. The practice of joining in church music [i.e. the psalms] has very much helped this. For as soon as they had once begun singing in public, in only one little church in London, immediately not only the churches in the neighbourhood, but even the towns far distant began to vie with each other in the same practice. You may now sometimes see at St Paul's Cross, after the service, six thousand persons, old and young, of both sexes, all singing together and praising God. This sadly annoys the Mass priests and the devil. For they perceive that by these means the sacred discourses sink more deeply into the minds of men, and that their kingdom is weakened and shakened at almost every note....

(*Zurich Letters*)

HENRY LIVINGS

Where there's music there's brass

The noblest sight of the year, on Whit Friday morning, is the Dobcross band. In scarlet and black, Nelson Peters in his drummer's apron, a knife-edge crease to his trousers and his uniform cap at a rakish angle over a face that a medieval craftsman would have carved in oak, detonates the big drum, and twenty-five players, plus snare drum, set off with 'Hail Smiling Morn' to join and lead the village procession and the Church and Congregational banners.

George Gibson, conductor, leads the band, a big man in every way, with the swift light movements bulky men sometimes have, a rosy face with baby-blue eyes that can catch you out with a sly wit, and a vast paunch; marching, as he puts it, 'in a smart and airmanlike manner', which somehow manages to convey a gleeful complicity at the same time. Better perhaps to leave this scene for the moment, until its significance has been filled out some.

First, a quick guide to the instruments, taking them in order of size: ten cornets. The cornet is a three-valved conical bore instrument, softer and more melodious than the trumpet, but similar in range and appearance. There are ten in a formal brass band, starting with the soprano, which has the highest pitch of any instrument in the band, and I sometimes wonder how come the player's knees don't rise up to his chin in certain pieces.

The rest of the cornets are slightly bigger and identical; there's the solo cornet – the 'leader' in orchestral terms, and three first cornets, the tutti, less elegantly known as bumpers-up. Then there's two each of the second and third cornets, for the texture and power; often scored for rhythmic

167

accompaniment to the firsts, the after-beats ('umchucks' to the vulgar). There's also a position of some importance occupied by the repiano cornet, which, together with the flugelhorn, can play the under-melody. The flugelhorn looks like a bigger cornet, and though it may share the same copy as the rep, is basically a solo instrument, with its own musical figures to make.

Next in ascending order of size, the three tenor horns: these you hold with the bell pointing up, and they link into the lower range of the flugel, with low notes at the upper end of the French horn's register.

Next the baritone horns, two of them; composers frequently neglect the virtuoso possibilities of this instrument (and murder the player with work in the ensemble), which can range from the cornet's register right down to the bass's. It's one of the hardest to play well, and rewards a good player with a fine, strong sound.

Next, the euphonium, the most melodious of brass band instruments. Often takes the French horn part in works adapted from orchestral scores, unjustly in my opinion, as it hasn't the rasp and force that the baritone has naturally. Marcus Cutts, the distinguished euphonium player from the Fairey Band, plays tuba occasionally with the Hallé, which is correct, as the other name for the euph is the tenor tuba. There's really almost no limit to the capacities of a great player: I heard Marcus one time play a solo piece which belonged rightly to the bassoon, and if you closed your eyes, you *heard* the distinctive tone of the woodwind. Next the trombones, first, second, and that magniloquent voice of the underworld, the bass trombone. I think it's safe to say that the most successful composers for brass band are the ones who respect the versatility of the trombone, which can give grandeur to a note which would merely be raucous on another instrument and then surprise you with a tender melody.

Finally, the E flat and the double B flat bombardons, known to us as the basses. The ground and foundation of the brass band sound: two of each, and a good bass section makes the floor tremble. All the instruments are usually silvered to keep them bright, but they're brass all right. This complement of twenty-five players, plus conductor ('who may not play' as they say in the contest rules) and percussion nowadays, has become conventional because of the need to have regular contest rules; there's nothing magical about it, and quartets, quintets, and octets sound fine; mind, this is not an argument likely to be accepted by a concert secretary who's booked you for a full band.

The clear, bright brassy sound used in orchestral works, and in dance band music, is not much sought in brass banding, where vibrato, properly controlled, is accepted and expected; in the context of fiddles violas etc, it would be foolish of a trumpet player to expect to distinguish himself by the softness of his tone, and useless on a dance-floor; whereas of course, in the brass band, brass is offering the full range of tone. John Ireland called them 'silver orchestras', which was friendly of him, but they're imitation nothing. A Victorian writer described the great Besses' o' th' Barn Band as having the 'sound of a mighty organ', which is fair, as instrument to instrument there is a blend, a homogeneity of sound; but it's also very flexible, it can give you contrasts of wit, vulgar hilarity, as well as schmaltz, oompah, deep nobility and fastidious musical balance. Most of all it needs to be *seen*: you need to see the cornets and trombones raised in fanfare, the lonely liquid soprano against the massed tapestry of the ensemble, the basses hoisted for their thunder. And moster than that, you need the privilege of knowing the bandsmen, of supporting your own band, because it's a social thing – if only for practical reasons: a set of instruments can cost over £5,000, and even a decent cornet is around the £100 mark.

(That the Medals and the Baton Be Put on View)

GEORGE MELLY

Bedsprings and Bechet on tour

Although we had a small public, and although we knew most of the musicians, Mick had not achieved any musical impact. Our first success was in Acton where we played the interval spot at the opening of a new club. The promoter and bandleader, Doug Whitton, had gone to a great deal of trouble to make it an important opening in the convention of the day. He had persuaded those jazz critics who had kept the flame alight in the dark days to come and drink at the club's expense, and, more importantly, the Marquis of Donegall to come and open it. This ensured that the opening would be covered in the musical Press....

'Frankie and Johnnie' has always been my most successful number, principally because of its dramatic story line, and, as I realize now but would have denied then, what talent I have is dramatic rather than vocal. At this period my version was comparatively uncluttered with special effects. Falling down, simulating two people making love, opening a kimono, standing on tip-toe to look over an imaginary transom, firing the little forty-four, etc; all these have gradually attached themselves to the song like barnacles to the bottom of an old ship. Even so it was always comparatively elaborate and theatrical.

Because of Acton, Mick felt ready to accept rather more ambitious jobs: not Humph's club – this he thought might kill our chances – but Cook's Ferry Inn for example.

Cook's Ferry Inn was one of London's earliest jazz clubs, and was the base of the Freddie Randall band. Freddie played a fiery trumpet, much influenced by Muggsy Spanier, and his band was decidedly 'white'. In consequence the New Orleans purists had little time for him, but he had a large following especially in North London. He was also one of the first Dixieland bandleaders to turn professional and go 'on the road'.

To reach the Ferry was a considerable labour. You caught the tube to Finsbury Park and then there was a long bus ride through the depressing suburbs with their chain-stores and second-hand car lots on the bomb sites. Finally there were half-hearted fields and factories making utility furniture or art metal work, and then a bridge over the canal in the style of the city of the future in the film of 'Things to Come'. The Ferry was on the far bank of this canal, a big 1935 pub in Brewers' Georgian with a hall attached. Its isolation had its advantages. The canal tow-path and the surrounding fields were suitable for knee-trembles and yet you could still hear the band.

The journey home was full of problems. For reasons either alcoholic or sexual it was always the *last* bus and its crawling progress put a terrible strain on the beer-filled bladder. On one occasion I had to stand on the bus platform and piss out into the reeling night. The god who looks after drunks stood by me, and I was neither caught by the conductor nor fell off into the road.

The central London jazz clubs in those years were all unlicensed. Jazz was the reason the audience were there. At the Ferry the public were mostly locals who liked jazz as a background to drinking and social intercourse.

Early in the band's history, 'Hermit', the tuba player, left us and was replaced by a sousaphone player called Owen Maddock, a tall man with a beard and the abrupt manner of a Hebrew Prophet who has just handed on the Lord's warning to a sinful generation. He was by profession a racing motor mechanic and designer and his hands, coat, clothes and face were always streaked with oil. His appetite was formidable. Thrusting bread and butter into his mouth with both hands he looked like the Goya of Satan devouring his children. As regards jazz he had a passion for the soprano sax of Sidney Bechet, which was so obsessive as to enter even into his erotic life. In his bedroom was an old-fashioned wind-up gramophone above which was suspended a weight through a pulley so adjusted as to lighten the pressure of the sound-arm on the record. On this antique machine he played Bechet records even while copulating. In fact the rather faded blonde with whom he was having an affair at that time told me she found it very disconcerting that, no matter what point they had reached, if the record finished, Owen would leap off and put on another. Now that there are a great many Bechet LPs available it must make his life easier.

Our first job out of town was on the south coast. I remember a castle on a cliff and the late sun going down over the water outside the glass wall of the dance hall. It was a perfectly ordinary job but we, having no truck or knowledge of professional ethics, carried our crates of beer on to the stand before we began to play. The manager was so amazed that he didn't even protest. It was, however, reported in the local newspaper.

Our first real success outside London was in Liverpool, and my mother was the cause.

Mick had been to Liverpool with me some months before on a purely social visit, and it had been fairly disastrous. We had been asked to give a lift to a coloured girl, also from Liverpool, who sang with Mike Daniels. Her name was Phyllis and she wished to visit her child who lived up there with her parents. For us the whole coloured race was sacred, but Phyllis tried our faith severely. The AA had advised us to go via Birkenhead. Our intention was to reach home in time to hear Beryl Bryden singing on 'Radio Rhythm Club'. We had, in the car, a gramophone and a number of records mostly by Jelly Roll Morton. We picked Phyllis up in Piccadilly and set off.

Every time we went over a bridge Phyllis said, 'Eh, me tits.' Every time we saw some cows in a field Phyllis said, 'All that meat and no potatoes!'

We were only on the Chester by-pass when it was time to listen to Beryl and had to go into a pub and ask the landlord to tune in for us.

As we were driving through the Mersey Tunnel Phyllis told us she didn't like New Orleans jazz really. She 'went more for modern like'. Sensibly enough she hadn't told us before. Faced with such blasphemy we might well have made her hitch-hike.

We dropped her by the Empire and drove home. My mother and Mick didn't really take to each other, although she thought him 'very attractive'. Both Mick and I have suffered throughout our whole relationship by people thinking that, in his case I was responsible for leading him astray, and, that in my case, he was responsible.

My father didn't help by saying the coffee tasted like ferret's piss. Somehow my mother thought that Mick was responsible for him saying this too. My mother was also certain we were an affair. 'Why didn't you tell

George Melly going pro

me?' she asked. I denied the whole thing, but she was by no means convinced. I can't really blame her for this. Although Mick is physically entirely hetero, he likes his men friends so much that it's an understandable fallacy.

Next morning at breakfast there was one fish-cake left over, and my mother pushed it on to my plate. Mick noticed and never forgot. The fish-cake became symbolic.

That afternoon Phyllis turned up. My mother didn't take to her either, not because she was coloured but because she was so Liverpool. She had her child with her. Both my grandmothers came to tea. They sat on each side of Phyllis as though she was a coloured Alice and they the Red and White Queens. Suddenly her child farted very loudly. Phyllis looked from one grandmother, severe and Jewish, to the other, severe and Christian. 'It wasn't me,' she said.

My mother's whole attitude towards jazz had been ambivalent. . . .

Even so it was my mother who arranged our first appearance in Liverpool. She was involved with a charitable institution and, following my self-interested advice, despite the active opposition of several reactionary members of the committee, she decided to raise funds during their appeals year by organizing a jazz concert. This took place at the Stadium, a huge building usually devoted to boxing and all-in wrestling. She contacted the Liverpool jazz promoters of that period, two brothers. They agreed to help and booked Freddy Randall, other name bands, and a few local groups. She insisted we were to appear. They'd never heard of us, and wanted to put us on the side stage with the local groups. She said no. Either we appeared 'in the ring', or the whole thing was off. This is typical of my mother. She might disapprove of what her children do, but if they insist on doing it, she will fight for them like a tiger. My father called it her 'partridge defending its young' act. It is, I suppose, a very Jewish characteristic.

She won, but even so we were booked to appear early on. There was a huge audience – traditional jazz was experiencing its first boom – but no Mick. My father was very worried. 'It's a good crowd,' I told him. 'Yes,' he said, 'but that's no use if Mick doesn't turn up.' We drove to Lime Street Station and found out that the train was late due to fog outside Rugby. At last it arrived. Up the platform strode Mick and the others, Owen's tuba gleaming fitfully through the steam. We were in time to go on in the best spot and went down a bomb. On the strength of it we were booked to do a concert at the Picton Hall. We had achieved an entrée in the provinces.

Manchester was the next step. There jazz was in the hands of a man called Paddy McKeirnan. Unlike most of the promoters in those days he believed in jazz *as a business*. He didn't just run a jazz club. He was the director of 'The Lancashire Society for the Promotion of Jazz Music'. He wrote to Mick offering him a contract to appear at the Grosvenor Hotel, Manchester. It was a real contract with clauses. Mick's acceptance began: 'Dear legal-minded sod, . . .'

We went down well in Manchester too. Paddy, in those days a decided puritan, was less happy about us personally. Mick asked him which of the girls fucked.

'In Manchester,' said Paddy, severely, 'we don't discuss things like that.'

(*Owning-Up*)

FELIX MENDELSSOHN

On accompanying Queen Victoria singing

Prince Albert had asked me to go to him on Saturday at two o'clock, so that I might try his organ before I left England; I found him alone, and as we were talking away the Queen came in, also alone, in a simple morning dress. She said she was obliged to leave for Claremont in an hour, and then, suddenly interrupting herself, exclaimed, 'But goodness, what a confusion!' for the wind had littered the whole room, and even the pedals of the organ (which, by the way, made a very pretty feature in the room), with leaves of music from a large portfolio that lay open. As she spoke she knelt down and began picking up the music; Prince Albert helped, and I too was not idle. Then Prince Albert proceeded to explain the stops to me, and she said that she would meanwhile put things straight.

I begged that the Prince would first play me something, so that, as I said, I might boast about it in Germany; and he played a Chorale, by heart; and the Queen, having finished her work, came and sat by him and listened, and looked pleased. Then it was my turn, and I began my chorus from 'St Paul' – 'How lovely are the messengers.' Before I got to the end of the first verse they both joined in the chorus. . . . Then the young Prince of Gotha [i.e. Prince Albert's brother Ernest] came in, and there was more chatting; and the Queen asked if I had written any new songs, and said she was very fond of singing my published ones. 'You should sing one to him,' said Prince Albert; and, after a little begging, she said she would try the 'Frühlingslied' in B flat – 'If it is still here,' she added, 'for all my music is packed up for Claremont.' Prince Albert went to look for it, but came back, saying it was already packed. 'But one might perhaps unpack it,' said I. 'We must send for Lady —,' she said. (I did not catch the name.) So the bell was rung, and the servants were sent after it, but without success; and at last the Queen went herself, and while she was gone Prince Albert said to

175

me, 'She begs you will accept this present as a remembrance,' and gave me a little case with a beautiful ring, on which is engraved 'V.R. 1842.'

Then the Queen came back, and said, 'Lady — is gone, and has taken all my things with her. It really is most annoying.' (You can't think how that amused me.) I then begged that I might not be made to suffer for the accident, and hoped she would sing another song. After some consultation with her husband he said, 'She will sing you something of Gluck's.' Meantime the Princess of Gotha [i.e. Prince Ernest's wife] had come in, and we five proceeded through various corridors and rooms to the Queen's sitting-room. The Duchess of Kent came in too, and while they were all talking I rummaged about amongst the music, and soon discovered my first set of songs. So, of course, I begged her rather to sing one of those than the Gluck, to which she very kindly consented; and which did she choose? – 'Schöner und schöner schmückt sich!' sang it quite charmingly, in strict time and tune, and with very good execution.... Then I was obliged to confess that Fanny [i.e. the musician's sister] had written the song (which I found very hard, but pride must have a fall), and to beg her to sing one of mine also. If I would give her plenty of help, she would gladly try, she said, and then she sang the Pilgerspruch 'Lass dich nur' really quite faultlessly, and with charming feeling and expression. I thought to myself, one must not pay too many compliments on such an occasion, so I merely thanked her a great many times; upon which she said, 'Oh, if only I had not been so frightened! generally I have such long breath.' Then I praised her heartily, and with the best conscience in the world; for just that part with the long C at the close she had done so well, taking it and the three notes next to it all in the same breath, as one seldom hears it done, and therefore it amused me doubly that she herself should have begun about it.

After this Prince Albert sang the Aerndtelied, 'Es ist ein Schnitter;' and then he said I must improvise something before I went, and they followed me with so much intelligence and attention that I felt more at my ease than I ever did in improvising to an audience. The Queen said several times she hoped I would soon come to England again and pay them a visit, and then I took leave; and down below I saw the beautiful carriages waiting, with their scarlet outriders, and in a quarter of an hour the flag was lowered, and the 'Court Circular' announced, 'Her Majesty left the Palace at twenty minutes past three.'

(From a letter to his mother, Frankfurt, 19 July 1842)

STANLEY MIDDLETON

From Calvary to cantata

John Chamberlain was in good health. He had played a lot of squash, walked by the sea, tanning face and hands, had cleared up his work and acquired something of a swagger. Compared with him Lynette was pale, quieter, slightly older, keeping herself in check, expecting trouble. By contrast he shouted boisterously, jumped out, made her run, acted with childish energy.

On the evening of Good Friday, sunny but cold still, they had driven to a Methodist church in Grantham to hear Boy McKay sing. He had discovered his voice in the last year or two, was taking lessons and this was his first engagement, in Maunder's *From Olivet to Calvary*. He himself was amused by his new 'talent', joked that the Law Society did not encourage artists, felt his life as an adulterer branded him as unfit for chapels, but put on his neatest grey three-piece. He talked to Lynette about it, seemed obsessed, sang snatches round the office. In the end, anti-climax, a coolish barn, not a fifth filled, the bunches of narcissi, the over-loud, under-soft wooden bourdon, the enthusiastic ruggedness of choir, exactly suited McKay's pale nervousness, tremor of hand and voice, odd contretemps with the organist.

John puzzled, mocked the enterprise. The building, the choral singing, the work itself belonged to a world he did not know, did not concern him. It was a survival, an atavism, seemingly genteel, among the working classes.

'There were women with flowers in their hats,' he said. 'And men with great red hands bawling away. You couldn't help laughing.'

'If you'd been back last week you could have heard the *St John Passion*,' his mother said.

'That hadn't got McKay in it, had it?'

'It had men with red hands. The women wore black, I'll grant you that. The cathedral bears looking at. The orchestra wasn't too bad. The soloists were, some of them, quite well known.'

'And what, Father, are you telling me this for?' John, lively, rash for argument.

'The place was full. Yet it made up a fraction of the population. You stop the man on the milk-float, cleaning windows, ask him to distinguish between Bach and Maunder, and he can't. And that at the end of a hundred years of universal education. They know neither.'

'You can't name pop-groups,' Elsa interrupted.

'I can. I needed a couple for my novel. I know where to look. Not that I understand a thing about them in any real sense. But I can give the appearance.'

'You're just a hypocrite.' John.

'That's what education's for. That's why I got out.'

'What was Mr McKay like, Lynette?' Elsa asked.

'Very nervous. Not himself, at all. More like a schoolboy or a choirboy. Pale and standing still, but wishing he could wriggle.'

'As if he'd peed himself.' John, confident.

Chamberlain lectured them, claiming that what his son would teach in schools was as irrelevant as that chapel, that oratorio.

'It's not a bad thing to be able to read,' John said.

'That's what you schoolmasters are not managing, if I understand it.'

'It's just come to the surface. There's always been a proportion of non-readers. Nobody bothered before. Now we're trying. Special classes. And we give 'em stuff to read that catches their interest. Based on their lives.'

'I know,' Chamberlain said. 'Low-grade Maunder and Stainer. Bach's too hard for 'em.'

'It might lead to Bach. That's the hope.'

'Don't tell me that. The bloody teachers are half illiterate themselves. Never read anything outside the magazines and the hot-breath paperbacks.'

'As provided by yourself?'

'Exactly. I'm no George Eliot.'

(*Ends and Means*)

ROGER NORTH

How music began

Nothing made so great a *denovement* in musick as the invention of horse hair, with rozin, and the gutts of animals twisted and dryed. I scarce think that the strings of the old Lyra used in either the Jewish or Greek times, which in latine are termed nerves, were such, becaus it was more or less piacular to deal in that manner with the *entra* of dead animalls. Nor is it any where, as I know, intimated of what materiall these strings were made, but I guess they were mettaline, as most sonorous, or of twisted silk; nor is there any hint when the Violl kind came first in use. Had the Greeks known it, some deity, for certain, had bin the inventor, and more worthily then Apollo of the Harp, for it draws a continuing sound, exactly tuneable to all occasions & compass, with small labour and no expence of breath. But as to the invention, which is so perfectly novel as not to have bin ever heard of before Augustulus, the last of the Roman Emperors, I cannot but esteem it perfectly gothick, and entred with those barbarous nations setled in Italy, and from thence spread into all the neighbour nations round about, and now is in possession, and like to hold it, as a principall squadron in the instrumentall navy.

I doe suppose that at first it was like its native country, rude and gross. And that at the early importation it was of the lesser kind, which they called Viola da Bracchia, and since the violin, and no better then as a rushy Zampogna used to stirr up the vulgar to dancing, or perhaps to solemnize their idolatrous sacrifices. These people made no scruple of handling gutts and garbages, and were so free with humane bodys as to make drinking cupps of their sculls. And when the discovery of the vertue of the bow was made, and understood, the *vertuosi* went to work, and modeled the use of it, and its subject the viol, with great improvement, to all purposes of musick, and brought it to a paralell state with the Organ it self. And by adapting sizes to the severall diapasons as well above E la as the doubles below, severall persons take their parts, and consorts are performed with small trouble, and in all perfection. The invention needs no enconium to recomend it to posterity; for altho' it hath bin in practise many hundred years, no considerable alterations of it in forme or application have bin made which any memoriall can account for. And now no improvement is thought of or desired, but in the choice of the materiall, & curiosity of the workmanship. I shall take leave of the Violl with a remembrance onely of a merry discovery of Kircher's in one of his windy volumes, which is a note added to the picture of a Lute and a Guittarre, that the old Hebrews used to sound them with the scratch of an horsetail bow!

As the Harpsicord or Spinett kind was a composition of the old harp and organ, so the Lute kind is a composition between the spinett and the violl. They are made of a shape not unlike a Tortois, which suits with some of the practises (if they are not fables) of the ancients, but so done now for convenience of handling. The stopps, or fretts, of all these instruments are a further improvement wholly unknown to the ancients, and make a distinct instrument with (almost) sufficient compass, of every string. But the Lute kind cannot spare the fretts as the Violl may, and in many shapes succeeds better, by plain stopps without them. The common Harp, by the use of gutt strings, hath received incomparable improvement, but cannot be a consort instrument becaus it cannot follow organs & violls in the frequent change of keys; and the wind musick, which by all stress of invention hath bin brought into ordinary consort measures, yet more or less labours under the same infirmity, especially the cheif of them, which is the Trumpet.

(*Memoires of Musick*)

JOHN NYREN

John Small, cricketer and fiddler

John Small the Elder was a remarkably well-made, and well-knit man, of honest expression, and as active as a hare. He was a good fiddler, and taught himself the double bass. The Duke of Dorset having been informed of his musical talent, sent him as a present a handsome violin, and paid the carriage. Small, like a true and simple-hearted Englishman, returned the compliment, by sending his Grace two bats and balls, also paying the carriage. We may be sure that on both hands the presents were choice of their kind.

Upon one occasion he turned his Orphean accomplishments to a good account. Having to cross two or three fields on his way to a musical party, a vivacious bull made at him; when our hero with the characteristic coolness and presence of mind of a good cricketer, began playing upon his bass, to the admiration and perfect satisfaction of the mischievous beast.

(*The Cricketers of my Time*)

WILLIAM MAKEPEACE THACKERAY

Mrs Mackenzie in pursuit of a catch

Mrs Mackenzie was, as the phrase is, 'setting her cap' so openly at Clive, that none of us could avoid seeing her play: and Clive laughed at her simple manœuvres as merrily as the rest. She was a merry little woman. We gave her and her pretty daughter a luncheon in Lamb Court, Temple; in Sibwright's chambers – luncheon from Dick's Coffee House – ices and dessert from Partington's in the Strand. Miss Rosey, Mr Sibwright, our neighbour in Lamb Court, and the Reverend Charles Honeyman sang very delightfully after lunch; there was quite a crowd of porters, laundresses, and boys to listen in the Court; Mr Paley was disgusted with the noise we made – in fact, the party was perfectly successful. We all liked the widow, and if she did set her pretty ribbons at Clive, why should not she? We all liked the pretty, fresh, modest Rosey. Why, even the grave old benchers in the Temple church, when the ladies visited it on Sunday, winked their reverend eyes with pleasure, as they looked at those two uncommonly smart, pretty, well-dressed, fashionable women. Ladies, go to the Temple church. You will see more young men, and receive more respectful attention there than in any place, except perhaps at Oxford or Cambridge. Go to the Temple church – not, of course, for the admiration which you will excite and which you cannot help; but because the sermon is excellent, the choral services beautifully performed, and the church so interesting as a monument of the thirteenth century, and as it contains the tombs of those dear Knights Templars! . . .

Whether the fair lady tried her wiles upon Colonel Newcome the present writer has no certain means of ascertaining: but I think another

Richard Doyle's drawing of 'Mr Honeyman At Home' in Thackeray's
The Newcomes

image occupied his heart: and this Circe tempted him no more than a score of other enchantresses who had tried their spells upon him. If she tried she failed. She was a very shrewd woman, quite frank in her talk when such frankness suited her. She said to me, 'Colonel Newcome has had some great passion, once upon a time, I am sure of that, and has no more heart to give away. The woman who had his must have been a very lucky woman: though I daresay she did not value what she had; or did not live to enjoy it – or – or something or other. You see tragedies in some people's faces. I recollect when we were in Coventry Island – there was a chaplain there – a very good man – a Mr Bell, and married to a pretty little woman who died. The first day I saw him I said, 'I know that man has had a great grief in life. I am sure that he left his heart in England.' You gentlemen who write books, Mr Pendennis, and stop at the third volume, know very well that the real story often begins afterwards. My third volume ended when I was sixteen, and was married to my poor husband. Do you think all our adventures ended then, and that we lived happy ever after? I live for my darling girls now. All I want is to see them comfortable in life. . . . (Enter Rosey.) 'Rosey, darling! I have been telling Mr Pendennis what a naughty, naughty child you were yesterday, and how you read a book which I told you you shouldn't read; for it is a very *wicked* book; and though it contains some sad sad truths, it is a great deal too misanthropic (is that the right word? I'm a poor soldier's wife, and no scholar, you know,) and a great deal too *bitter*, and though the reviews praise it, and the clever people – *we* are poor simple country people – *we* won't praise it. Sing, dearest, that little song' (profuse kisses to Rosey) 'that pretty thing that Mr Pendennis likes.'

'I am sure that I will sing any thing that Mr Pendennis likes,' says Rosey, with her candid bright eyes – and she goes to the piano and warbles Batti, Batti, with her sweet fresh artless voice.

More caresses follow. Mamma is in a rapture. How pretty they look – the mother and daughter – two lilies twining together. The necessity of an entertainment at the Temple – lunch from Dick's (as before mentioned), dessert from Partington's, Sibwright's spoons, his boy to aid ours, nay, Sib himself, and his rooms, which are so much more elegant than ours, and where there is a piano and guitar: all these thoughts pass in rapid and brilliant combination in the pleasant Mr Pendennis's mind. How delighted the ladies are with the proposal! Mrs Mackenzie claps her pretty hands, and kisses Rosey again. If osculation is a mark of love, surely

Mrs Mack is the best of mothers. I may say, without false modesty, that our little entertainment was most successful. The champagne was iced to a nicety. The ladies did not perceive that our laundress, Mrs Flanagan, was intoxicated very early in the afternoon. Percy Sibwright sang admirably, and with the greatest spirit, ditties in many languages. I am sure Miss Rosey thought him (as indeed he is) one of the most fascinating young fellows about town. To her mother's excellent accompaniment Rosey sang her favourite songs (by the way her stock was very small – five, I think, was the number). Then the table was moved into a corner, where the quivering moulds of jelly seemed to keep time to the music; and whilst Percy played, two couple of waltzers actually whirled round the little room. No wonder that the court below was thronged with admirers, that Paley the reading man was in a rage, and Mrs Flanagan in a state of excitement. Ah! pleasant days, happy old dingy chambers illuminated by youthful sunshine! merry songs and kind faces – it is pleasant to recall you. Some of those bright eyes shine no more: some of those smiling lips do not speak. Some are not less kind, but sadder than in those days: of which the memories revisit us for a moment, and sink back into the grey past. The dear old Colonel beat time with great delight to the songs; the widow lit his cigar with her own fair fingers. That was the only smoke permitted during the entertainment – George Warrington himself not being allowed to use his cutty-pipe – though the gay little widow said that she had been used to smoking in the West Indies, and I daresay spoke the truth. Our entertainment lasted actually until after dark; and a particularly neat cab being called from St Clement's by Mr Binnie's boy, you may be sure we all conducted the ladies to their vehicle: and many a fellow returning from his lonely club that evening into chambers must have envied us the pleasure of having received two such beauties.

The clerical bachelor was not to be outdone by the gentlemen of the bar; and the entertainment at the Temple was followed by one at Honeyman's lodgings, which, I must own, greatly exceeded ours in splendour, for Honeyman had his luncheon from Gunter's; and if he had been Miss Rosey's mother, giving a breakfast to the dear girl on her marriage, the affair could not have been more elegant and handsome. We had but two bouquets at our entertainment; at Honeyman's there were four upon the breakfast-table, besides a great pine-apple, which must have cost the rogue three or four guineas, and which Percy Sibwright delicately cut up. Rosey thought the pine-apple delicious. 'The dear thing does not remember the pine-apples in the West Indies!' cries Mrs Mackenzie; and she gave us many exciting narratives of entertainments at which she had been present at various colonial governors' tables. After luncheon, our host hoped we should have a little music. Dancing, of course, could not be allowed. 'That,' said Honeyman, with his 'soft-bleating sigh,' 'were scarcely clerical. You know, besides, you are in a *hermitage*; and (with a glance round the table) must put up with Cenobite's fare.' The fare was, as I have said, excellent. The wine was bad, as George, and I, and Sib agreed; and in so far we flattered ourselves that *our* feast altogether excelled the parson's. The champagne especially was such stuff, that Warrington remarked on it to his neighbour, a dark gentleman, with a tuft to his chin, and splendid rings and chains.

The dark gentleman's wife and daughter were the other two ladies invited by our host. The elder was splendidly dressed. Poor Mrs Mackenzie's simple gimcracks, though she displayed them to the most advantage, and could make an ormolu bracelet go as far as another woman's emerald clasps, were as nothing compared to the other lady's gorgeous jewellery. Her fingers glittered with rings innumerable. The head of her smelling-bottle was as big as her husband's gold snuff-box, and of the same splendid material. Our ladies, it must be confessed, came in a modest cab from Fitzroy Square; these arrived in a splendid little open carriage with white ponies, and harness all over brass, which the lady of the rings drove with a whip that was a parasol. Mrs Mackenzie, standing at Honeyman's window, with her arm round Rosey's waist, viewed this arrival perhaps with envy. 'My dear Mr Honeyman, whose are those beautiful horses?' cries Rosey, with enthusiasm.

The divine says with a faint blush – 'It is – ah – it is Mrs Sherrick and Miss Sherrick, who have done me the favour to come to luncheon.'

'Wine merchant. Oh!' thinks Mrs Mackenzie, who has seen Sherrick's brass-plate on the cellar-door of Lady Whittlesea's chapel; and hence, perhaps, she was a trifle more magniloquent than usual, and entertained us with stories of colonial governors and their ladies, mentioning no persons, but those who 'had handles to their names,' as the phrase is.

Although Sherrick had actually supplied the champagne which Warrington abused to him in confidence, the wine-merchant was not wounded; on the contrary, he roared with laughter at the remark, and some of us smiled who understood the humour of the joke. As for George Warrington, he scarce knew more about the town than the ladies opposite to him; who, yet more innocent than George, thought the champagne very good. Mrs Sherrick was silent during the meal, looking constantly up at her husband, as if alarmed and always in the habit of appealing to that gentleman, who gave her, as I thought, knowing glances and savage winks, which made me augur that he bullied her at home. Miss Sherrick was exceedingly handsome: she kept the fringed curtains of her eyes constantly down; but when she lifted them up towards Clive, who was very attentive to her (the rogue never sees a handsome woman, but to this day he continues the same practice) – when she looked up and smiled, she was indeed a beautiful young creature to behold, – with her pale forehead, her thick arched eyebrows, her rounded cheeks, and her full lips slightly shaded, – how shall I mention the word? – slightly pencilled, after the manner of the lips of the French governess, Mademoiselle Lenoir.

Percy Sibwright engaged Miss Mackenzie with his usual grace and affability. Mrs Mackenzie did her very utmost to be gracious; but it was evident the party was not altogether to her liking. Poor Percy, about whose means and expectations she had in the most natural way in the world asked information from me, was not perhaps a very eligible admirer for darling Rosey. She knew not that Percy can no more help gallantry than the sun can help shining. As soon as Rosey had done eating up her pine-apple, artlessly confessing (to Percy Sibwright's inquiries) that she preferred it to the rasps and hinnyblobs in her grandmamma's garden, 'Now, dearest Rosey,' cries Mrs Mack, 'now, a little song. You promised Mr Pendennis a little song.' Honeyman whisks open the piano in a moment. The widow takes off her cleaned gloves (Mrs Sherrick's were new, and of the best Paris make), and little Rosey sings, No. 1 followed by No. 2, with very great applause. Mother and daughter entwine as they quit the piano. 'Brava! brava!' says Percy Sibwright. Does Mr Clive Newcome say nothing? His back is turned to the piano, and he is looking with all his might into the eyes of Miss Sherrick.

Percy sings a Spanish seguidella, or a German lied, or a French romance, or a Neapolitan canzonet, which, I am bound to say, excites very little attention. Mrs Ridley is sending in coffee at this juncture, of which Mrs Sherrick partakes, with lots of sugar, as she has partaken of numberless things before. Chickens, plover's eggs, prawns, aspics, jellies, creams, grapes, and what-not. Mr Honeyman advances, and with deep respect asks if Mrs Sherrick and Miss Sherrick will not be persuaded to sing? She rises and bows, and again takes off the French gloves, and shows the large white

187

hands glittering with rings, and, summoning Emily her daughter, they go to the piano.

'Can she sing?' whispers Mrs Mackenzie, 'can she sing after eating so much?' Can she sing, indeed! O, you poor ignorant Mrs Mackenzie! Why, when you were in the West Indies, if you ever read the English newspapers, you must have read of the fame of Miss Folthorpe. Mrs Sherrick is no other than the famous artist, who, after three years of brilliant triumphs at the Scala, the Pergola, the San Carlo, the opera in England, forsook her profession, rejected a hundred suitors, and married Sherrick, who was Mr Cox's lawyer, who failed, as every body knows, as manager of Drury Lane. Sherrick, like a man of spirit, would not allow his wife to sing in public after his marriage; but in private society, of course, she is welcome to perform: and now with her daughter, who possesses a noble contralto voice, she takes her place royally at the piano, and the two sing so magnificently that everybody in the room, with one single exception, is charmed and delighted; and that little Miss Cann herself creeps up the stairs, and stands with Mrs Ridley at the door to listen to the music.

Miss Sherrick looks doubly handsome as she sings. Clive Newcome is in a rapture; so is good-natured Miss Rosey, whose little heart beats with pleasure, and who says quite unaffectedly to Miss Sherrick, with delight and gratitude beaming from her blue eyes, 'Why did you ask me to sing, when you sing so wonderfully, so beautifully yourself? Do not leave the piano, please, do sing again.' And she puts out a kind little hand towards the superior artist, and, blushing, leads her back to the instrument. 'I'm sure me and Emily will sing for you as much as you like, dear,' says Mrs Sherrick, nodding to Rosey good-naturedly. Mrs Mackenzie, who has been biting her lips and drumming the time on a side-table, forgets at last the pain of being vanquished in admiration of the conquerors. 'It was cruel of you not to tell us, Mr Honeyman,' she says, 'of the – of the treat you had in store for us. I had no idea we were going to meet professional people; Mrs Sherrick's singing is indeed beautiful.'

'If you come up to our place in the Regent's Park, Mr Newcome,' Mr Sherrick says, 'Mrs S. and Emily will give you as many songs as you like. . . .'

(*The Newcomes*)

ANTHONY TROLLOPE

Septimus Harding's solace

Mr Harding is a small man, now verging on sixty years, but bearing few of the signs of age; his hair is rather grizzled, though not grey, his eye is very mild, but clear and bright, though the double glasses which are fixed upon his nose, show that time has told upon his sight: his hands are delicately white, and both hands and feet are small; he always wears a black frock coat, black knee-breeches, and black gaiters, and somewhat scandalises some of his more hyper-clerical brethren by a black neck-handkerchief.

Mr Harding's warmest admirers cannot say that he was ever an industrious man; the circumstances of his life have not called on him to be so; and yet he can hardly be called an idler. Since his appointment to his precentorship, he has published, with all possible additions of vellum, typography, and gilding, a collection of our ancient church music, with some correct dissertations on Purcell, Crotch, and Nares. He has greatly improved the choir of Barchester, which, under his dominion, now rivals that of any cathedral in England. He has taken something more than his fair share in the cathedral services, and has played the violoncello daily to such audiences as he could collect, or, *faute de mieux*, to no audience at all.

We must mention one other peculiarity of Mr Harding. As we have before stated, he has an income of eight hundred a year, and has no family but his one daughter; and yet he is never quite at ease in money matters. The vellum and gilding of *Harding's Church Music*, cost more than anyone knows, except the author, the publisher, and the Rev. Theophilus

Grantly, who allows none of his father-in-law's extravagances to escape him. . . .

[John] Bold at once repaired to the hospital. The day was now far advanced, but he knew that Mr Harding dined in the summer at four, that Eleanor was accustomed to drive in the evening, and that he might therefore probably find Mr Harding alone. It was between seven and eight when he reached the slight iron gate leading into the precentor's garden, and though, as Mr Chadwick observed, the day had been cold for June, the evening was mild, and soft, and sweet. The little gate was open. As he raised the latch he heard the notes of Mr Harding's violoncello from the far end of the garden, and, advancing before the house and across the lawn, he found him playing: and not without an audience. The musician was seated in a garden-chair just within the summer-house, so as to allow the violoncello which he held between his knees to rest upon the dry stone flooring; before him stood a rough music desk, on which was open a page of that dear sacred book, that much-laboured and much-loved volume of church music, which had cost so many guineas; and around sat, and lay, and stood, and leaned, ten of the twelve old men who dwelt with him beneath old John Hiram's roof. The two reformers were not there. I will not say that in their hearts they were conscious of any wrong done or to be done to their mild warden, but latterly they had kept aloof from him, and his music was no longer to their taste.

It was amusing to see the positions, and eager listening faces of these well-to-do old men. I will not say that they all appreciated the music which they heard, but they were intent on appearing to do so; pleased at being where they were, they were determined, as far as in them lay, to give pleasure in return; and they were not unsuccessful. It gladdened the precentor's heart to think that the old bedesmen whom he loved so well admired the strains which were to him so full of almost ecstatic joy; and he used to boast that such was the air of the hospital, as to make it a precinct specially fit for the worship of St Cecilia.

Immediately before him, on the extreme corner of the bench which ran round the summer-house, sat one old man, with his handkerchief smoothly laid upon his knees, who did enjoy the moment, or acted enjoyment well. He was one on whose large frame many years, for he was over eighty, had made small havock, – he was still an upright, burly, handsome figure, with an open, ponderous brow, round which clung a few, though very few, thin grey locks. The coarse black gown of the hospital, the breeches, and buckled shoes became him well; and as he sat with his hands folded on his staff, and his chin resting on his hands, he was such a listener as most musicians would be glad to welcome.

This man was certainly the pride of the hospital. It had always been the custom that one should be selected as being to some extent in authority over the others; and though Mr Bunce, for such was his name, and so he was always designated by his inferior brethren, had no greater emoluments than they, he had assumed, and well knew how to maintain, the dignity of his elevation. The precentor delighted to call him his sub-warden, and was not ashamed, occasionally, when no other guest was there, to bid him sit down by the same parlour fire, and drink the full glass of port which was placed near him. Bunce never went without the second glass, but no entreaty ever made him take a third.

'Well, well, Mr Harding; you're too good, much too good,' he'd always say, as the second glass was filled; but when that was drunk, and the half-hour over, Bunce stood erect, and with a benediction which his patron valued retired to his own abode. He knew the world too well to risk the comfort of such halcyon moments, by prolonging them till they were disagreeable.

Mr Bunce, as may be imagined, was most strongly opposed to innovation. Not even Dr Grantly had a more holy horror of those who would interfere in the affairs of the hospital; he was every inch a Churchman, and though he was not very fond of Dr Grantly personally, that arose from there not being room in the hospital for two people so much alike as the doctor and himself, rather than from any dissimilarity in feeling. Mr Bunce was inclined to think that the warden and himself could manage the hospital without further assistance; and that, though the bishop was the constitutional visitor, and as such entitled to special reverence from all connected with John Hiram's will, John Hiram never intended that his affairs should be interfered with by an archdeacon.

At the present moment, however, these cares were off his mind, and he was looking at his warden, as though he thought the music heavenly, and the musician hardly less so.

As Bold walked silently over the lawn, Mr Harding did not at first perceive him, and continued to draw his bow slowly across the plaintive wires; but he soon found from his audience that some stranger was there, and looking up, began to welcome his young friend with frank hospitality.

191

'Pray, Mr Harding; pray don't let me disturb you,' said Bold; 'you know how fond I am of sacred music.'

'Oh! it's nothing,' said the precentor, shutting up the book and then opening it again as he saw the delightfully imploring look of his old friend Bunce. 'Oh, Bunce, Bunce, Bunce, I fear that after all thou art but a flatterer. Well, I'll just finish it then; it's a favourite little bit of Bishop's; and then, Mr Bold, we'll have a stroll and a chat till Eleanor comes in and gives us tea.' And so Bold sat down on the soft turf to listen, or rather to think how, after such sweet harmony, he might best introduce a theme of so much discord, to disturb the peace of him who was so ready to welcome him kindly.

Bold thought that the performance was soon over, for he felt that he had a somewhat difficult task, and he almost regretted the final leave-taking of the last of the old men, slow as they were in going through their adieus.

Bold's heart was in his mouth, as the precentor made some ordinary but kind remark as to the friendliness of the visit.

'One evening call,' said he, 'is worth ten in the morning. It's all formality in the morning; real social talk never begins till after dinner. That's why I dine early, so as to get as much as I can of it.'

'Quite true, Mr Harding,' said the other; 'but I fear I've reversed the order of things, and I owe you much apology for troubling you on business at such an hour; but it is on business that I have called just now.'

Mr Harding looked blank and annoyed; there was something in the tone of the young man's voice, which told him that the interview was intended to be disagreeable, and he shrank back at finding his kindly greeting so repulsed.

'I wish to speak to you about the hospital,' continued Bold.

'Well, well, anything I can tell you I shall be most happy – '

'It's about the accounts.'

'Then, my dear fellow, I can tell you nothing, for I'm as ignorant as a child. All I know is, that they pay me £800 a year. Go to Chadwick, he knows all about the accounts; and now tell me, will poor Mary Jones ever get the use of her limb again?'

'Well, I think she will, if she's careful; but, Mr Harding, I hope you won't object to discuss with me what I have to say about the hospital.'

Mr Harding gave a deep, long-drawn sigh. He did object, very strongly object, to discuss any such subject with John Bold; but he had not the business tact of Mr Chadwick, and did not know how to relieve himself from the coming evil; he sighed sadly, but made no answer.

'I have the greatest regard for you, Mr Harding,' continued Bold; 'the truest respect, the most sincere – '

'Thank ye, thank ye, Mr Bold,' interjaculated the precentor somewhat impatiently; 'I'm much obliged, but never mind that; I'm as likely to be in the wrong as another man – quite as likely.'

'But, Mr Harding, I must express what I feel, lest you should think there is personal enmity in what I'm going to do.'

'Personal enmity! Going to do! Why, you're not going to cut my throat, nor put me into the Ecclesiastical Court – '

Bold tried to laugh, but he couldn't. He was quite in earnest, and determined in his course, and couldn't make a joke of it. He walked on awhile in silence before he recommenced his attack, during which Mr Harding, who had still the bow in his hand, played rapidly on an imaginary violoncello. 'I fear there is reason to think that John Hiram's will is not carried out to the letter, Mr Harding,' said the young man at last; 'and I have been asked to see into it.'

(*The Warden*)

BETSEY WYNNE

Betsey Wynne (1779–1857) was one of the most prolific and liveliest diarists of
the period, even against the competition of the Burney family. Her chronicle
started at 1789 when she was ten and ended with her death. Her sister Eugenia
was almost as assiduous. Their father was Riccardo Gulielmo Casparo Melchior
Balthazaro Wynne (better known as Richard). By a happy coincidence for the
purposes of this anthology, his sister was Giustiniana, the mysterious Countess of
Rosenberg, another of the young ladies whom Casanova included in his *Memoirs*
as 'Mlle. X.C.V.' and who is discussed at length by his biographers. The family's
cosmopolitan tastes ensured that Betsey's musicality was appreciated, and 'Mon.
Pleyel' was engaged as music master to the Misses Wynne. Hence Betsey's
keyboard competence. As Anne Fremantle (who married into the family in 1930
and edited the diaries) wrote: 'Betsey was very much the elder sister, witty,
self-assured, brilliant, of really scintillating intelligence, and a little unfeminine for
all her charm whilst Eugenia, with less superabundant vitality, thought and felt
more deeply, was kinder, more merciful, less hard.'

Eugenia had a turbulent love affair with a wild Scot in volume 3, while in
the marriage stakes Betsey did better: she captured Captain (later Admiral)
Fremantle, one of Nelson's chief friends and colleagues: indeed, she was married
from Lady Hamilton's house in 1798. He died in 1819 and she remained as
the matriarch of the family during her long widowhood. Some of the musical
occasions recorded have been extracted from the three published volumes
(some 1200 pages), which Anne Fremantle had already reduced from 62 manu-
script volumes. Not much escaped the sisters' lively commentary, at home and
abroad.

Hoisting a harpsichord aboard

February 1, 1791, Venice: We dined today at the Ambassadress of Spain where we had an excellent diner we had to return to the Ambassadress of France for the Musick and the Ball she gave for the Count d'Artois. He came, as also all the Polignac family except the children, all the French and a quantity of ladies that I don't know. The Countess of Rosenberg was there, I played 2 sonatas. Eugenia sang, the dutchess of Guiche sang also a duet with Miss Idalie this last executed a piece for the harpsichord by Clementi that was very difficult perfectly well. After we dansed Miss Idalie dansed the minuet perfectly she has had Vestris for master, I dansed several country danses, and the Russian and the Cossacke these two were infinitely admired, the Count d'Artois kissed Eugenia which I think was very flattered although she says that it did not please her.

July 29, 1796, off Toulon, on board the Britannia: Sir John Jervis wrote a note at four oclock in the morning to ask us to dine with him. We accepted with infinite pleasure of his kind invitation and . . . we dressed to go to the Victory . . . the Admiral was on Deck to receive us with the greatest civility and kindness nothing stiff or formal about him and we were not at all embarrassed as I feared we should be. He desired we should pay the tribute that wass due to him at our entering his Cabin, this was to kiss him which the Ladies did very willingly. . . . The good Admiral has a very high opinion of me. He told me that I should make the best wife in England. And indeed he made me so many such fine compliments that I was quite at a loss how to answer them. All the gentlemen that had been to see us in the morning dined with us. It was a large party and we were very gay, laughed much and made a monstrous noise at table. . . . We were obliged to sing a duet after dinner. We did not stay late for as Admiral Jervis gets up at two oclock in the morning he goes to bed at halfpast eight. We got into the Barge to come to the Britannia at seven very much pleased with the kind reception we had met with from the Admiral and the kindly manner he treated us with. The victory is a much finer ship than the Britannia, the same size but the apartments not by half as good and comfortable. On our return to our ship we stopped near the Courageous to hear some very pretty musick. Captain Hallow who commands that 74 (taken from the french the war before the last) has a very good band. They played the charming tunes and the flutes and Bugle horns [flugelhorns] made a most delightful effect. We had a dance in the evening on board the Britannia.

[In January 1797, Captain (later Admiral) T. F. Fremantle, whose own terse diary of the period also survives, married Betsey Wynne. By virtue of his command, he was able to take not only Betsey but her harpsichord on board on peaceful voyages. Five years later he wrote to his wife ('June 22nd, 1804, at Sea off Ferrol']:

My Dearest Betsey,

I wish you would by some means endeavour to procure and send me a Sonata I believe of Mozart with an accompanyment of the violin, if you recolect it as one played by Miss Tate at our house in Clifford Street, and I have frequently requested you to play it since, it is pretty that I wish to give it to the Consul's daughters. I hope you recolect it, I am now singing it.

[The sonata clearly arrived, for there is a scornful reference in Fremantle's letter from the same station, August 19]:

... I have received the box with the tooth powder and brushes, and thank you for the Sonata, which will now not be of as much consequence as it would some time ago, for the Damsel to whom I meant to present it, sixteen years of age, has thought fit to fall in Love with an ugly, ill-looking officer, a Lieut. without a shilling and with a very bad character, and contrary to the advice of her parents is determined to marry him ...

May 7, 1805: Fremantle came home to dress with us but just received a Letter from lord Garlies (who is now one of the Lords of the Admiralty) to inform him Ld. Barham had this day appointed him to the Neptune 98 guns, which is coming into Plymouth in a few days. I fear he will be obliged to join her very soon.

May 8: We were very busily employed in preparing for our little Concert – & poor Fremantle in getting information about his ship & making arrangements for his departure. He dined at his Brother William's & came to our music late. Dragonetti dined with us another very good second violin & Bartolozzi came to play Quatuors & accompany. Our company did not come till near ten & the party was very select & brilliant – about 130 in all. The Amateur performers were Mrs W Jerningham on the Harp, myself on the Piano, the chevalier La Caema who really sung delightfully, Mrs Peploe, Miss Fanny Cornewall, Eugenia & Mr Mercer. We had asked all our best acquaintance & very charitably left out the Quizzes. Our party ended very dismally as after every body was gone poor Fremantle who had looked very unhappy all the evening announced to us he should be obliged

196

to sett out to morrow for Plymouth to join his Ship. I wish he had not been employed so soon but at any time it happen'd I should have disliked it, therefore it is perhaps better while we are in Town than had he left after my return to Swanbourne.

May 11: I heard to day from Fremantle from Portsmouth where he made every arrangement about his Wine & Cabin Furniture, & expected to get to Plymouth to morrow. His ship is quite ready for sea, so that he will sail immediately. We all stayed at home, I feel low & not quite well.

[Her depression was understandable. Four months later, the diary records her delivery of a daughter on September 7. On October 1, Lord Nelson gave the news to her husband, captain of the Neptune and third in the line of battle, over dinner on the Victory off Cadiz. Three weeks later, Trafalgar was fought, leaving Fremantle unscathed in spite of his ship's fierce engagement with the Santissima Trinidad, whose marksman in the shrouds mortally wounded Nelson on Victory.]

(*The Wynne Diaries*)

4
VIBRATIONS IN THE MEMORY

ANON

An elegy for Anacreon

Anacreon of Teos, the imperishable fount sprung from the Muses, loved boys like honey and his desires were sped by the Graces. In the dark realm, his heart is heavy, not for lost sunlight and fading memories but for the passion he cherished for handsome Megistheus and the pleasure he had in Smerdies the Thracian. For he never had to forgo his sweet joy in melody; nor could he ever put his lyre to bed, even in death.

(*Palatine Anthology*)

NEVILLE CARDUS

A child's tonic sol-fa tone-row

It was strange but not marvellous that a poor boy with a frail physique and a shy, nervous disposition and of extreme short sight should in time have come to play cricket; for after all this is our national game. Sooner or later everybody belonging to England will be tempted to succumb to its allurements. But I can attribute the music discovered in me late in my teens only to some obscure hereditary influence. There was no piano in my home, or any other instrument; the radio was not yet a universal dissemi-nator of music, and the phonograph remained more or less experimental and sepulchral. The piano was, indeed, in these days the privilege of the middle and upper-classes; I was at least eighteen years old before I entered a house containing a piano; and the top of it was covered with family portraits. The only music taught in the Board school was tonic-solfa – doh: ray, me – which I found more than useful when I began really to learn to read a score; I once transposed or translated nearly a whole piano arrange-ment of 'Tristan and Isolde' into tonic-solfa (the last sharp to the right a 'te'; the last flat to the right a 'fah'). Four-part songs were sung in school a half an hour or so a week, conducted by one of the corsetted yellow faces; sometimes we had to read tonic-solfa at sight, not only from the black-board but from various signs made by the teacher's hand. 'Doh' was a fist clasped strenuously; 'ray' was the right hand slightly aslant, as though in disapproval; and so on. The songs we sang included 'As pants the hart for cooling streams' and Balfe's 'Excelsior.'

When the music was written in tonic-solfa on the blackboard, coloured chalks denoted the different voices, alto and treble. And when the singing-

Miss Glover's tonic sol-fa, as sabotaged by the young Neville Cardus

class was at an end the blackboard would be turned over and the reverse side used for other and more practical studies, such as long division. Once I was hauled out of class for some misdemeanour, and hidden out of the sight of my kind, girls as well as boys, segregated in two groups; and I was put behind this blackboard. The teacher left the class-room for a while, and I took some coloured chalks from her desk and altered at random the tonic-solfa notation, changing 'fahs' to 'rays,' or 'tes' to 'lahs.' The following week, when the class sang 'As pants the hart' at sight, empirical efforts in atonalism were heard for the first time in England. I was easily identified as the cause of the dissonances, and I was – probably fairly and with justice for once in a way – prodigiously flogged.

(Second Innings)

TRISTRAM CARY

My mother, the inspired faker

My mother could have been a professional pianist if she had studied more methodically, but as it was she was a versatile natural artist on both piano and 'cello, and sang very musically, with true feeling and excellent intonation. By natural I mean that her practical ability transcended her theoretical knowledge – for example she could transpose quite complex music at sight without really knowing how she did it, and she was an inspired 'faker' in difficult song accompaniments, knowing exactly how to simplify the performance while sacrificing the minimum energy, tempo or richness.

She started us all on the piano at about five years old, and saw that we practised, but when we came under the school music teacher she confined her role to supervising practice. We were frequently made to play for visitors, giving us a sense of occasion and improving continuity of performance (keep going and finish at all costs!).

She played a fairly small repertoire of piano solos, mostly those she had learned as a girl, and mainly in the Beethoven Brahms bracket. She sometimes played Bach and Mozart, but not often. She accompanied her own singing a lot, particularly singing to my father, but she also enjoyed singing to our accompaniment. She sang some Handel, but mostly Lieder – Schubert, Schumann, Brahms, Wolf. She adored Wagner but did not often sing his music. As a patriotic Briton she was very hurt to hear that she was accused of disloyalty in singing Lieder in German during the war. For her (as far as most people) German is the only language you can sing these songs in, but she was very upset by the fatuous innuendoes.

For my mother the last word about music was said by Wagner and Brahms, she never really got interested in the 20th century repertoire, except Elgar and a little Debussy and Ravel. Stravinsky, Bartok, Schoenberg and the young British school she was not fond of on the whole. Trudy sang a lot of choral music, mainly in the Bach Choir (under Hugh Allen) but sometimes she played the 'cello in Bach Choir concerts instead of singing.

We had irregular but fairly frequent chamber music at home and around Oxford up to 1939, but it dropped to very little in the war. Her 'cello playing had lovely warmth but she did not like playing high – she was always unhappy in thumb-position and never learnt to sight read properly from treble clef. In piano chamber music she always played 'cello and recruited another pianist – from the family or outside. A favourite work was Schubert's Trout Quintet, for which a lady bass player would bring her instrument in an old pram. She played bass very badly, but my mother for some reason felt good not being the bottom line. As a small child I would occasionally be invited down to chamber music in the evening (after official bedtime), and remember sitting underneath the Steinway (which I now have at home), enjoying the thunderous sounds.

('Trudy Cary as a Musician')

ERIC COATES

A clerical goose in Brahms

About half-way through the term, Ellenberger [my teacher] asked me if I would like to join a special quartet he was forming to play on Friday evenings at his house. The maestro himself was going to lead, I was to be second violin, Mrs Ellenberger viola, and a local musician, Fred Hodgkinson, the 'cello. Of course I was delighted to have the opportunity of studying the Great Masters under such conditions, and to have the privilege of being admitted into the 'Inner Circle'. And so it was arranged, and the trains between Hucknall and Nottingham saw me more frequently than ever.

I usually left my home after what we call in the Midlands a 'high tea' (it took me years to break myself of this old custom, but to-day I can fortunately pass that magic hour without a pang) and arrived at my professor's house just as they were finishing their dinner ('high tea' in the Ellenberger *ménage* was not considered 'the thing') and in time for a very acceptable cup of coffee. A cigarette, and then, the stands arranged and the music set out, the evening would begin. A quartet of Haydn's and then some Brahms; a quartet of Mozart and then again Brahms; a quartet of Beethoven's and yet again Brahms; it did not matter which of the Masters was omitted from our practices provided it was not Brahms. I am sure these delightful evenings were responsible for my love of Brahms to-day, especially his quartets, quintets and sextets and, finally, the Clarinet Quintet in B Minor. I have cause to remember this work in particular, for it was to be the means of great changes for me in my musical career. Ellenberger had for a long time been endeavouring to find a local clarinettist who was willing to spend an evening playing the Brahms Quintet 'for love'. Now, I wish to state quite clearly that I am not criticising clarinet players as a body, and I am sure there are artists to-day who enjoy playing for the love of it, but in those days clarinettists were far too often of what I call the 'beery' type. You would find them in the interval at any orchestral concert playing nap on a beer-barrel, or some such other type of receptacle, in the evil-smelling band-room under the stage. And would they play their clarinet for nothing? Certainly not! It was bad enough anyhow, playing professionally. Now do you wonder that there were few really good clarinet players, when they were so mercenary? But, one day, Ellenberger met a charming old clergyman, the rector of some parish on the Fosse Way, outside Nottingham (I cannot recall his name, but perhaps that may be as well), who considered himself a clarinettist of some ability. It was too good to be true. And so one Friday evening Fred Hodgkinson and I arrived at the charming house in Burns Street to find the reverend gentle-man already installed with the maestro and his wife, and beaming with good-will. Everyone was very happy. Evidently the dinner had been beyond reproach, and excitement over the impending performance of the Brahms Quintet ran high. Once again the stands were arranged (five this time), the music set out, the chairs placed in position, one more cigarette and a last cup of coffee, followed by much tuning-up of instruments, and then Ellenberger raised his bow and the two violins began that lovely introduction to one of the Master's greatest achievements in chamber music. I can recall the scene even now. The pretty drawing-room with the soft-coloured lamp-shades, the soft-coloured curtains, the soft-coloured rugs on the parquet floor; an effect of pastel blue throughout. Even the pale blue night outside seemed in harmony, with the garden showing a misty blue through the open french windows. A large standard-lamp in the centre of the players, throwing a pleasant light on to the music and five very serious people intent on the work in hand. At the entrance of the clarinet I realised that all was not well. A quick glance at Fred over the top of the music-stand – but he was absorbed in a technical passage; and then an alarming 'quawk' from the old clergyman. He had blown what is known among orchestral players as a 'goose' – an unearthly note in the high register of the instrument, due to faulty lip-pressure. Again I looked across at Fred and unfortunately our eyes met. Ellenberger and his wife appeared unmoved – this made matters worse, as far as the 'cello and the second fiddle were concerned. Another unearthly 'goose' followed by another and yet another (all the notes sounded like 'geese') finished the proceedings. Hysterical attempts on the part of Fred and myself to prevent ourselves from laughing merely brought us to the verge of complete collapse; we cried, silently and helplessly, and nothing could stop us. The music ceased. The Ellenbergers were furious – at the time we did not know whether their fury was directed at the old clergyman for his 'quawks' or at us for showing such deplorable lack of self-control. But what could they have expected? To see the old boy with his eyes standing out of his head, sucking at the mouthpiece of his clarinet and vainly trying to keep the thing in order, was ludicrous beyond description. Fred and I had him in full view, so we knew. Murmuring something about the keys having seized up through the instrument's lying for too long in its case, the old fellow closed his music, saying he would like a little longer to practise before playing the work again ensemble. By this time we were feeling sorry for the old man, for he had really taken it very well, and now that our mirth had subsided we both felt ashamed of ourselves for our display of bad manners. Apologies were duly made, strong drink was forthcoming, and after half a dozen glasses of good old port, our clarinettist was laughing at himself.

And so the Clarinet Quintet in B Minor by Brahms was put on one side, until one day Ellenberger discovered that the clarinet part had been arranged (I believe by the composer himself) for solo viola. Mrs Ellenberger was not up to it – what did I think about having a try to see if I could play it? So, with my father's consent, I called on my friend, Mr Waterfield, to find out if he had a viola to sell. He had – several.

(*Suite in Four Movements*)

SAMUEL TAYLOR COLERIDGE

Lines Composed in a Concert-Room

Nor cold, nor stern, my soul; yet I detest
    These scented rooms, where, to a gaudy throng,
Heaves the proud harlot her distended breast
    In intricacies of laborious song.

These feel not Music's genuine power, nor deign
    To melt at Nature's passion-warbled plaint;
But when the long-breathed singer's uptrilled strain
    Bursts in a squall – they gape for wonderment.

Hark! the deep buzz of vanity and hate!
    Scornful, yet envious, with self-torturing sneer
My lady eyes some maid of humbler state,
    While the pert captain, or the primmer priest,
Prattles accordant scandal in her ear.

O give me, from this heartless scene released,
    To hear our old musician, blind and gray,
(Whom stretching from my nurse's arms I kissed,)
    His Scottish tunes and warlike marches play,
By moonshine, on the balmy summer night.
    The while I dance amid the tedded hay
With merry maids, whose ringlets toss in light.

D. R. DAVIES

How musical was my valley (1)

It was during my life in Clydach that there awoke in me two interests that were to influence considerably my intellectual development. These were music and history.

As I have already indicated, my father had no mean musical talent. As choirmaster of the chapel, he was responsible for many musical activities, so that I lived in an atmosphere of music. Hardly a night passed that he did not have somebody at home for musical tuition of some kind. My two sisters and brother were gifted with good voices. My younger sister had the making of a first-rate soprano; my elder sister had a beautiful contralto voice; and my brother was a tenor and sang for a while in the Moody Manners Opera Company. I was the only one without a singing voice. That did not mean I was exempt from instruction.

My father had the idea that no one could be really educated without a knowledge and appreciation of music and he did his best to inculcate in his children a deep love of it. He taught me the rudiments of tonic sol-fa, which, to this day, I can read more easily than staff notation. A score written in sol-fa I can hear with my eyes. I have an idea of the harmony from reading it. But my father was not really a good teacher. He was too impatient. The need for repeated or varied explanations made him angry, and then my brain ceased to function. But he pulled me through the examinations of the Tonic Sol-Fa College. He also taught me to appreciate vocal music – good music, too. I quite early knew the difference, not only between good and bad singing, but also between good and bad music. I was constantly listening to Bach, Handel, Mozart, Mendelssohn and Schubert – oratorios, cantatas and masses.

I had to learn an instrument. I chose the violin. In spite of poverty, money was found to pay for lessons. As my younger sister and brother had voice training, a goodly proportion of the family income must have been spent on music. I never became really proficient, however, though I played in different orchestras at different times, and even played first violin. What it did for me chiefly was to create an ear for tone, which is an indispensable minimum for the appreciation especially of chamber and orchestral music....

My love of music, which my father first inculcated in those far-off days, has also continued to grow in spite of the fact that I have completely neglected it for long periods. For instance, during my first year in London..., when I could not earn a penny, I sold part of my library in order to buy a season ticket for the Promenade Concerts, and did not miss a single concert. I then had to walk from Palmers Green to Queen's Hall and back again after the concert, each night, for pennies were too scarce for bus fares. Oh! Those nights with their ache and loneliness! There must have been some deep hunger in my soul for music. It began in Clydach when I was nine or ten years of age, when hymns in the minor key made me weep. Indeed, music has brought me great suffering. There are some works to which I can hardly bear to listen, particularly the second part of Tchaikovsky's Swan Lake ballet music. But Tchaikovsky's is supremely the music of man unredeemed, his despair and frustration.

The third thing that happened to me in this Clydach phase was the awakening of romance, a divinely ecstatic experience. It was pure joy. It had none of the pain of adolescent and adult passion. It was a fleeting, momentary dawn which dissolved, not into day with its inevitable shadow and oppression, but into nothingness: an experience that bore no congruity to its objective stimulus. It happened one Christmas night, when a girl many years my senior unexpectedly kissed me under the mistletoe – and then vanished. It was pure ecstasy. If I have ever had a perfect experience, that was it. I was not more than twelve years old. It was as though body spontaneously became spirit, and for a moment my perceptions became ethereal.

I mention it here because of its spiritual significance. I took not the slightest interest in the girl. It did not occur to me to go in search of her. I didn't even connect the kiss with the mistletoe. But it gave me, I believe, a hint of perfection, an idea of the sexes before the Fall. I think it was from that experience that the intimation awakened in my consciousness that spirit is a greater factor in sex than the physical. I should be a miserable humbug were I to try to persuade the reader that that has been my predominating experience. It has not.

In 1900 or 1901, calamity fell upon our household. The pit at which my father worked closed down, and he became unemployed. Owing to his physical disability he could perform no heavy labour. His occupation had to be very light employment. None could be found in the district. Days of hardship returned. At length, my father was offered the post of underground lampman at a colliery in Maesteg, the manager of which was an old friend. So we moved there. For me it meant a great deal. I had just won a scholarship for the county school at Ystalyfera and I was destined not to enjoy it.

(*In Search of Myself*)

EDWARD ELGAR AND CHARLES BUCK

Dr Buck's grumble tub

In summer 1932 Elgar wrote to one of his oldest friends, Dr Buck. The British Medical Association had returned to Worcester once more to honour their founder, Sir Charles Hastings (a native of the city). It was during a similar commemorative visit in 1882 that the two young men had met: and there had followed the first of all Elgar's visits to his friend in Yorkshire.

Marl Bank, Worcester
19th August 1932

My dear Buck:

I have thought much of you & the dear old days lately. Your British Medical Socy. have been here, as you will know, unveiling a window in the Cathedral to Sir C. Hastings: it is just fifty(!) years since you were here & played in the orch: – what a lovely time we had; the first of many adventures. In this August weather I always live over again the holidays I had with you & the taste of *potted Ribble trout* comes with ineffaceable relish: nothing so good in eating or company has occurred to me since 1882.

Best regards
Yours very sincerely
Edward Elgar

'Cravendale',
Giggleswick, Settle.
Aug 22

My dear Elgar

You cannot think how your cheery letter has brightened me up, for I am 'hors de combat' with stoppage of the Bile duct & consequently assume the colour of the shade Ace Guinea, but I ought not to grumble seeing that on Wednesday Aug 30 I shall be 81 and my dear [daughter] Monica has come from town [i.e., London] to 'wakken me up a bit'

I am one of those 'quem olim meminisse juvabit' and I fly back mentally to 1882 when we played with Uncle Henry [Elgar] and after the orgy Louis d'Egville tore out old Mr Hopkins Bell pull by the roots, and I shall never forget you & I carrying my parrot over to Settle with a stick pushed through the cage when the bottom fell out on Settle bridge & we nearly lost the birds

I believe 1882 was the only time I saw your good mother, who told us she had saved all your youthful lucubrations and that they were stored in a box in the attic above the old shop. Is Frank [Elgar] still in statu quo?

My dear niece whom you carried on your back from Clapham [Yorkshire] – died last year from Pneumonia at Penarth[.] Her husband – Commander Back – has just retired & I was there when I developed Gastroduodenal Catarrh – the commencement of my present trouble.

What a good time we had when poor old Jack Baguley pianised for us in Trio work[.] He died on the banks of Lake Titicaca (Peru)

I still get out my old grumble tub (Nicholas Amati [cello]) and with Monica played a Sammartini Sonata – but my old fingers won't go as fast as my brain.

In one thing I am very fortunate viz a good nurse – hospital trained, who also manages my chateau, so I have much to be thankful for

It will be delightful to see you again in the old home, if ever you are in the district & no one would be more welcome to my frugal hospitality.

With affectionate greetings

Yours in sincerity
C W Buck

Lord Chamberlain's Office, St James's Palace, London, S.W.1.
23 Augt 1932

My dear Buck:

It is splendid to hear you are still enjoying life in spite of livers and ducts – or something: you may remember that I never could learn anything about the human form & to this day if you offered me £1,000,000,000 I cd. not tell you where my liver, or Kidneys, or any damn thing lies.

It is marvellous that you remember the gorgeous doings after that Soirée; – it was not *Louis* d'Egville but his cousin *Wm.* – it was a grand wind-up to a woolly concert.

Changes amany have been among us: poor old Frank departed this life three years ago.

I fear there is small chance of my travelling north again but I still hope for it.

Warm regards
Yours ever
Edward Elgar

[The old friends were not to meet again. As Dr Buck's letter hinted, it was a last greeting: for he was fatally ill, and he died three months later.]

(*Letters of a Lifetime*)

GEORGE EWART EVANS

How musical was my valley (2)

Gwilym Williams ... had the makings of a fine pianist and was always looking for a place where there was a piano. Llanfabon was such a place. It was a typical traditional Welsh village on top of the hill, with just a church, a house opposite, and the pub. The pub had no piano, but in the house where the verger once lived I had heard the sound of one. The house had a shop in the front room: I thought a policeman lived there. It was on the route we had travelled when we were delivering goods to the farms, and I had often looked in the open door and had seen a policeman's helmet hanging in the passage. It was not until we penetrated into the house that we found that the lady who lived there was a widow and the policeman's helmet was a device to deter undesirable customers. The old lady served soft drinks; and in her middle room was a well tuned upright piano. Gwilym played well – Schubert, Beethoven, Liszt – and it was a delight to listen to him.

The walks to Llanfabon were enjoyable and although the entertainment was not wildly exciting, being with 'the boys' was sufficiently satisfying. On a fine frosty night when the stars stood out like flashing diamonds and our singing voices sent out rippling waves of sound in the quiet country-side, we got a tremendous sense of expanse. In the valleys we had a limited view of the night sky; only when we got on to the hills did we understand what we were being deprived of by living down below. One night as we passed Llanfabon cemetery on our way home Joe Matthews, a young miner, put it into words: '*Duw annwyl!*' (Dear God) 'They put the dead 'uns on the hills where the live 'uns ought to be!' Joe was often one of the company: he had a beautiful tenor voice that could charm a bird out of a tree. When he was with us in a pub or singing walking back over the hills at night, Joe could lift our attempt at harmony to a new level, and make our day most memorable, worthy to be noted, as the old Roman said, with the whitest of white pebbles.

I have often wondered about this faculty, found in the Welsh, of being able to harmonize spontaneously, without musical training or understanding in the ordinary sense at all. This puzzled me for a long time and when I met one of the foremost authorities on folk music in Britain I asked him if he could explain the prevalence of the spontaneous love of harmony in the singing of the Welsh. His answer, as I found out later, was just 'off the top of his head': 'Oh, the Welsh learned to harmonize during the religious revival of the eighteenth century. They sang hymns which they had to learn by heart because they had no text. And of course many of them couldn't read – that, by the way, is why they repeated the last two lines of the hymns.' It was clear, however, that 'harmonizing' was a much older accomplishment than the eighteenth century. Giraldus Cambrensis, the Norman Welshman, raised the same question in the twelfth century about the Welsh love of harmony in their singing. He observed: 'In their musical concerts they do not sing in unison like the inhabitants of other countries, but in many different parts; so that in a company of singers, which one frequently meets with in Wales, you will hear as many different parts and voices as there are performers who all at length unite with organic melody in one consonance and the softness of B flat ... and the practice is so firmly rooted in them that it is unusual to hear a simple and single melody well sung; and, what is still more wonderful, the children, even from their infancy, sing in the same manner.'

(*The Strength of the Hills*)

THOMAS HARDY

A Musical Incident

When I see the room it hurts me
  As with a pricking blade,
Those women being the memoried reason why my cheer
deserts me. –
  'Twas thus. One of them played
  To please her friend, not knowing
  That friend was speedily growing,
  Behind the player's chair,
  Somnolent, unaware
  Of any music there.

  I saw it, and it distressed me,
  For I had begun to think
I loved the drowsy listener, when this arose to test me
  And tug me from love's brink.
  'Beautiful!' said she, waking
  As the music ceased. 'Heart-aching!'
  Though never a note she'd heard
  To judge of as averred –
  Save that of the very last word.

  All would have faded in me,
  But that the sleeper brought
News a week thence that her friend was dead. It stirred within me

Sense of injustice wrought
That dead player's poor intent –
So heartily, kindly meant –
As blandly added the sigher:
'How glad I am I was nigh her,
To hear her last tune!' – 'Liar!'
I lipped. – This gave love pause,
And killed it, such as it was.

In the Nuptial Chamber

'O that mastering tune!' And up in the bed
Like a lace-robed phantom springs the bride;
'And why?' asks the man she had that day wed,
With a start, as the band plays on outside.
'It's the townsfolk's cheery compliment
Because of our marriage, my Innocent.'

'O but you don't know! 'Tis the passionate air
To which my old Love waltzed with me,
And I swore as we spun that none should share
My home, my kisses, till death, save he!
And he dominates me and thrills me through,
And it's he I embrace while embracing you!'

JAMES JOYCE

James Joyce was musical on both sides of the family. His father John was a comic singer and had 'the best tenor in Ireland', according to Barton McGuckin, the leading tenor with the Carl Rosa company, thinly disguised in Joyce's long story 'Dead'. His mother May had lessons in piano and voice from the age of five to nineteen – but, by Shaw's own account, there was only one singing teacher in Dublin of the period who really knew his craft and he ran off with Shaw's mother.

There are rich family echoes in 'Dead', written in 1905–6 and published in *Dubliners* (1914). 'The Misses Flynn school', run by Joyce's great-aunts; his grandmother's sullen opposition to his parents' marriage; his seldom-sober father carving the goose and making the Christmas party speech; his future wife Nora Barnacle and her first singing lover in Connacht who died of consumption or a broken heart: they are all there, transcribed or transmuted.

Joyce's own voice was mellifluous but weak, compared with that of his friend and contemporary John McCormack, who became the best theatrical tenor outside Italy. Joyce won a scholarship in Dublin, treasured complimentary concert notices and once appeared with McCormack himself. In 1904 he rashly wrote to Arnold Dolmetsch to ask the price of a lute. Dolmetsch was discouraging and suggested a spinet instead: '£30 to £60 would get one.' But, already, Joyce knew that he would be a virtuoso in words, rather than notes: 'Chamber Music' rather than 'Farewell and adieu to you, Spanish Ladies.' That famous episode with Gogarty and Jenny, the merry widow, pissing behind the curtain, belongs to that period remembered by Bloom in Ulysses: 'Chamber music. Could make a kind of pun on that. It is a kind of music I often thought when she. Acoustics that is. Tinkling. Empty vessels make most noise. Because the acoustics, the resonance changes according as the weight of the water is equal to the law of falling water.'

Mozart would have relished both the glass harmonica technique and the joke.

James Joyce

The singers and the song

Gabriel could not listen while Mary Jane was playing her Academy piece, full of runs and difficult passages, to the hushed drawing-room. He liked music, but the piece she was playing had no melody for him and he doubted whether it had any melody for the other listeners, though they had begged Mary Jane to play something. Four young men, who had come from the refreshment-room to stand in the doorway at the sound of the piano, had gone away quietly in couples after a few minutes. The only persons who seemed to follow the music were Mary Jane herself, her hands racing along the key-board or lifted from it at the pauses like those of a priestess in momentary imprecation, and Aunt Kate standing at her elbow to turn the page.

Gabriel's eyes, irritated by the floor, which glittered with beeswax under the heavy chandelier, wandered to the wall above the piano. A picture of the balcony scene in *Romeo and Juliet* hung there and beside it was a picture of the two murdered princes in the Tower which Aunt Julia had worked in red, blue and brown wools when she was a girl. Probably in the school they had gone to as girls that kind of work had been taught for one year. His mother had worked for him as a birthday present a waistcoat of purple tabinet, with little foxes' heads upon it, lined with brown satin and having round mulberry buttons. It was strange that his mother had had no musical talent, though Aunt Kate used to call her the brains carrier of the Morkan family. Both she and Julia had always seemed a little proud of their serious and matronly sister. Her photograph stood before the pier-glass. She held an open book on her knees and was pointing out something in it to Constantine who, dressed in a man-o'-war suit, lay at her feet. It was she who had chosen the names of her sons, for she was very sensible of the dignity of family life. Thanks to her, Constantine was now senior curate in Balbriggan and, thanks to her, Gabriel himself had taken his degree in the Royal University. A shadow passed over his face as he remembered her sullen opposition to his marriage. Some slighting phrases she had used still rankled in his memory; she had once spoken of Gretta as being country cute and that was not true of Gretta at all. It was Gretta who had nursed her during all her last long illness in their house at Monkstown.

He knew that Mary Jane must be near the end of her piece, for she was playing again the opening melody with runs of scales after every bar, and

221

while he waited for the end the resentment died down in his heart. The piece ended with a trill of octaves in the treble and a final deep octave in the bass. Great applause greeted Mary Jane as, blushing and rolling up her music nervously, she escaped from the room. The most vigorous clapping came from the four young men in the doorway who had gone away to the refreshment-room at the beginning of the piece but had come back when the piano had stopped.

Lancers were arranged. Gabriel found himself partnered with Miss Ivors. She was a frank-mannered, talkative young lady, with a freckled face and prominent brown eyes. She did not wear a low-cut bodice, and the large brooch which was fixed in the front of her collar bore on it an Irish device and motto.

When they had taken their places she said abruptly:

'I have a crow to pluck with you.'

'With me?' said Gabriel.

She nodded her head gravely.

'What is it?' asked Gabriel, smiling at her solemn manner.

'Who is G.C.?' answered Miss Ivors, turning her eyes upon him.

Gabriel coloured and was about to knit his brows, as if he did not understand, when she said bluntly:

'O, innocent Amy! I have found out what you write for *The Daily Express*. Now, aren't you ashamed of yourself?'

'Why should I be ashamed of myself?' asked Gabriel, blinking his eyes and trying to smile.

'Well, I'm ashamed of you,' said Miss Ivors frankly. 'To say you'd write for a paper like that. I didn't think you were a West Briton.'

A look of perplexity appeared on Gabriel's face. It was true that he wrote a literary column every Wednesday in *The Daily Express*, for which he was paid fifteen shillings. But that did not make him a West Briton surely. The books he received for review were almost more welcome than the paltry cheque. He loved to feel the covers and turn over the pages of newly printed books. Nearly every day when his teaching in the college was ended he used to wander down the quays to the second-hand booksellers, to Hickey's on Bachelor's Walk, to Webb's or Massey's on Aston's Quay, or to O'Clohissey's in the by-street. He did not know how to meet her charge. He wanted to say that literature was above politics. But they were friends of many years' standing and their careers had been parallel, first at the University and then as teachers: he could not risk a grandiose phrase with her. He continued blinking his eyes and trying to smile and murmured lamely that he saw nothing political in writing reviews of books.

When their turn to cross had come he was still perplexed and inattentive. Miss Ivors promptly took his hand in a warm grasp and said in a soft friendly tone:

'Of course, I was only joking. Come, we cross now.'

When they were together again she spoke of the University question and Gabriel felt more at ease. A friend of hers had shown her his review of Browning's poems. That was how she had found out the secret: but she liked the review immensely. Then she said suddenly:

'O, Mr Conroy, will you come for an excursion to the Aran Isles this summer? We're going to stay there a whole month. It will be splendid out in the Atlantic. You ought to come. Mr Clancy is coming, and Mr Kilkelly and Kathleen Kearney. It would be splendid for Gretta too if she'd come. She's from Connacht, isn't she?'

'Her people are,' said Gabriel shortly.

'But you will come, won't you?' said Miss Ivors, laying her warm hand eagerly on his arm.

'The fact is,' said Gabriel, 'I have just arranged to go –'

'Go where?' asked Miss Ivors.

'Well, you know, every year I go for a cycling tour with some fellows and so –'

'But where?' asked Miss Ivors.

'Well, we usually go to France or Belgium or perhaps Germany,' said Gabriel awkwardly.

'And why do you go to France and Belgium,' said Miss Ivors, 'instead of visiting your own land?'

'Well,' said Gabriel, 'it's partly to keep in touch with the languages and partly for a change.'

'And haven't you your own language to keep in touch with – Irish?' asked Miss Ivors.

'Well,' said Gabriel, 'if it comes to that, you know, Irish is not my language.'

Their neighbours had turned to listen to the cross-examination. Gabriel glanced right and left nervously and tried to keep his good humour under the ordeal, which was making a blush invade his forehead.

'And haven't you your own land to visit,' continued Miss Ivors, 'that you know nothing of, your own people, and your own country?'

'O, to tell you the truth,' retorted Gabriel suddenly, 'I'm sick of my own country, sick of it!'

'Why?' asked Miss Ivors.

Gabriel did not answer, for his retort had heated him.

'Why?' repeated Miss Ivors.

They had to go visiting together and, as he had not answered her, Miss Ivors said warmly:

'Of course, you've no answer.'

Gabriel tried to cover his agitation by taking part in the dance with great energy. He avoided her eyes, for he had seen a sour expression on her face. But when they met in the long chain he was surprised to feel his hand firmly pressed. She looked at him from under her brows for a moment quizzically until he smiled. Then, just as the chain was about to start again, she stood on tiptoe and whispered into his ear:

'West Briton!'

When the lancers were over Gabriel went away to a remote corner of the room where Freddy Malins' mother was sitting. She was a stout, feeble old woman with white hair. Her voice had a catch in it like her son's and she stuttered slightly. She had been told that Freddy had come and that he was nearly all right. Gabriel asked her whether she had had a good crossing. She lived with her married daughter in Glasgow and came to Dublin on a visit once a year. She answered placidly that she had had a beautiful crossing and that the captain had been most attentive to her. She spoke also of the beautiful house her daughter kept in Glasgow, and of all the friends they had there. While her tongue rambled on Gabriel tried to banish from his mind all memory of the unpleasant incident with Miss Ivors. Of course the girl, or woman, or whatever she was, was an enthusiast, but there was a time for all things. Perhaps he ought not to have answered her like that. But she had no right to call him a West Briton before people, even in joke. She had tried to make him ridiculous before people, heckling him and staring at him with her rabbit's eyes.

He saw his wife making her way towards him through the waltzing couples. When she reached him she said into his ear:

'Gabriel, Aunt Kate wants to know won't you carve the goose as usual. Miss Daly will carve the ham and I'll do the pudding.'

'All right,' said Gabriel.

'She's sending in the younger ones first as soon as this waltz is over so that we'll have the table to ourselves.'

'Were you dancing?' asked Gabriel.

'Of course I was. Didn't you see me? What row had you with Molly Ivors?'

'No row. Why? Did she say so?'

'Something like that. I'm trying to get that Mr D'Arcy to sing. He's full of conceit, I think.'

'There was no row,' said Gabriel moodily, 'only she wanted me to go for a trip to the west of Ireland and I said I wouldn't.'

His wife clasped her hands excitedly and gave a little jump.

'O, do go, Gabriel,' she cried. 'I'd love to see Galway again.'

'You can go if you like,' said Gabriel coldly.

She looked at him for a moment, then turned to Mrs Malins and said: 'There's a nice husband for you, Mrs Malins.'

While she was threading her way back across the room Mrs Malins, without adverting to the interruption, went on to tell Gabriel what beautiful places there were in Scotland and beautiful scenery. Her son-in-law brought them every year to the lakes and they used to go fishing. Her son-in-law was a splendid fisher. One day he caught a beautiful big fish and the man in the hotel cooked it for their dinner.

Gabriel hardly heard what she said. Now that supper was coming near he began to think again about his speech and about the quotation. When he saw Freddy Malins coming across the room to visit his mother Gabriel left the chair free for him and retired into the embrasure of the window. The room had already cleared and from the back room came the clatter of plates and knives. Those who still remained in the drawing-room seemed tired of dancing and were conversing quietly in little groups. Gabriel's warm, trembling fingers tapped the cold pane of the window. How cool it must be outside! How pleasant it would be to walk out alone, first along by the river and then through the park! The snow would be lying on the branches of the trees and forming a bright cap on the top of the Wellington Monument. How much more pleasant it would be there than at the supper-table!

He ran over the headings of his speech: Irish hospitality, sad memories, the Three Graces, Paris, the quotation from Browning. He repeated to himself a phrase he had written in his review: 'One feels that one is listening to a thought-tormented music.' Miss Ivors had praised the review. Was she sincere? Had she really any life of her own behind all her propagandism? There had never been any ill-feeling between them until that night. It unnerved him to think that she would be at the supper-table, looking up at him while he spoke with her critical quizzing eyes. Perhaps she would not be sorry to see him fail in his speech. An idea came into his mind and gave him courage. He would say, alluding to Aunt Kate and Aunt Julia: 'Ladies and Gentlemen, the generation which is now on the wane among us may have had its faults, but for my part I think it had certain qualities of hospitality, of humour, of humanity, which the new and very serious and hypereducated generation that is growing up around us seems to me to lack.' Very good: that was one for Miss Ivors. What did he care that his aunts were only two ignorant old women?

A murmur in the room attracted his attention. Mr Browne was advancing from the door, gallantly escorting Aunt Julia, who leaned upon his arm, smiling and hanging her head. An irregular musketry of applause escorted her also as far as the piano and then, as Mary Jane seated herself on the stool, and Aunt Julia, no longer smiling, half turned so as to pitch her voice fairly into the room, gradually ceased. Gabriel recognized the prelude. It was that of an old song of Aunt Julia's – *Arrayed for the Bridal.* Her voice, strong and clear in tone, attacked with great spirit the runs which embellish the air, and though she sang very rapidly she did not miss even the smallest of the grace notes. To follow the voice, without looking at the singer's face, was to feel and share the excitement of swift and secure flight. Gabriel applauded loudly with all the others at the close of the song, and loud applause was borne in from the invisible supper-table. It sounded so genuine that a little colour struggled into Aunt Julia's face as she bent to replace in the music-stand the old leather-bound song-book that had her initials on the cover. Freddy Malins, who had listened with his head perched sideways to hear her better, was still applauding when every one else had ceased and talking animatedly to his mother, who nodded her head gravely and slowly in acquiescence. At last, when he could clap no more, he stood up suddenly and hurried across the room to Aunt Julia whose hand he seized and held in both his hands, shaking it when words failed him or the catch in his voice proved too much for him.

'I was just telling my mother,' he said, 'I never heard you sing so well, never. No, I never heard your voice so good as it is to-night. Now! Would you believe that now? That's the truth. Upon my word and honour that's the truth. I never heard your voice sound so fresh and so … so clear and fresh, never.'

Aunt Julia smiled broadly and murmured something about compliments as she released her hand from his grasp. Mr Browne extended his open hand towards her and said to those who were near him in the manner of a showman introducing a prodigy to an audience:

'Miss Julia Morkan, my latest discovery!'

He was laughing very heartily at this himself when Freddy Malins turned to him and said:

'Well, Browne, if you're serious you might make a worse discovery. All I can say is I never heard her sing half so well as long as I am coming here. And that's the honest truth.'

'Neither did I,' said Mr Browne. 'I think her voice has greatly improved.'

Aunt Julia shrugged her shoulders and said with meek pride:

'Thirty years ago I hadn't a bad voice as voices go.'

'I often told Julia,' said Aunt Kate emphatically, 'that she was simply thrown away in that choir. But she never would be said by me.'

She turned as if to appeal to the good sense of the others against a refractory child, while Aunt Julia gazed in front of her, a vague smile of reminiscence playing on her face.

'No,' continued Aunt Kate, 'she wouldn't be said or led by anyone, slaving there in that choir night and day, night and day. Six o'clock on Christmas morning! And all for what?'

'Well, isn't it for the honour of God, Aunt Kate?' asked Mary Jane, twisting round on the piano-stool and smiling.

Aunt Kate turned fiercely on her niece and said:

'I know all about the honour of God, Mary Jane, but I think it's not at all honourable for the pope to turn out the women out of the choirs that have slaved there all their lives and put little whipper-snappers of boys over their heads. I suppose it is for the good of the Church, if the pope does it. But it's not just, Mary Jane, and it's not right.'

She had worked herself into a passion and would have continued in defence of her sister, for it was a sore subject with her, but Mary Jane, seeing that all the dancers had come back, intervened pacifically.

'Now, Aunt Kate, you're giving scandal to Mr Browne, who is of the other persuasion.'

Aunt Kate turned to Mr Browne, who was grinning at this allusion to his religion, and said hastily:

'O, I don't question the pope's being right. I'm only a stupid old woman and I wouldn't presume to do such a thing. But there's such a thing as common everyday politeness and gratitude. And if I were in Julia's place I'd tell that Father Healey straight up to his face . . .'

'And besides, Aunt Kate,' said Mary Jane, 'we really are all hungry and when we are hungry we are all very quarrelsome.'

'And when we are thirsty we are also quarrelsome,' added Mr Browne.

'So that we had better go to supper,' said Mary Jane, 'and finish the discussion afterwards.'

(*Dubliners*)

D. H. LAWRENCE

Piano

Softly, in the dusk, a woman is singing to me;
Taking me back down the vista of years, till I see
A child sitting under the piano, in the boom of the tingling strings
And pressing the small, poised feet of a mother who smiles as she sings.

In spite of myself, the insidious mastery of song
Betrays me back, till the heart of me weeps to belong
To the old Sunday evenings at home, with winter outside
And hymns in the cosy parlour, the tinkling piano our guide.

So now it is vain for the singer to burst into clamour
With the great black piano appassionato. The glamour
Of childish days is upon me, my manhood is cast
Down in the flood of remembrance, I weep like a child for the past.

LAURIE LEE

At least it's over

The vicar rose to his feet.... 'And now, my friends, comes the – er – feast for the soul. If you would care to – ah – take the air a moment, willing hands are waiting to clear the hall and prepare for the – um – Entertainment....'

We crowded outside and huddled in the snow while the tables were taken away. Inside, behind curtains, the actors were making up – and my moment, too, was approaching. The snow whirled about me and I began to sweat, I wanted to run off home. Then the doors reopened and I crouched by the stove, shivering and chattering with nerves. The curtains parted and the Entertainment began with a comic I neither saw nor heard....

'For the next item, ladies and gentlemen, we have an instrumental duet, by Miss Brown and – er – young Laurie Lee.'

Smirking with misery I walked to the stage. Eileen's face was as white as a minim. She sat at the piano, placed the music crooked, I straightened it, it fell to the ground. I groped to retrieve it; we looked at one another with hatred; the audience was still as death. Eileen tried to give me an A, but struck B instead, and I tuned up like an ape threading needles. At last we were ready, I raised my fiddle; and Eileen was off like a bolting horse. I caught her up in the middle of the piece – which I believe was a lullaby – and after playing the repeats, only twice as fast, we just stopped, frozen motionless, spent.

Some hearty stamping and whistling followed, and a shout of 'Give us another!' Eileen and I didn't exchange a glance, but we loved each other now. We found the music of 'Danny Boy' and began to give it all our emotion, dawdling dreamily among the fruitier chords and scampering over the high bits; till the audience joined in, using their hymn-singing voices, which showed us the utmost respect. When it was over I returned to my seat by the stove, my body feeling smooth and beautiful. Eileen's mother was weeping into her hat, and so was mine, I think . . . .

Now I was free to become one of the audience, and the Entertainment burgeoned before me. What had seemed to me earlier as the capering of demons now became a spectacle of human genius. Turn followed turn in variety and splendour. Mr Crosby, the organist, told jokes and stories as though his very life depended on them, trembling, sweating, never pausing for a laugh, and rolling his eyes at the wings for rescue. We loved him, however, and wouldn't let him go, while he grew more and more hysterical, racing through monologues, gabbling songs about shrimps, skipping, mopping, and jumping up and down, as though humouring a tribe of savages.

Major Doveton came next, with his Indian banjo, which was even harder to tune than my fiddle. He straddled a chair and began wrestling with the keys, cursing us in English and Urdu. Then all the strings broke, and he snarled off the stage and started kicking the banjo round the cloakroom. He was followed by a play in which Marjorie, as Cinderella, sat in a goose-feathered dress in a castle. While waiting for the pumpkin to turn into a coach, she sang 'All alone by the telephone'.

Two ballads came next, and Mrs Pimbury, a widow, sang them both with astonishing spirit. The first invited us to go with her to Canada; the second was addressed to a mushroom:

> Grow! Grow! Grow little mushroom grow!
> Somebody wants you soon.
> I'll call again tomorrow morning –
>   See!
> And if you've growen bigger you will just suit ME!
> So Grow! Grow! Grow little mushroom – Grow!

Though we'd not heard this before, it soon became part of our heritage, as did the song of a later lady. This last – the Baroness von Hodenburg – sealed our entertainment with almost professional distinction. She was a guest star from Sheepscombe and her appearance was striking, it enshrined all the mystery of art. She wore a loose green gown like a hospital patient's, and her hair was red and long. 'She writes,' whispered Mother. 'Poems and booklets and that.'

'I am going to sink you,' announced the lady, 'a little ditty I convected myself. Bose vords und music, I may say, is mine – und zey refer to ziss pleasant valleys.'

With that she sat down, arched her beautiful back, raised her bangled wrists over the keyboard, then ripped off some startling runs and trills, and sang with a ringing laugh:

> Elfin volk come over the hill!
> Come und dance, just vere you vill!
> Brink your pipes, und brink your flutes,
> Brink your sveetly soundink notes!
> Come avay-hay! Life is gay-hay!
> Life – Is – Gay!

We thought this song soppy, but we never forgot it. From then on, whenever we saw the Baroness in the lanes we used to bawl the song at her through the hedges. But she would only stop, and cock her head, and smile dreamily to herself....

(*Cider with Rosie*)

BORIS PASTERNAK

First memories of piano and strings

Facing the wicket-gate of a small garden shaded by ancient trees, the annexe where we lived rose above the sheds and offices in the yard. Hot lunches were served to students in the basement, and an everlasting smell of fried cutlets and pasties cooked in batter hung over the stairs. Our flat was on the first landing....

Half a century later, I read the following under the heading '1894' [in] *Moscow in the Life and Work of Leo Tolstoy* by N.S. Rodionov:

On the 23rd November, Tolstoy and his daughters went to a concert given at the flat of the painter Leonid Pasternak... The musicians were Pasternak's wife, the 'cellist Brandukov and the violinist Grzhimaldi, both Professors at the Conservatoire.

... I remember that evening perfectly. I had been put to bed, but late in the night I was aroused by such a sweet, nostalgic torment as I had not experienced in the same degree before. I cried out and wept in fear and anguish. But the music drowned my cries and it was not until the end of the movement that anyone heard me. Then the curtain which hung across the room, dividing it in two, was pushed aside. My mother came in, bent over me and soon calmed me down. She may have carried me into the drawing-room, or perhaps I only saw it through the open door. The air was filled with cigarette smoke; the candles blinked as if it stung their eyes. They shone on the red varnished wood of the 'cello and of the violin. The piano loomed black. The men were in black frock-coats. Women leaned out of their shoulder-high dresses like flowers out of flower baskets. Like smoke rings, the grey-ringed heads of two or three old men drifted together. One of them was the painter Gué, whom I was later to know well and see often. The image of another has been present to me, as to most people, all my life: to me especially because my father illustrated his work, went to see him, honoured him, and indeed our whole house was permeated by his spirit. This was Lev Nikolayevich [Tolstoy]....

Why then did I cry so bitterly and why do I remember my anxiety so well? I was used to the sound of the piano – my mother was an accomplished pianist; to me it was inseparable from that of music itself. But the voices of strings – particularly strings combined in chamber music – were unfamiliar and as disturbing as if they had been real voices carried through the open window from the street, calling for help and announcing a disaster....

That evening marked for me the end of my unconscious early childhood. From then on, my memory functioned and my consciousness was active and unbroken by long gaps, as in an adult.

(An Essay in Autobiography)

FRITZ SPIEGL

Who diddled Sherlock Holmes?

Whenever you read in the tabloids about a person or subject you are familiar with, you know that they invariably get something wrong, if only the person's name or age. The same goes for authors who like to add expert colour to their fiction but are less knowledgeable on the subject than they like to think they are.

Sir Arthur Conan Doyle's Sherlock Holmes stories often mention music, including actual performers active at the time (Sarasate, Lady Hallé, etc.), information he probably garnered from the papers. He makes it clear that Holmes is not only musical (as every educated man would have been expected to be 100 years ago) but also an expert violinist. Moreover, one lucky enough to possess a Stradivarius. Dr Watson says (in *A Study in Scarlet*) '... at my request he has played me some of Mendelssohn's *Lieder*...' This is not totally implausible, as there must have been plenty of arrangements for fiddle and piano, though surely not for unaccompanied violin?

But Holmes's playing posture was nothing if not eccentric. 'Leaning back in his armchair of an evening', says Watson, 'he would close his eyes and scrape carelessly at the fiddle which was thrown across his knee. Sometimes the chords were sonorous and melancholy. Occasionally they were fantastic and cheerful.'

All the while, no doubt, thinking about his latest case. And when some flash of intuition struck him, he leapt to his feet and 'threw the fiddle into a corner'; or, elsewhere simply 'flung down the instrument'. What a way to treat a Strad. But don't worry. It was clearly an instrument built to

Sherlock Holmes's mahogany Strad?

withstand such treatment. For you see it was – 'made of mahogany'. Solid all the way through, I expect, and therefore not needing a soundpost. Holmes (we read in *The Cardboard Box*) had bought this heavy-duty Strad 'from a Jew broker in the Tottenham Court Road for fifty-five shillings.'

I think he was done.

(*Classic CD Magazine*)

EUDORA WELTY

Two cultures at a Southern wedding

Everybody for miles around came to the reception. Troy said he did not know there could be so many people in the whole Delta; it *looked* like it was cotton all the way. The mayor of Fairchilds and his wife were driven up with the lights on inside their car, and they could be seen lighted up inside reading the Memphis paper (which never quite unrolled when you read it); in the bud vases on the little walls beside them were real red roses, vibrating, and the chauffeur's silk cap filled with air like a balloon when they drove over the cattle guard. Shelley's heart pounded as she smiled; indeed this was a grand occasion for everybody, their wedding was really eventful.... Lady Clare came down once – pitiful indeed, her spots all painted over with something, and for some reason clad in a nightgown with a long tear. 'I'm exposing you! I'm exposing you all!' cried Lady Clare fiercely, but was rushed back upstairs. More champagne was opened, buffet was carried out, and all started being served under the trees.

Then Dabney changed from her wedding gown to her going-away dress and the new Pierce-Arrow was brought up to the door. Dabney began kissing the family and the bridesmaids all around; she ran up and kissed Lady Clare. When she kissed Aunt Shannon, the old lady said, 'Now who do you think you are?'

A brown thrush in a tree still singing could be heard through all the wild commotion, as Dabney and Troy drove away, scattering the little shells of the road. Ellen waved her handkerchief, and all the aunts lifted theirs and waved. Shelley began to cry, and Ranny ran down the road after the car and followed it as long as it was in hearing, like a little puppy. Unlike the mayor's car that had come up alight like a boat in the night, it went away dark. The full moon had risen.

Then the party nearly all moved outdoors, where the lanterns burned in the trees. 'I hear the music coming,' said Laura, coming up and taking Ellen around the knees for a moment. The band came playing – 'Who?' coming out over the dark and brightening fields above the sound of their rackety car – a little river band, all very black Negroes in white coats, who were banjo, guitar, bass fiddle, trumpet and drum – and of course saxophone, that was the owner. Horace flagged them down with his flashlight. Howard showed them their chairs which he had fixed by the dance platform like a place for a select audience to come and watch a performance of glory. The dancing began.

At midnight, Shelley came in by herself for a drink of cool water. On the back porch the moths spread upon the screens, the hard beetles knocked upon the radius of light like an adamant door. She drank still swaying a little to the distant music. 'Whispering' turned into 'Linger Awhile.'

Only that morning, working at the wedding flowers with Dabney, she had thought to herself, hypnotically, as though she read it in her diary, Why do you look out thinking nothing will happen any more? Why are you thinking your line of trees the indelible thing in the world? There's the long journey yo're going on, with Aunt Tempe, leading out . . . and you can't see it now. Even closing your eyes, you see only the line of trees at Shellmound. Is it the world? If Shellmound were a little bigger, it would be the same as the world entirely. . . . Perhaps that was the real truth. But she had been dancing with George, with his firm, though (she was certain) reeling body so gaily leading her, so solicitously whirling her round. 'Bridesmaid,' he called her. 'Bridesmaid, will you dance?' She felt it in his cavorting body – though she danced seriously, always moved seriously – that he went even among the dancers with some vision of choice. Life lay ahead, he might do anything . . . . She followed, she herself had a vision of choice, or its premonition, for she was much like George. They played 'Sleepy Time Gal,' turning it into 'Whispering.' Only the things had not happened to her yet. They would happen. Indeed, she might not be happy either, wholly, and she would live in waiting, sometimes in terror. But Dabney's marriage, ceasing to shock, was like a door closing to her now. Entering into a life with Troy Flavin seemed to avow a remote, an unreal world – it came nearest to being real for Shelley only in the shock, the challenge to pride. It shut a door in their faces. Behind the closed door, what? Shelley's desire fled, or danced seriously, to an open place – not from one room to another room with its door, but to an opening wood, with weather – with change, beauty...

There was a scratch at the back door, and Shelley unlatched it. Her old cat, Beverley of Graustark, came in. He had been hunting; he brought in a mole and laid it at her feet.

In the music room, with some of the lingering guests there, Tempe and Primrose sang two-part songs of their girlhood, arch, full of questions and answers – and Tempe was in tears of merriment at the foolishness she had lived down. Primrose with each song remembered the gestures – of astonishment, cajolery – and Tempe could remember them the next instant. The sisters sang beckoning and withdrawing like two little fat mandarins, their soft voices in gentle, yielding harmony still. But soon Tempe, who had only come inside looking for her fan, was back where the dancing was.

(*Delta Wedding*)

DAVID WRIGHT

The Musician

In the south aisle of the abbey at Hexham
I turned to make a remark on its Roman
Tomb; but she did not hear me, for the organ
Was playing in the loft above the rood-screen,
Laying down tones of bronze and gold, a burden
Of praise-notes, fingerings of a musician
There at the keys, a boy, his master by him,
Whose invisible sound absorbed my saying.

Music inaudible to me, barbarian.
But legible. I read in my companion
Its elation written in her elation.
'He is so young he can be only learning,
You would not have expected to hear such playing.
It's like a return to civilization.'
Unable to hear, able to imagine
Chords pondering decline, and then upwelling

There in that deliberate enclave of stone,
I remembered music was its tradition;
Its builder, Acca, taught by one Maban
To sing; who may have been the god of song,
Mabon the god of music and the young;
That another bishop of this church, St John,
Taught here a dumb man speech, says Bede; became
Patron and intercessor of deaf men.

240

5

WE'D LOVE TO ACCEPT, BUT . . .

KINGSLEY AMIS

Even if Kingsley Amis had never written in his own person about music, both jazz and classical, his novels (and the odd poem) themselves let fall musical drops of prejudice and precision that reveal his tastes. When a character refers to an enemy singing 'filthy Mozart' one can be sure – even if he had not told us – that Mozart touches the author's heart most nearly. Similarly, to convey the full horror of a Round House pop audience out of control, Sir Roy Vandervane in *Girl, 20* (1971) attempts to play 'Elevation 9' and then has to watch his beloved Strad being smashed to matchwood.

Professor Welch's madrigal party in *Lucky Jim* is deliciously observed, and since Amis has owned up to his childhood as a chorister he must have been obliged to utter a few rebellious hey-nonny-no's in his time. But there are even more recondite musical pleasures elsewhere. The late Andor Foldes, for instance, identified Jim Dixon's favourite curse or 'Welch tune', a rondo from an unnamed piano concerto, solely from the stresses of the words Amis's text supplies: '"You ignorant clod, you stupid old sod, you havering slavering get…" Here intervened a string of unmentionables, corresponding with an oom-pah sort of effect in the orchestra. "You wordy old turdy old scum, you griping old piping old bum…"' No prizes – but start singing in E flat.

Similarly, I have often wondered how the name 'P. Racine Fricker' (a promising Fifties composer who went to California early and died in 1990) strayed into that Welch musical evening, just as Jim Dixon was bowing out. What an evocative name for a modernist composer, Amis must have thought – unless it were Peter Schat, the Dutchman.

Kingsley Amis

Professor Welch's madrigals

'Of course, this sort of music's not intended for an audience, you see,' Welch said as he handed the copies round. 'The fun's all in the singing. Everybody's got a real tune to sing – a real tune,' he repeated violently. 'You could say, really, that polyphony got to its highest point, its peak, at that period, and has been on the decline ever since. You've only got to look at the part-writing in things like, well, *Onward, Christian Soldiers*, the hymn, which is a typical ... a typical ...'

'We're all waiting, Ned,' Mrs Welch said from the piano. She played a slow arpeggio, sustaining it with the pedal. 'All right, everybody?'

A soporific droning filled the air round Dixon as the singers hummed their notes to one another. Mrs Welch rejoined them on the low platform that had been built at one end of the music-room, taking up her stand by Margaret, the other soprano. A small bullied-looking woman with un-abundant brown hair was the only contralto. Next to Dixon was Cecil Goldsmith, a colleague of his in the College History Department, whose tenor voice held enough savage power, especially above middle C, to obliterate whatever noises Dixon might feel himself impelled to make. Behind him and to one side were three basses, one a local composer, another an amateur violinist occasionally summoned at need by the city orchestra, the third Evan Johns.

Dixon ran his eye along the lines of black dots, which seemed to go up and down a good deal, and was able to assure himself that everyone was going to have to sing all the time. He'd had a bad setback twenty minutes ago in some Brahms rubbish which began with ten seconds or so of unsupported tenor – more accurately, of unsupported Goldsmith, who'd twice dried up in face of a tricky interval and left him opening and shutting his mouth in silence. He now cautiously reproduced the note Goldsmith was humming and found the effect pleasing rather than the reverse. Why hadn't they had the decency to ask him if he'd like to join in, instead of driving him up on to this platform arrangement and forcing sheets of paper into his hand?

The madrigal began at the bidding of Welch's arthritic forefinger. Dixon kept his head down, moved his mouth as little as possible consistent with being unmistakably seen to move it, and looked through the words the others were singing. 'When from my love I looked for love, and kind affections due,' he read, 'too well I found her vows to prove most faithless

243

and untrue. But when I did ask her why . . .' He looked over at Margaret, who was singing away happily enough – she turned out regularly during the winter with the choir of the local Conservative Association – and wondered what changes in their circumstances and temperaments would be necessary to make the words of the madrigal apply, however remotely, to himself and her. She'd made vows to him, or avowals anyway, which was perhaps all the writer had meant. But if he'd meant what he seemed to mean by 'kind affections due', then Dixon had never 'looked for' any of these from Margaret. Perhaps he should; after all, people were doing it all the time. It was a pity she wasn't a bit better-looking. One of these days, though, he would try, and see what happened.

'Yet by, and by, they'll arl, deny, arnd say 'twas *bart* in jast,' Goldsmith sang tremulously and very loudly. It was the last phrase; Dixon kept his mouth open while Welch's finger remained aloft, then shut it with a little flick of the head he'd seen singers use as the finger swept sideways. All seemed pleased with the performance and anxious for another of the same sort. 'Yes, well, this next one's what they called a ballet. Of course, they didn't mean what we mean by the similar . . . Rather a well-known one, this. It's called *Now is the Month of Maying*. Now if you'll all just . . .'

A bursting snuffle of laughter came from Dixon's left rear. He glanced round to see Johns's pallor rent by a grin. The large short-lashed eyes were fixed on him. 'What's the joke?' he asked. If Johns were laughing at Welch, Dixon was prepared to come in on Welch's side.

'You'll see,' Johns said. He went on looking at Dixon. 'You'll see,' he added, grinning.

In less than a minute Dixon did see, and clearly. Instead of the customary four parts, this piece employed five. The third and fourth lines of music from the top had *Tenor I* and *Tenor II* written against them; moreover, there was some infantile fa-la-la-la stuff on the second page with numerous gaps in the individual parts. Even Welch's ear might be expected to record the complete absence of one of the parts in such circumstances. It was much too late now for Dixon to explain that he hadn't really meant it when he'd said, half an hour before, that he could read music 'after a fashion'; much too late to transfer allegiance to the basses. Nothing short of an epileptic fit could get him out of this.

'You'd better take first tenor, Jim,' Goldsmith said; 'the second's a bit tricky.'

Dixon nodded bemusedly, hardly hearing further laughter from Johns.

Before he could cry out, they were past the piano-ritual and the droning and into the piece. He flapped his lips to: 'Each with his bonny lass, a-a-seated on the grass: fa-la-la la, fa-la-la-la-la-la la la-la ...' but Welch had stopped waving his finger, was holding it stationary in the air. The singing died. 'Oh, tenors,' Welch began; 'I didn't seem to hear ...'

An irregular knocking on the door at the far end of the room was at once followed by the bursting-open of this door and the entry of a tall man wearing a lemon-yellow sport-coat, all three buttons of which were fastened, and displaying a large beard which came down further on one side than on the other, half-hiding a vine-patterned tie. Dixon guessed with surging exultation that this must be the pacifist painting Bertrand whose arrival with his girl had been heralded, with typical clangour, by Welch every few minutes since tea-time. It was an arrival which must surely prove an irritant sooner or later, but for the moment it served as the best possible counter-irritant to the disastrous madrigals. Even as Dixon thought this, the senior Welches left their posts and went to greet their son, followed more slowly by the others who, perhaps finding the chance of a break not completely unwelcome, broke into conversation as they moved. Dixon delightedly lit a cigarette, finding himself alone: the amateur violinist had got hold of Margaret; Goldsmith and the local composer were talking to Carol, Goldsmith's wife, who'd refused, with enviable firmness, to do more than sit and listen to the singing from an armchair near the fireplace; Johns was doing something technical at the piano. Dixon moved down the room through the company and leaned against the wall at the end by the door where the bookshelves were. Placed here, savouring his cigarette, he was in a good position to observe Bertrand's girl when she came in, slowly and hesitantly, a few seconds later, and stood unnoticed, except by him, just inside the room.

In a few more seconds Dixon had noticed all he needed to notice about this girl: the combination of fair hair, straight and cut short, with brown eyes and no lipstick, the strict set of the mouth and the square shoulders, the large breasts and the narrow waist, the premeditated simplicity of the wine-coloured corduroy skirt and the unornamented white linen blouse. The sight of her seemed an irresistible attack on his own habits, standards and ambitions: something designed to put him in his place for good. The notion that women like this were never on view except as the property of men like Bertrand was so familiar to him that it had long since ceased to appear an injustice. The huge class that contained Margaret was destined to provide his own womenfolk: those in whom the intention of being attractive could sometimes be made to get itself confused with perform-ance; those with whom a too-tight skirt, a wrong-coloured, or no, lipstick, even an ill-executed smile could instantly discredit that illusion beyond apparent hope of renewal. But renewal always came: a new sweater would somehow scale down the large feet, generosity revivify the brittle hair, a couple of pints site positive charm in talk of the London stage or French food.

The girl turned her head and found Dixon staring at her. His diaphragm contracted with fright; she drew herself up with a jerk like a soldier standing easy called to the stand-at-ease position. They looked at each other for a moment, until, just as Dixon's scalp was beginning to tingle, a high, baying voice called 'Ah, there you are, darling; step this way, if you please, and be introduced to the throng' and Bertrand strode up the room to meet her, throwing Dixon a brief hostile glance. Dixon didn't like him doing that; the only action he required from Bertrand was an apology, humbly offered, for his personal appearance . . . .

A maidservant was now collecting the used crockery, and the company was moving about. The next stage of the evening was clearly imminent . . . . At Welch's summons, Dixon left Margaret to help arrange some chairs. 'What's the next item on the programme, Professor?' he asked.

Welch's heavy features had settled into their depressive look after the manic phase of the last hour and a half. He gave Dixon a mutinous glare. 'Just one or two instrumental items.'

'Oh, that'll be nice. Who's first on the list?'

The other brooded, his slab-like hands on the back of a ludicrously low chair that resembled an inefficiently converted hassock. In a moment he disclosed that the local composer and the amateur violinist were going to 'tackle' a violin sonata by some Teutonic bore, that an unstated number of recorders would then perform some suitable item, and that at some later time Johns might be expected to produce music from his oboe. Dixon nodded as if pleased.

He returned to Margaret to find her in conversation with Carol Gold-smith. This woman, aged about forty, thin, with long straight brown hair, Dixon regarded as one of his allies, though sometimes she overawed him a little with her mature air.

'Hallo, Jim, how's it going?' she asked in her abnormally clear voice.

SONATA

I

P. RACINE FRICKER, Op. 12

Lucky Jim vs *P. Racine Fricker*

'Badly. There's at least an hour of scraping and blowing in front of us.'...

The amateur violinist nodded the top half of his body and, supported by the local composer, burst into some scurrying tunelessness or other. Bertrand leaned over towards Dixon. 'What the hell do you mean?' he asked in a loud undertone.

'Who's your alienist?' Dixon said, broadening his field of fire.

'Look here, Dixon, you're talking as if you want a bloody good punch on the nose, aren't you?'

Dixon, when moved, was bad at ordering his thoughts. 'If I did, you don't think you're the one to give me one, do you?'

Bertrand screwed up his face at this enigma. 'What?'

'Do you know what you look like in that beard?' Dixon's heart began to race as he switched to simplicity.

'All right; coming outside for a bit?'

The latest of this string of questions was drowned by a long rumbling shake in the bass of the piano. 'What?' Dixon asked.

Mrs Welch, Margaret, Johns, the Goldsmiths and the contralto woman all seemed to turn round simultaneously. 'Ssshh,' they all said. It was like a railway engine blowing out steam under a glass roof. Dixon got up and tip-toed to the door. Bertrand half rose to follow, but his girl stopped him.

Before Dixon could reach the door, it opened and Welch entered. 'Oh, you've started, have you?' he asked without dropping his voice at all.

'Yes,' Dixon whispered. 'I think I'll just...'

'Pity you couldn't have waited a little longer. I've been on the phone, you see. It was that chap from the ... from the...'

'See you later.' Dixon began edging past to the doorway.

'Aren't you going to stay for the P. Racine Fricker?'

'Shan't be long, Professor. I just think I'll...' Dixon made some gestures meant to be indecipherable. 'I'll be back.'

He shut the door on Welch's long-lived, wondering frown.

(*Lucky Jim*)

ANON ('K.M.S.')

Amateur Rehearsal: Der Fussy Clarinetist

Der Meyer plays die Clarinet
Bei uns mit in der Band.
He's alvays tooteling arount
Or fooling mit his Shtand.
Und v'en our Leader lifts his Shtick
Und we're subbosed to play
Denn Meyer shpits upon his reed
Und says, 'Giff me vonce *A*.' –

He makes such funny Mout's dabei
Shust wie a Tsherman Carp,
Und v'en die Oboe sounds das *A*
He says, 'Tchee, ain't I sharp?
I haff to pull dot Mout'piece out
A tiny liddle vay.
Now – led me see if dot's on tune –
Shust giff me vonce more *A*.

'By golly, she vent down too far.
Dat sounts like almost flet.
Vell, nefer mind, v'en she gets warm
She might come up. Shust let
Me blow a couple runs und shcales.
Dot von't make much delay.

So – now if you vould be so kind
Und giff me yet vonce *A*.' –

'Vot! *A* und *A* und wieder *A*,
It makes me red im face!'
Our Leader yells. 'Dot's all I hear!
It don't giff no more *A's!*
You shust play nodding but der Rests,
Und let me dell you v'itch:
If you had der whole Alphabet
You shtill von't be on pitch!'

ANGELA BRAZIL

Mutual Improvement Friday at St Chad's

'One wouldn't expect it from Flossie Taylor!' said Honor contemptuously, as she hurried off to her music lesson.

I am afraid Honor's scales that day were anything but a satisfaction to Fräulein Bernhardt, the piano teacher. Her mind was so abstracted that she kept continually playing wrong fingering, or even an occasional wrong note in the harmonic minors. Her study was little better, and her piece a dead failure. The mistress, with characteristic German patience, set her to work to try to conquer a couple of difficult phrases, through which Honor stumbled again and again, each time with the same old mistakes, until the end of the half-hour.

'I find you not yet fit to take share in ze evening pairformance!' sighed poor Fräulein, whose musical ear had been much distressed by this mangling of her favourite tarantella. 'Zere must be more of improvement before ve render ze piece to Mees Maitland. You say you not vish to play in publique? Ach, so! Zat is vat zey all say; but it is good to begin young to get over ze fear – vat you call ze "shyness" – is it not so?'

Fräulein Bernhardt was an excellent teacher – patient, conscientious, and enthusiastic. She tried to inspire all her pupils with her own love for music, and with some indeed she succeeded, though with others it proved a more difficult task.

'I'm almost impossible!' avowed Lettice Talbot. 'I believe I'm nearly as bad as the old fellow who declared he only knew two tunes – one was "God Save the King", and the other wasn't.'

'You certainly have a particularly leaden touch,' agreed Dorothy

Arkwright. 'The way you hammer out Mendelssohn is enough to try my nerves, so I'm sure it must be an offence to Fräulein.'

'I think it's stupid to be obliged to learn the piano when you've absolutely no taste for it,' yawned Lettice. 'I'm going to ask Father to let me give it up next term.'

'Don't!' interposed Vivian Holmes, who happened to overhear Lettice's remark. 'I went through that same phase myself, when I was fourteen. I implored my mother to allow me to stop music, and she had nearly consented when I met a lady who advised me most strongly to go on. She said she couldn't play herself, and regretted it immensely now she was grown-up, and would be thankful if she could manage even a hymn tune. So I did go on, and now I'm very glad. I'm certain you'll like it better, Lettice, when you've got over more of the drudgery.'

'Perhaps it will never be anything but drudgery for me!'

'Oh, yes, it will! We shall have you taking part in the "Friday firsts" yet.'

On the first Friday in every month Miss Maitland held a 'Mutual Improvement Evening', at which all who were sufficiently advanced were expected to contribute by playing, singing, or reciting. These were quite informal gatherings, only Chaddites being present. Miss Cavendish considered it good for teachers and pupils to meet thus socially, and a similar arrangement obtained at each house. To many of the girls, however, it was more of an ordeal to be obliged to perform before their schoolfellows than it would have been to play to strangers.

'I'm always nervous, in any case,' said Pauline Reynolds; 'but strangers don't criticize one openly afterwards, whatever they may think in private. I feel it's perfectly dreadful to have Fräulein and Miss Maitland and Miss Parkinson sitting on one side, and all of you in a row on the other!'

'But we're very polite,' urged Lettice. 'We say, "Thank you?"'

Honor had not yet been considered proficient enough to take an active part in the monthly entertainment, but Flossie's name was one of the first on the list. She played the violin remarkably well, better than almost anybody else at Chessington; and as she was seldom nervous, her pieces were generally very successful. The day following Evelyn Fletcher's fright happened to be 'Mutual Improvement Friday'. The girls only spent a short time at preparation, and then went upstairs to change their dresses. The meetings were always held in the drawing-room, and were rather festive in character. Miss Maitland tried to make them as much as possible like ordinary parties; she received the girls as guests, encouraged them to converse with herself and the other teachers, and had coffee served to them during the evening.

On this particular occasion Flossie made a very careful toilet, and she certainly looked nice in her pretty, embroidered white muslin dress, her fair hair tied with big bows of palest blue ribbon. She took a last glance at herself in the looking-glass, then, seizing her violin, which she had brought to her cubicle, she prepared to go downstairs.

In passing Miss Maitland's bedroom on the lower landing, she noticed that the door stood open, and that no one was within. There was a large mirror in the wardrobe, and, catching a glimpse of her own reflection as she went by, she stopped suddenly, and could not resist the temptation to run in for a moment and take a full-length view of herself as she would appear when she was playing her piece. She raised her violin and struck a suitable attitude, and was immensely pleased with the result that faced her – the dainty dress, the blue bows, the coral cheeks, flaxen hair, and bright eyes all made a charming picture, and the position in which she held her instrument was particularly graceful. She drew her bow gently over the strings, to observe the curve of her slender wrist and well-shaped arm. It was gratifying to know that she would make such a good appearance before her schoolfellows. Once again she played a few notes, for the sheer satisfaction of watching her slim, white fingers in the glass.

Alas for Flossie! That single bar of Schubert's *Serenade* was her un-doing. Honor chanced to be passing the door at the identical moment, and, hearing the strain of music, peeped inside. She grasped the situation at a glance.

'Oho, Miss Flossie! So I've caught you prinking!' she said to herself. 'You're evidently practising your very best company smile for this evening. What a disappointment it would be to you, now, if you were not able to play that piece after all!'

Honor had a resourceful mind. Very gently she put her hand inside the door and abstracted the key, which, with equal caution, she fitted into the keyhole on the outside; then, quickly shutting the door, she locked it, and ran away before Flossie had even discovered that anybody was there. The latter naturally noticed the slight noise and turned round, but she was too late; and though she rattled the handle, and knocked and called, it was of no avail. Honor, as it happened, had been the last girl to go downstairs, and there was nobody left on either landing to hear even the most frantic thumps. Flossie rushed to the electric bell, hoping to bring a servant to her assistance; but it was out of order, and would not ring. She was in a terrible dilemma: if she made too much noise one of the teachers, or even Miss Maitland herself, might come upstairs to see what was the matter; on the other hand, there she was locked up fast and secure, missing the 'evening', and with an equal chance of being found out in the end, and asked to give some explanation of her presence in the mistress's room.

In the meantime, Honor went downstairs chuckling. She entered the drawing-room in the highest of spirits, paid her respects to Miss Maitland, and found a seat close to the door. The musical part of the performance, she ascertained, was to come first, and after coffee there were to be recitations, and a dialogue in French. A neat programme had been written out and was laid on the top of the piano, so that it could be referred to by Vivian Holmes, who was conductress of the ceremonies.

It was late already, and the proceedings began immediately. The room was crowded, and amongst the forty girls nobody seemed to have particularly remarked Flossie's absence, and no enquiry was made for her, until the close of the song that preceded her violin solo.

'Where is Flossie Taylor?' whispered Vivian then, with a look of marked annoyance on her face. 'Her *Serenade* comes next. She ought to be standing by the piano. Has anybody seen her? Please pass the question on.'

She paused a moment or two in great impatience; then, as no Flossie put in an appearance, she turned to Meta Fletcher and May Turner, who followed on the programme, and asked them to begin their duet.

'I can't wait for anybody,' she remarked. 'If Flossie isn't ready, I must simply miss her out. We've almost too many pieces to get through in the time.'

The rest of the music went off successfully. Nobody broke down, or even made a bad stumble, a subject of much self-congratulation to several nervous performers and of great relief to Vivian, who, as monitress of the house, always arranged the little concerts as a surprise for Miss Maitland, the latter preferring that the girls should settle all details amongst themselves, instead of leaving matters to a teacher.

Coffee was brought in at eight o'clock, after which the recitations began immediately. At this stage of the entertainment Honor felt magnanimous. She did not want to involve Flossie in serious trouble, so, slipping quietly away, she ran upstairs, unlocked the door of Miss Maitland's bedroom, and released her prisoner.

The disappointed violinist emerged looking decidedly glum.

'It's a nasty, mean trick you've played me, Honor Fitzgerald!' she burst out.

'No meaner than you played on Evelyn Fletcher – not half so bad, in my opinion. I'm sorry to say you're too late for your solo. The music's over long ago, and they're hard at work reciting Shakespeare at present.'

'Just what I expected! And it's all your fault!'

'You're very ungrateful! You ought to be most relieved to be let out before Miss Maitland caught you,' retorted Honor. 'What an opportunity to point a moral on the fatal consequences of vanity!' Then, as Flossie flounced angrily away: 'You've never thanked me for unlocking this door yet. I thought we were supposed to cultivate manners at St Chad's....'

(*The New Girl at St Chad's*)

CHARLES BURNEY

Dutch music as perceived by Italians

Wednesday 31 October. This morning I went with young Oliver to his conservatorio of S. Onofrio, and visited all the rooms, where the boys practice, sleep and eat. On the 1st flight of stairs was a trumpeter screaming upon his instrument till he was ready to burst – on the 2nd a French horn bellowing in the same manner – in the common practicing room was a dutch concert,* consisting of 7 or 8 harpsichords, more than as many fiddles, and several voices all performing different things in different keys – other boys were writing in the same room, but it being holiday time not near all were there who study and practice in the same room. This method of jumbling them all together may be convenient for the house and may teach the boys to stand fire, by obliging them to attend their own parts with firmness whatever else may be going forward at the same time. It may likewise give them force, in obliging them to play loud in order to hear themselves, for nothing but noise can pervade noise, but in the midst of such jargon and continued dissonance it is wholly impossible to acquire taste, expression or delicacy – there can be no polish or finishing given to their performance and that seems to account for the slovenliness and coarseness remarkable in their public exhibitions, and for the total want of taste, neatness and expression in these young performers till they have acquired it elsewhere. The beds which are in the same room serve for seats to the harpsichords etc. Out of 30 or 40 boys who were practicing I could discover but 2 that were playing the same piece. Some of those who were practicing on the violin seemed to have a great deal of hand. The

* A concert in which every performer plays a different tune.

violoncellos are in another room and the wind instruments, such as the flutes, hautbois etc in a 3rd. – The trumpets and horns either fag on the stairs or top of the house. – There are in this college 16 castrati, and these lye by themselves in a warmer appartment upstairs than the other boys for fear of colds, which might endanger or injure the voice. This is the only vacation time in the whole year, but on Monday term begins, and I shall then return and hear them take lessons of the masters. They then begin the winter practice of rising 2 hours before daylight, from which time they continue their exercise, an hour and ½ at dinner excepted till 8 o'clock at night, and this constant perseverance for a number of years, must, with genius and good teaching produce great musicians.

(*An Eighteenth-Century Musical Tour in France and Italy*)

FANNY BURNEY (MME D'ARBLAY)

La! What a crush

... How ridiculous to invite so many more people than could be accommodated!

Lord Mulgrave was soon sick of the heat, and finding me distressed what to do with my cup, he very good-naturedly took it from me, but carried not only that, but himself also, away, which I did not equally rejoice at.

You may laugh, perhaps, that I have all this time said never a word of the music, but the truth is I heard scarce a note. There were quartettos and overtures by gentlemen performers whose names and faces I know not, and such was the never ceasing tattling and noise in the card-room, where I was kept almost all the evening, that a general humming of musical sounds, and now and then a twang, was all I could hear.

Nothing can well be more ridiculous than a concert of this sort; and Dr Harrington told me that the confusion amongst the musicians was equal to that amongst the company; for that, when called upon to open the concert, they found no music. The Miss C——'s had prepared nothing, nor yet solicited their *dilettanti's* to prepare for them. Miss Harrington, his daughter, who played upon the harpsichord, and by the very little I could sometimes hear, I believe very well, complained that she had never touched so vile an instrument, and that she was quite disturbed at being obliged to play upon it.

About the time that I got against the door, as I have mentioned, of the music room, the young ladies were preparing to perform, and with the assistance of Mr Henry, they sang catches. Oh, such singing! worse squalling, more out of tune, and more execrable in every respect, never did I hear. We did not get away till late.

(*The Diary and Letters of Madame D'Arblay*)

Opposite: *The actual players caricatured at Dr Burney's Sunday concerts, 1782*

PHILIP STANHOPE,
EARL OF CHESTERFIELD

Gentlemen don't fiddle or pipe

To his Son:
Dear Boy,   April 19, 1749

This letter will, I believe, still find you at Venice, in all the dissipation of masquerades, ridottos, operas, &c: with all my heart; they are decent evening amusements, and very properly succeed that serious application to which I am sure you devote your mornings. There are liberal and illiberal pleasures as well as liberal and illiberal arts. . . . As you are now in a musical country, where singing, fiddling, and piping are not only the common topics of conversation, but almost the principal objects of attention; I cannot help cautioning you against giving in to those (I will call them illiberal) pleasures, (though music is commonly reckoned one of the liberal arts,) to the degree that most of your countrymen do when they travel in Italy. If you love music, hear it; go to operas, concerts, and pay fiddlers to play to you; but I insist upon your neither piping nor fiddling yourself. It puts a gentleman in a very frivolous, contemptible light; brings him into a great deal of bad company; and takes up a great deal of time, which might be much better employed. Few things would mortify more, than to see you bearing a part in a concert, with a fiddle under your chin, or a pipe in your mouth . . .

(*The Letters of Philip Dormer Stanhope, Earl of Chesterfield*)

FRYDERYK CHOPIN

A letter about the English

To Albert Grzymala, 1848

...I am quite lost in London. What with twenty years in Poland and seventeen in Paris, it's not surprising that I am getting on slowly here, particularly as I don't speak the language. They don't chatter while I am playing and they apparently all speak well of my music, but my little colleagues are usually treated with such scant respect that I appear to be a kind of amateur, and I shall soon be regarded as a kind of *nobleman*, for I have clean shoes and I don't carry around visiting-cards inscribed: 'Private lessons given. Evening engagements accepted.'

Old Mme Rothschild asked me how much I *cost* ['Combien coûtez-vous?'], as some lady who had heard me was making inquiries. Since Sutherland gave me twenty guineas, the fee fixed for me by Broadwood on whose piano I play, I answered, 'Twenty guineas'. She, so obviously trying to be kind and helpful, replied that of course I play very beautifully, but that she advised me to take less, as one had to show greater 'moderayshon' this season.

I gather from this that they are not so open-handed and money is tight everywhere. To please the middle class you need something sensational, some technical display which is out of my sphere. The upper classes who travel abroad are proud, but educated and fair – when they deign to take notice of anything. But their attention is frittered away so much on a thousand different trifles, they are so hemmed in by tiresome conventions, that it's all the same to them whether the music is good or bad, for they are compelled to listen to it from morning till night. There is music at every

261

flower-show, music at every dinner, every sale is accompanied by music. The street-singers, Czechs and my pianist-colleagues are as numerous as dogs – and all mixed up together. I am writing all this as if you didn't know London!

To Wojciech Grzymala in Paris

[Hamilton Palace] 21 October [1848]

By 'art' they mean here painting, sculpture and architecture. Music is not an art, and is not called by that name; and if you say 'artist' these English think you mean a painter, sculptor or architect. But music is a *profession*, not an art, and no one ever calls any musician an artist or uses the word in such a sense in print. In their language and customs music is something different from an art – it is a profession. Ask any Englishman you like and he will tell you the same; and Neukomm has assured me of it. Of course musicians have only themselves to blame, but just you try to alter such things! They play the most fantastic pieces, supposing them to be beautiful, but it's absurd to try to teach them decent things. Lady ..., one of the most important ladies here, at whose castle I spent a few days, is said to be both a *grande dame* and a musician. Well, after I had played and other Scottish ladies had sung various songs, they brought out a sort of accordion [a concertina!] and she, with the utmost gravity, began to play the most dreadful tunes on it. But what can you expect? It seems to me that every one of these creatures has a screw loose.

Another lady, showing me her album, said: 'I stood beside the Queen while she looked at it.' A third declares that she is 'the thirteenth cousin of Mary Stuart'. Another one, always to be original of course, accompanies herself *standing* at the piano while she sings a French romance with an English accent: 'J'aie aiimaiie' which she pronounces: J'ay ay-may!!!

The Princess of Parma told me that one of them *whistled* for her, with guitar accompaniment! The ones who know my compositions ask [in French]: 'Play me your Second Sigh [Nocturne in G major] ... I love your bells.' And every comment ends with the words: 'Leik water', meaning that the music flows like water. I have never yet played to an Englishwoman without her saying: 'Leik WATER!!' They all look at their hands and play wrong notes most soulfully. What a queer lot! God preserve them!

(*Selected Correspondence of Fryderyk Chopin*)

CURIO (RICHARD HOLMES)

The Wiggins's musical party

After many and repeated invitations and promises on either side, it was at length agreed, with my friend Tom Gossett, that Christmas of—— should not be suffered to pass without my paying a visit to his recently adopted domicile in the vicinity of that pretty village of E——, which those at all acquainted with the county of Devonshire can hardly fail to have visited. I had often looked forward with pleasure to this promised relaxation from the turmoil of professional life, and the grateful exchange of the exciting cares and responsibilities of business for the luxurious independence of a week's holiday in that delightful locality, combined with the additional enjoyment of the society of one of the most accomplished and amiable of men. Tom was one of my oldest and most intimate friends, and his wife was just the sort of person to make such a guest as myself happy and comfortable under her husband's roof.

The day at length arrived when I felt myself at liberty to take my departure, and, on the 23d of December, of the year above-mentioned, I had the satisfaction of presenting myself at the door of my good host, and was speedily confronted with the family party, consisting of no more, in fact, than my old friend, his wife, and a young person who was introduced to me as Tom's nephew.

'That lad,' said Tom to me in a whisper, as he showed me to my apartment, – 'that lad whom you saw in the drawing-room——'

'Your nephew?'

'Yes – he has, he has indeed——'

'What?'

'Genius!'

Well it's no worse, thought I; but was forthwith brought again under the infliction of my friend's mysterious revelations touching the singular endowments of his *protégé*. Too tired after my journey on the one hand, and too content with anticipating the grateful repose that awaited me on the other, to enter with any peculiar interest into the merits of this *rara avis*, my demonstrations were confined to the conventional style of response which a helpless spirit of resignation to the will of my interpreter alone could enable me to adopt.

We descended to the drawing-room, and were very soon summoned to dinner, during which ceremony I had an opportunity of observing, among other things, the characteristics of the youthful prodigy in behalf of whom my passive sympathies had already been enlisted by his admiring uncle. It was very soon observable, that one subject, and one alone, engaged the thoughts and feelings of this interesting scion. It was music – or rather the art of 'fiddling,' with its concomitant pedantries. The boy was evidently a pet with his indulgent relatives, and they not only countenanced to excess his aspirations after the artistic excellence which he appeared to regard as the *summum bonum* of life, but were betrayed into the error too common with enthusiastic parents and guardians, of so far misinterpreting his promise as to confound the restlessness of undisciplined boyhood with the throes of incipient genius, and to view the pertinacious ardour with which he clung to his infatuation as evidence of undoubted inspiration. The consequence was that the most unrestrained license was accorded to this youth in the indulgence of his particular, or rather absorbing pursuit. As dinner advanced, I discovered that the scion, as we must call him, had been just imported into his present enviable quarters, in consequence of an invitation which had been sent to my friend and his estimable partner by an inimitable couple residing in the vicinity, couched in the following terms:

'MR AND MRS WIGGINS request the pleasure of Mr and Mrs Gossett's company at a musical *soirée*, on the 29th instant, at eight o'clock precisely.'

The invitation was accompanied by a private note from Mrs Wiggins to the lady, which ran as follows:

'MY DEAR MRS GOSSETT, – You have often heard of our musical *soirées*; you will now have an opportunity of appreciating them. We do not ask any but *musical* people, notwithstanding they are so few; but I tell you candidly we shall this time surpass ourselves; for the selection will not merely be of the most classical description, but the performers will all be very superior. Our great Kanteler is coming (this, however, amongst ourselves). By the by, would you like to bring your nephew with you? I mean the one with such precocious musical talent. We shall be delighted to see him.

'Believe me, yours sincerely,
'LIZZY WIGGINS.'

Upon this hint it appears the prodigy was duly summoned, and as duly arrived, and such was the occasion of the young gentleman's presence within the hospitable walls which had just received me as an inmate for at least six days to come.

I am thankful in being able to avow myself one of those persons who are so happily constituted as seldom to be enslaved or distracted by any predominating train of thought when in the society of others, and, consequently, was enabled at this moment to listen to the conversation which, by reason of the presence of the scion, bore chiefly on the all-absorbing topic of music. It will not be necessary to detail that conversation, – suffice it, that it embraced allusions which were new to me, and appeared to possess little interest for one of the uninitiated. Of course, having been tolerably familiarized with the formulæ of ordinary society, and of musical entertainments in the metropolis, I had heard about Mozart and Beethoven, *cum multis aliis* of the same illustrious fraternity, – in fact, possess a fair average acquaintance with matters musical, so far as they are expounded by our popular caterers to the requirements of a superficial public, have a tolerable ear, can join in a chorus, and have experienced the legitimate unbiassed sensations on listening to the infelicities of a bad vocalist or fiddler, although not identifying the cause of such sensation with the analytic skill of a connoisseur. But the technicalities connected with composition, and the paraphernalia of the concert-room, the strange investiture of the choice passages with a meaning and intelligence which I had not only never been guilty of imputing, but had never before heard imputed, to those respectable phenomena, the contrarieties of taste, and the heating discussions and dissensions arising therefrom, and above all – But this is anticipating.

The day arrived – the evening approached. I, of course, was to be one of the party. Tom was unusually erratic; his wife was equally unsettled, and the scion was like a ball of wildfire. Of necessity, everything went wrong during the day; there was an utter suspension of domestic routine; the ceremony of breakfast lasted, with sundry intermissions, upwards of two hours; dinner was a perfect farce, – in fact, I was an isolated being, and thrown upon my own resources during the entire day. At seven o'clock we were summoned by the appearance at the door of a snug vehicle, which was exactly large enough to hold four, and then off we were whirled to the cottage of the renowned Wigginses.

'Mr and Mrs Gossett,' proclaimed the servant, and in we all walked into a spacious room, presenting a collection of neat and respectable-looking individuals, some of whose appearance may be cursorily described. Our valued host and hostess, Mr and Mrs Wiggins, claim precedence in this enumeration. Wiggins was a round, shortish, florid, smiling, nice old fellow, presenting an exterior of almost professional respectability, comprising the characteristic blackness and whiteness, and tightness and cleanness, with, in addition, an amiable and shining naturalness, individually and particularly his own. The temperament of our friend was of the most genial description, presenting an attractiveness which only the most unaffected simplicity of character, and the most exuberant goodness of heart, can, with other minor combinations, secure. His fault was that he was an amateur violin-player.

Mrs Wiggins was one of those persons who please everybody, – in fact, just the sort of character that her husband deserved as a wife. Like him, she had devoted herself assiduously to the cultivation of musical art, and was, as may be supposed, to officiate as the pianiste of this eventful evening. Mrs Wiggins was stout, but winning.

The *salon* was arranged with all the needful appliances for an amateur concert. The pianoforte was turned inside out, and was surrounded by a number of musical desks, garnished each with wax-candles, and a chair attached, upon or against which lay or stood a musical instrument of one description or other, together comprising violins of the required different sizes, flutes, clarionet, &c. The first thing the scion did, on entering the room, was to go and fumble about among the fiddles: he flew to them with instinctive impetuosity, and was soon imbedded in the little orchestra. The party further consisted of Mr and Mrs Simpson, the former tall, thin, and intellectual; the latter an animated pincushion in appearance, but possessing, as Mrs Wiggins informed my friends, 'great soul.' Mr Simpson was to take the second violin. Major Starkie and his daughter next presented themselves: the major was one of those benevolent people who are always forward to impart edification to all sorts of their fellow-creatures, and, without pretending himself to be a performer, made up for the deficiency by extemporising verbally and volubly upon the subject uppermost in the general mind upon this occasion: 'instructor-general' was written on his brow, and with the manner of a gentleman and the heart of a wiseacre, he took me aside, soon after the introduction, and conferred some oracular communications which I was conscientiously bound to respect, inasmuch as they were upon the various points referred to corroborative of the stereotyped dogmas of the day. His daughter was a perfect specimen of the English lady, – quiet, graceful, observant, and conversible, and evidently qualified to enjoy to its utmost extent the intellectual repast in store for us.

Mrs Wiggins was indefatigable in dispensing the needful *agrémens* among her guests, especially to our party, to whom she was remarkably solicitous in conveying an adequate appreciation of the several personages assembled. Mr Wiggins himself had enough to do in superintending the order of the entertainments. Our revered host was to be the viola of the evening: the violoncello was undertaken by Mr Scott Bell, and the flute by Mr Pinkerton.

The general attention was directed to the performers, all of whom, however, were in a state of suspense and uneasiness in consequence of the non-appearance of the first violin, Mr Kanteler, the most important character. At length, after some considerable delay, the lion of the evening was announced, and in walked the great Kanteler. His entrance was the signal for general recognition, and he was at once hailed as the central functionary of the musical circle. He was a spare, middle-sized man, with great apparent elaboration of costume. His head was well shaped, visage thin – hair the same – rather pock-marked, large goggle eyes, the merest modicum of languid whisker, underhung mouth, long chin; and 'the inheritor himself,' encompassed in a blue coat with brass buttons, protecting an embroidered waistcoat, and an interior confluence of costly embellishment in quality of studs, chains, and divers intricate appendages, betokening the eccentricity of taste which usually marks the provincial lion: his lower proportions, which, under the restrictive authority of modern fashion were denied the privilege of illustrating the gentleman's taste in decorative art, were, nevertheless, punctilio itself; and his cravat was a perfect picture – white, inflexible, and of uncompromising depth, and consequently height, to the extent of invading the lower extremities of his ears, each of which curled up from the encroachment with an effect entirely unique. His most remarkable peculiarity, however, was the breadth and prominence of his wristbands, which bore undeniable evidence to the daring inveteracy with which he had equipped himself for the all-important *rôle* assigned to him by his devoted compeers. He walked up to Mrs Wiggins, and seated himself beside her, when a series of whispering mutualities ensued, marked by irrepressible emphasis and anxiety on the one part, and the most imperturbable and dignified coolness on the other. As the lady poured into his ears the burthen of all her secret solicitudes at that critical moment, and as the depth of feeling with which her musical soul was preparing to be agitated was apparent in the gentle undulations of her respected breast, the great Kanteler maintained the immoveable aspect which he wore on first entering the room. At the termination of this portentous *tête-à-tête*, Major Starkie walked up to the accomplished man, and addressed him in a delightful tone of confraternity, which Kanteler returned with the same stolid serenity as before. The Major indulged his propensity to impart knowledge in his interview with Kanteler, not to the extent of presuming to offer anything acceptable to the latter in the way of connoisseurship, which would, in all probability, have been received with withering disdain, but contented himself with at once asserting his originality, and exempting the lion from any wound to his vanity, by simply discoursing to him on the subject of some newly-imported fiddlestrings, which a friend of his had, as cigar-smokers often confess to you, just obtained with great difficulty and by very particular favour. The Major's daughter then accosted Kanteler, upon which the latter rose, and a similar abortive attempt on the part of that lady was made to 'draw him out.' The mind was evidently pre-occupied; and a quiet signal from Mr Wiggins withdrew him to the orchestra, where he was forthwith installed as leader. Whereupon commenced the tuning business, introduced with a series of whimp'rings and gruntings of the short duration desirable by reason of the extreme agony they appeared to express, and assimilating at last to what might be expected from a chorus of guinea-pigs trying to get up a rational conversation. The word was given by the scion, who stood behind Kanteler for the purpose of turning over the leaves of the 'master' as occasion required.

The first burst was the signal for the deadest silence among the audience, and the most lively noisiness on the part of the performers. It was the first out-and-out thing of the kind I had ever witnessed, and I must in candour avow that the effect of the first piece was to excite me irresistibly to laughter: especially as the constant pattering of the digital department, with its graduated tones, first from the first violin, with its intermittent scream, then from his junior brother the second violin, then with the sonorous accents of uncle tenor (Wiggins), and capped by the climax of old grandfather grumbletonian, whose freaks of ponderous agility had the effect of representing the violoncello, to my unpractised observation, as one of the funniest old fellows I had ever met with. The performers seemed, I thought, all to understand each other, and managed to inspire the audience, at least, with a due sense of the untiring perseverance displayed by the composer in chasing an idea in a circle whenever he got hold of one. The finale to the first quintette went off with exceedingly audible *éclat*, and the performers, one and all (excepting the leader), looked pretty considerably burnished up by their exertions. Mr Wiggins smoothed his glowing frontispiece, and looked for all the world like a good boy who had had a pommelling and felt the better for it; there was a happy, tearful expression which implied exultation at having confronted

A rustic concert in a rotten borough

A Country Concert: — or — an Evenings Entertainment in Sussex.

danger, and joy at having honourably escaped from it: he looked first at Kanteler and smiled, but that obdurate hero was sympathy-proof still. The look went round to the others, and was by them congenially met, especially by Pinkerton, who feeling very proud of what he had himself achieved, indulged in a self-eulogy in shape of a hearty panegyric on the efficiency pretended to have been displayed by the benign Wiggins. Upon scrutinizing further, it was apparent that the harmony of the entertainment was not altogether free from alloy. Mr Simpson, the second violin, somehow or other, in his executive capacity, had had the misfortune to forfeit the confidence of Kanteler; the melancholy fact was evinced by the peculiar flush visible on Simpson's cheek. Unlike the glow of honourable acquittal which garnished the countenances of the others, it clearly evidenced that consuming feeling of heat which a sense of shame produces: he attempted to speak to the leader, but a guilty falter impeded every effort; whilst, on the other hand, the offended chief kept him inexorably at bay. An interval then followed, during which some low-toned intercommunications passed among the amateurs, and some casual interchanges of opinion among the rest of the party. The flute went and sat by his sister, an unmarried-looking lady, whose first impression on an ordinary mind would be 'twere best to have nothing to do with her, but who, nevertheless, improved on acquaintance; for I found in her conversation more than I had given her credit for, both of amiability and intelligence. I was altogether the better for my colloquy with her, as it certainly relieved in me a sort of painful feeling of incapacity to appreciate the performances of the evening as they might deserve; a feeling which has, doubtless, often been experienced by others similarly situated to myself.

The next performance was a duet between Pinkerton and Mrs Wiggins. The lady took her seat at the piano, the scion stood at her right, Mrs Simpson (the great soul) at her left, and the shepherd in the background with his solitary pipe. The piece consisted of a splashing introduction, which seemed to illustrate a game of blindman's-buff set to music, the one groping after something and never catching anything, accompanied by a din and clamour from the other, productive of that sort of harmony called 'singing in the ears,' which went far to excuse the ineffectiveness of the struggling Mr P., resulting from such very noisy co-operation. Nevertheless, *some* more significant impression was produced. Mrs Simpson, during 'the slow movement,' as it was called, made a slow movement with her head from ear to ear, and looked like a person in all the ecstasies of weeping without the indecorous intrusion of a tear, forcibly illustrating the sentiment that

> 'To some, the meanest flute that blows
> Gives thoughts that lie almost too deep for tears.'

The scion went fiercely to work with turning over the leaves, and conducted that operation with a singleness of purpose gracefully tempered with an affecting gurgle or two wherever the finer emotions were appealed to. Major Starkie, too, found something in the performance to be excited about, and showers of compliments were lavished upon both artists at the conclusion. Mr Wiggins looked nicer now than ever; his general pleasing expression gaining the accession of a new charm indicating the conjugal pride which he felt at witnessing the success achieved by his wife, and the warm acknowledgment which it secured. Nothing particular occurred until the subsequent performance; the only thing that excited my notice being the frequent furtive glances cast at Kanteler by the disgraced Simpson, who looked so very much as if he couldn't help it, that I really couldn't help looking very much at the cruel oppressor, hoping, by the fixedness of my gaze, and what I flattered myself to be the severity of my frown, to elicit from him something like an indication of remorse for the inhumanity he had exhibited, – but no, the stern heart was impenetrable.

The next invocation was the scion on the violin. This outpouring presented the concentrated essence of the young genius's moral, intellectual, and sentient energies. The mechanical faculties of the brain, the sympathy, such as it was, which essayed to interpret the train of thought or strain of rhapsody, or combination of both, or of neither, such as they might be, – the fervour of youthful ambition – the misgiving intensity of the tyro – were all and each displayed here in the full tide of operation. My friend Gossett and his wife were, of course, charmed; and, so far as the plaudits of the general company could contribute, the scion's success was complete; but a smile from Kanteler would have transcended them all – one kind look, one encouraging glance from the icy autocrat, would have 'outweighed' a 'whole theatre of others.' The youngster was standing in a misty state of involuntary self-gratulation by Major Starkie, who happened to be speaking to Kanteler and said, 'That youngster *can* play.' 'No, he can't,' was the answer, 'and never will. See,' added he, with crushing contempt, 'see how he places his thumb upon the neck.' Unhappily the youth overheard this; the consequence was, he was a piping ninepin for the evening. No more turning over leaves for Kanteler –

> 'No more his soul a charm in fiddling finds,
> Fiddling hath charms alone for peaceful minds.'

To relieve his bursting heart, he imparted this to Simpson, to whom it afforded evident relief. Companionship in sorrow at once elicits and destroys the power of suffering: Simpson's growing vindictiveness towards his persecutor assumed a less selfish character; he forgot his own ignominy in his friend's, and from being the victim of Kanteler he had now risen to be the champion of the scion. The performances proceeded, and instead of producing that enjoyment which is, or should be, the object of such assemblages, it was evident that disappointments, frustrations, indignities, wanton opposition, 'faint praise,' and other acrimonious niceties, too numerous to specify, were here invading the musical *sanctum* to the destruction of that harmony which in a social *réunion* ought always to exist; more especially where the pretensions are really all of one class, as on this occasion; for, as I learned from Miss Pinkerton, in a second interchange of ideas, just before the finale, this Kanteler was, as a violin-player, *very much below mediocrity!* He possessed, it appeared, great flexibility, and could do some of the most 'difficult tricks' on the instrument. He could make a great noise in lieu of extracting a fine tone, finger with rapidity, but not with articulateness, could stop in time but not in tune, and could distinguish between the *adagio* and *allegro* better than between the sublime and the ridiculous, minute not comprehensive, precise without soul or imagination, his interpretation of the effusions of a composer worthy of better celebration might without disparagement be compared to the far-famed poulterer's description of the phœnix, 'It was green and yellow, red and blue. He did not let us off for a single feather.'

By the time we sat down to supper I was fairly beaten. We had been for four mortal hours listening, as I at last gathered, to villainously bad music, compelled to sit still and not speak a word, excepting at lucid intervals; witness the very inharmonious exhibitions of jealousy, temper, and pride, which had so sadly marred what I had anticipated as a scene of rare enjoyment, – and all for what? For the indulgence (so I reasoned), for the indulgence of a mania which is unprofitable enough when confined to the infected few, but when regarded in connexion with the silent sufferings of thousands of unwilling votaries, such as I was at this Wiggins's musical party, may be emphatically pronounced to be a grievance and a pest.

(Sketches)

THE BOOK OF DANIEL

Nebuchadnezzar's compulsory orchestra

Nebuchadnezzar the king made an image of gold, whose height *was* threescore cubits, *and* the breadth thereof six cubits: he set it up in the plain of Dura, in the province of Babylon....

Then an herald cried aloud, To you it is commanded, O people, nations, and languages,

That at what time ye hear the sound of the cornet, flute, harp, sackbut, psaltery, dulcimer, and all kinds of musick, ye fall down and worship the golden image that Nebuchadnezzar the king hath set up:

And whoso falleth not down and worshippeth shall the same hour be cast into the midst of a burning fiery furnace.

Therefore at that time, when all the people heard the sound of the cornet, flute, harp, sackbut, psaltery, and all kinds of musick, all the people, the nations, and the languages, fell down *and* worshipped the golden image that Nebuchadnezzar the king had set up.

Wherefore at that time certain Chaldeans came near, and accused the Jews.

They spake and said to the king Nebuchadnezzar, O king, live for ever.

Thou, O king, hast made a decree, that every man that shall hear the sound of the cornet, flute, harp, sackbut, psaltery, and dulcimer, and all kinds of musick, shall fall down and worship the golden image:

And whoso falleth not down and worshippeth, *that* he should be cast into the midst of a burning fiery furnace.

12 There are certain Jews whom thou hast set over the affairs of the

province of Babylon, Shadrach, Meshach, and Abed-nego; these men, O king, have not regarded thee: they serve not thy gods, nor worship the golden image which thou hast set up.

Then Nebuchadnezzar in *his* rage and fury commanded to bring Shadrach, Meshach, and Abed-nego. Then they brought these men before the king.

Nebuchadnezzar spake and said unto them, *Is it* true, O Shadrach, Meshach, and Abed-nego, do not ye serve my gods, nor worship the golden image which I have set up?

Now if ye be ready that at what time ye hear the sound of the cornet, flute, harp, sackbut, psaltery, and dulcimer, and all kinds of musick, ye fall down and worship the image which I have made; *well*: but if ye worship not, ye shall be cast the same hour into the midst of a burning fiery furnace; and who *is* that God that shall deliver you out of my hands?

Shadrach, Meshach, and Abed-nego, answered and said to the king, O Nebuchadnezzar, we *are* not careful to answer thee in this matter.

If it be *so*, our God whom we serve is able to deliver us from the burning fiery furnace, and he will deliver *us* out of thine hand, O king.

But if not, be it known unto thee, O king, that we will not serve thy gods, nor worship the golden image which thou hast set up.

Then was Nebuchadnezzar full of fury, and the form of his visage was changed against Shadrach, Meshach, and Abed-nego: *therefore* he spake, and commanded that they should heat the furnace one seven times more than it was wont to be heated.

And he commanded the most mighty men that *were* in his army to bind Shadrach, Meshach, and Abed-nego, *and* to cast *them* into the burning fiery furnace.

(*Authorized Version*)

CHARLES DICKENS

The Master's flute

I sat down to my brown loaf, my egg, and my rasher of bacon, with a basin of milk besides, and made a most delicious meal. While I was yet in the full enjoyment of it, the old woman of the house said to the Master:

'Have you got your flute with you?'

'Yes,' he returned.

'Have a blow at it,' said the old woman coaxingly. 'Do!'

The Master, upon this, put his hand underneath the skirts of his coat, and brought out his flute in three pieces, which he screwed together, and began immediately to play. My impression is, after many years of consideration, that there never can have been anybody in the world who played worse. He made the most dismal sounds I have ever heard produced by any means, natural or artificial. I don't know what the tunes were – if there were such things in the performance at all, which I doubt – but the influence of the strain upon me was, first, to make me think of all my sorrows until I could hardly keep my tears back; then to take away my appetite; and lastly, to make me so sleepy that I couldn't keep my eyes open. They begin to close again, and I begin to nod, as the recollection rises fresh upon me. Once more the little room, with its open corner cupboard, and its square-backed chairs, and its angular little staircase leading to the room above, and its three peacock's feathers displayed over the mantelpiece – I remember wondering when I first went in, what that peacock would have thought if he had known what his finery was doomed to come to – fades from before me, and I nod, and sleep. The flute becomes inaudible, the wheels of the coach are heard instead, and I am on my journey. The coach jolts, I wake with a start, and the flute has come back again, and the Master at Salem House is sitting with his legs crossed, playing it dolefully, while the old woman of the house looks on delighted. She fades in her turn, and he fades, and all fades, and there is no flute, no Master, no Salem House, no David Copperfield, no anything but heavy sleep.

I dreamed, I thought, that once while he was blowing into this dismal flute, the old woman of the house, who had gone nearer and nearer to him in her ecstatic admiration, leaned over the back of his chair and gave him an affectionate squeeze round the neck, which stopped his playing for a moment. I was in the middle state between sleeping and waking, either then or immediately afterwards; for, as he resumed – it was a real fact that he had stopped playing – I saw and heard the same old woman ask Mrs Fibbitson if it wasn't delicious (meaning the flute), to which Mrs Fibbitson replied, 'Ay, ay! yes!' and nodded at the fire : to which, I am persuaded, she gave the credit of the whole performance.

When I seemed to have been dozing a long while, the Master at Salem House unscrewed his flute into the three pieces, put them up as before, and took me away.

(*David Copperfield*)

W. S. GILBERT

The 'Bandoline' Player

A troubadour, young, brave, and tall,
    One morning might be seen,
A singing under COLTER's hall
    Upon the village green.

He went through all the usual forms,
    And rolled his eyes of blue,
As dying ducks in thunderstorms
    Are often said to do.

For COLTER had a daughter, she
    Was barely twenty-two.
Why sang that minstrel party? He
    Adored her – so would you.

He played upon a what's-its-name –
    You know the thing I mean –
The *Pall Mall* critics call the same
    A 'dainty bandoline.'

And COLTER's daughter, wrapt in joy
    (A sweet, romantic maid),
She smiled upon that guileless boy
    As gracefully he played.

'Oh, person in the crimson legs,'
    She modestly exclaimed,
'A bashful maiden coyly begs
    You'll tell her how you're named.

'For, oh, you feed a tender flame
    In playing on the green,
And, oh, she loves what critics name
    The dainty bandoline!'

That troubadour he tore his hair
    And sent a sigh above,
To think his bandoline should share
    That maiden's wealth of love.

He hied him to his village shed,
    Wept village tears in quarts,
Then laid him on his village bed,
    And thought these village thoughts:

'I must be worshipped all in all –
    For what I've always been –
And not for what the critics call
    My dainty bandoline.

'To which of us her loving may
    Be due, I'll thus detect –
Upon the fiddle I can play
    With singular effect.

'To-morrow, with its graceful aid,
    Her moments I'll beguile,
That maiden I will serenade
    In JOACHIM's finest style.'

And so he did, that gallant boy,
    But never came the maid;
He, hoping she was only coy,
    Still sang to her and played.

BEETHOVEN, GLUCK, PICCINNI, SPOHR –
    He gave her for a while;
And other masters, even more,
    'Dot-touch-and-go' in style.

For hours that patient boy he played
    At FATHER COLTER's farm –
Behind his noble shoulder-blade,
    And underneath his arm –

Below his leg – behind his back –
    He played till he was red –
Between his knees, with dainty knack,
    And then above his head.

With musico-gymnastic tricks
    He warbled forth her name;
From half-past nine till half-past six,
    But, ah! no maiden came.

(For MARY had been sent away
    To Weston-super-Mare –
A fact of which that minstrel gay
    Was wholly unaware.)

But FATHER COLTER rose at nine,
    His wrath it also rised,
For fiddle, voice, and bandoline
    He equally despised.

'I have,' said he, 'some bellows *here* –
    A fine young noddle *there* –
It would but be politeness mere
    To introduce the pair!'

No sooner was it said than done,
    And as above I've shown,
Upon the sconce he fetched him one –
    One for himself alone!

'Ah, MARY,' said the simple lad,
    'I know thy gentle touch.
Upon my word this is too bad,
    I feel it very much.

'That you don't care for me at all
    Is easy to be seen –
You love what *Pall Mall* critics call
    My dainty bandoline!'

(But MARY had been sent away
    To Weston-super-Mare –
A fact of which that minstrel gay
    Was wholly unaware.)

GEORGE AND WEEDON GROSSMITH

Mrs Pooter out of voice

Mrs Cummings sang five or six songs, 'No, Sir' and 'The Garden of Sleep', being best in my humble judgment; but what pleased me most was the duet she sang with Carrie – classical duet, too. I think it is called, 'I would that my love!' It was beautiful. If Carrie had been in better voice, I don't think professionals could have sung it better.

(*The Diary of a Nobody*)

LADY MARY WORTLEY MONTAGU

The gentry invading the opera

Dear Child, – I am now in a place the most beautifully romantic I ever saw in my life: it is the Tunbridge of this part of the world, to which I was sent by the doctor's order, my ague often returning, notwithstanding the loads of bark I have taken. To say truth, I have no reason to repent my journey, though I was very unwilling to undertake it, it being forty miles, half by land and half by water; the land so stony I was almost shook to pieces, and I had the ill luck to be surprised with a storm on the lake, that if I had not been near a little port (where I passed a night in a very poor inn), the vessel must have been lost. A fair wind brought me hither next morning early. I found a very good lodging, a great deal of good company, and a village in many respects resembling Tunbridge Wells, not only in the quality of the waters, which is the same, but in the manner of the buildings, most of the houses being separate at little distances, and all built on the sides of hills, which indeed are far different from those of Tunbridge, being six times as high: they are really vast rocks of different figures, covered with green moss, or short grass, diversified by tufts of trees, little woods, and here and there vineyards, but no other cultivation, except gardens like those on Richmond-hill. The whole lake, which is twenty-five miles long, and three broad, is all surrounded with these impassable mountains, the sides of which, towards the bottom, are so thick set with villages (and in most of them gentlemen's seats), that I do not believe there is anywhere above a mile distance one from another, which adds very much to the beauty of the prospect.

We have an opera here which is performed three times in the week. I was at it last night, and should have been surprised at the neatness of the scenes, goodness of the voices and justness of the actors, if I had not remembered I was in Italy. Several gentlemen jumped into the orchestra, and joined in the concert, which I suppose is one of the freedoms of the place, for I never saw it in any great town. I was yet more amazed (while the actors were dressing for the farce that concluded the entertainment) to see one of the principal among them, and as errant a *petit maître* as if he had passed all his life at Paris, mount the stage, and present us with a cantata of his own performing. He had the pleasure of being almost deafened with applause. The ball began afterwards, but I was not witness of it, having accustomed myself to such early hours, that I was half asleep before the opera finished: it begins at ten o'clock, so that it was one before I could get to bed, though I had supped before I went, which is the custom.

I am much better pleased with the diversions on the water, where all the town assembles every night, and never without music; but we have none so rough as trumpets, kettle-drums, and French horns: they are all violins, lutes, mandolins, and flutes doux. Here is hardly a man that does not excel in some of these instruments, which he privately addresses to the lady of his affections, and the public has the advantage of it by his adding to the number of the musicians.

The fountain where we drink the waters rises between two hanging hills, and is overshadowed with large trees, that give a freshness in the hottest time of the day. The provisions are all excellent, the fish of the lake being as large and well tasted as that of Geneva, and the mountains abounding in game, particularly blackcocks, which I never saw in any other part of Italy: but none of the amusements here would be so effectual to raising my spirits as a letter from you.

(*Letter to the Countess of Bute, Lovere, 24 July 1747*)

ROGER NORTH

Organ vs. bowls at midnight

Roger North, the historian of music

The doctor [my elder brother] had no favourite diversion, or manual exercise, to rest his mind a little, which he held bent with continual thinking. His parents, who were much addicted to music, recommended that to him for a diversion, and particularly the noble organ, as the fullest, and not only a complete solitary concert, but most proper for an ecclesiastic. And indeed, if study had not had the upper hand of all his intendments, he must of course have taken up in that way, his parents themselves being so fond of it. For after the care of prayers and meals, nothing was more constant and solemn than music was in that family. He was sensible the advice was very good, and accordingly got a small organ into his chamber at Jesus College, and suffered himself to be taught a lesson or two, which he practised over when he had a mind to be unbent; but he made no manner of advance, and one accident put him out of all manner of conceit of it. His under neighbour was a morose and importune master of arts; and one night the doctor could not sleep; and thought to fit himself for it by playing upon his organ. The bellows knocking on the floor, and the hum of the pipes, made a strange din at midnight, and the gentleman below, that never heard it so before, could not tell what to make of it; but, at length, he found it out to be his neighbour's organ. And thereupon, to retaliate this night's work, got out of his bed, and, with his two couple of bowls, went to bowls by himself. This made a much louder noise than the organ, and the doctor was as much at a loss to know what that meant, but, suspecting how the case stood, he left off, and scarce ever touched his organ after. The pleasure of music is like that of books, never true and good, unless easily and familiarly read, and performed; and then nothing is more medicinal to a crazy and fatigued mind than that.

(*The Lives of the ... North[s]*)

GEORGE BERNARD SHAW

In the past century there have been many great composers, and thousands of fine performers. But great music critics in English occur once or twice in a generation. This remark can be guaranteed to enrage, so rather than attempting to defend my contemporaries in music criticism – daily or periodical; caustic or indulgent; learned or trivial – it may be wiser to state the qualifications: an exacting ear, an analytical mind, curiosity about five centuries of music, a retentive memory for five decades of live music (recording is not enough), and above all, lucid, witty prose that can charm phrases out of the rafters and keep the reader's toast burning. Critics of theatre, television, opera and food have it easy by comparison: music criticism is direct translation from the wordless to the word.

My pleasure in this craft is catholic, I hope, from Dr Burney to Neville Cardus or from Samuel Pepys to my *Guardian* colleague who is known in the music trade as 'the Lancashire Ripper'. But for Desert Island purposes my critic has to be Shaw. As Robert Anderson puts it in *The New Grove*: 'Shaw's collected writings on music stand alone in their mastery of English and compulsive readability. He made many foes, if only on the ground that to him poor performance was a personal insult to be treated accordingly; but an exact knowledge of the law of libel earned for his pen a subjective licence without parallel in music criticism.'

Note the word 'subjective'. No critic is worth heeding unless he prints the odd thumping misjudgement, as Shaw did with Brahms, notably with his scathing account of the German Requiem. But anyone who knows London amateur orchestras in the 1990s, as player or listener, can hardly withhold a smile of recognition. Little has changed from a century ago when 'Corno di Bassetto', the self-taught Dubliner, took the train down to Richmond and observed the reticent technique used by elegant ladies in the second fiddle section when asked to play tremolando...

George Bernard Shaw

A ladylike tremolando in Richmond

In the eye of an inconsiderate public, concerts given by amateur orchestral societies hardly seem worth the serious attention of a critic who is busy watching the symptoms of the Philharmonic, the Crystal Palace, the London Symphony, the Richter, and the Hallé orchestras. Yet to me the amateur orchestra is all-important; for out of every ten people who support music in England, at least nine and three-quarters must have acquired their knowledge of it as amateurs and from amateurs. The musician of professional antecedents is an incorrigible deadhead: whether he performs or listens, music has to support him, instead of being supported by him.

It is clear that a man cannot cultivate a taste for orchestral music by listening once a week to a church service accompanied by the combination of pan-pipes and accordion which has replaced the old-fashioned village church band, or even by occasionally patronizing a travelling dramatic company in the town-hall, and studying the efforts of a pianist, backed by three fiddles and a cornet, to give a satisfactory account of the overture to William Tell, Mascagni's intermezzo, and a twenty-year-old waltz by Waldteufel. The moment you step outside the circle of London, Birmingham, Manchester, Bristol, Glasgow, and towns of their calibre, you have to choose between amateur music and no music at all; whilst even in these big towns music is really kept alive by professional musicians who as teachers discover amateur talent, and as conductors and concert-givers organize it for the performance of the masterpieces of modern music.

The professional orchestral conductor who is a conductor and nothing else, and who conducts professional singers and players exclusively, only exists in great capitals. It takes London and Vienna combined to keep Richter in this position, and Glasgow and the Crystal Palace combined to keep Manns in it; and both these eminent conductors have to depend on amateurs for the performance of choral works. Had Destiny buried them in a small provincial town, they would, whilst they remained there, have had to put up with an amateur band, and amateur principal singers into the bargain. And there are suburbs of London which are in darkness more deplorable than any country town.

Under these circumstances, it seems to me that the critic who considers an amateur orchestra beneath his notice stamps himself as a hopeless

Cockney – that is, a man who does not know the country because he has never lived there, and does not know London because he has never lived anywhere else. Last week Mr James Brown, the conductor of the Richmond Orchestral Society, had the gumption to surmise that a stroll out to Richmond Hill to hear what his Society can do might seem to me at least as tempting a way of spending an evening as a visit to Steinway or Prince's Hall to hear the annual concert of Miss Smith or Miss Brown, aided by more or less distinguished artists singing exactly what they have sung on similar occasions for a whole generation of miscellaneous concerts. I accepted his invitation, and arrived at sundown on the terrace, where I mused over the site of that Wagner Theatre which yet remains unbuilt, until it was time to go into the 'Star and Garter' and get to business.

The program was of the usual amateur kind: that is to say, it would have taxed the finest qualities of the best band in the world. Mozart's G Minor symphony, the Lohengrin prelude, Mendelssohn's Athalie overture and his violin concerto: only such works as these can inspire the mighty craving and dogged perseverance which carry a man through that forlorn hope, the making of an orchestra out of nothing. When you start you are received with enthusiasm by men who can play the posthorn, the banjo, the concertina, and every other instrument not used in the orchestra. You enlist trombone-players only to find that though they can 'vamp' they cannot read, and propose to assist you by improvising a bass continuously to whatever may be going on. You can choose the two least execrable out of twenty cornet-players at the cost of making eighteen bitter enemies in the neighborhood; but you are lucky if you find one horn-player, although you require four. Flutes, too, are comparatively plentiful; whilst clarionets are scarce, oboes all but unknown, and bassoons quite out of the question (though there is a lady-bassoonist at Richmond).

In the string department the same difficulty arises. Young ladies who can play much better than the average professional 'leader' of twenty years ago are discoverable with a little research in sufficient abundance nowadays (chiefly because Madame Neruda proved at that time that the violin shews off a good figure); and the violoncello, for some less obvious reason, fascinates tiny women sufficiently to keep itself fairly alive in amateur circles. But nobody will touch the double bass; and the viola comes to grief almost as signally as it used to do in the professional band in the old days, when only worn-out violinists scraped the tenor, and when such viola parts as those in Tristan or Harold, and such players as Hollander condescending to the instrument, were unknown.

When trying to get an orchestra together the conductor stops at nothing, except at houses whence come sounds of practising on an orchestral instrument. I have known a man, on catching this doleful noise at midnight on his way home from rehearsal, listen at the area-railings, take a note of the address, and call next day to kidnap the practiser by reckless flatteries. I have known valuable appointments, involving the transfer of learned professors from the Metropolis to provincial towns, decided by the frantic efforts of a local conductor to secure the election of a candidate who was said to be a proficient player on one of the scarcer instruments. But it is when the orchestra is actually formed and set to work that its creator tastes the full bitterness of his position.

The unredeemed villainy of the amateur nature is not easy to describe adequately. Its outrageous frivolity, to which no engagement is sacred, and its incredible vanity, to which art is nothing and the lower self everything, baffle my powers of description, and make me for once regret that I do not wield one of those bitter, biting pens which were made to lash offenders on whom mercy is thrown away – for instance, those two amateur extremes, the man who never attends a rehearsal but always turns up at the concert, and the man who attends all the rehearsals and blenches from the concert. Even your leader will miss a rehearsal to go to a dance, or will coolly tell you on the morning of the concert that he cannot play because his father is dead, or some such frivolous excuse. Then there is the incompetent wind-player who has a bit of solo which he cannot execute, and who, at the last moment, must have his part doubled by a professional to save public disgrace and break-down.

On such occasions the professional, regarding all amateurs as blacklegs, is offensive; objects to having his part doubled; says, 'Look here! Who's going to play this – me or you?' etc., etc. The amateur sulks, broods over his injuries, leaves the orchestra, and probably tries to establish a rival society for the performance of wind-instrument chamber-music. The difficulties are endless, and the artistic results agonizing, since the progress made by the people who stick to the rehearsals is always spoiled at the last moment by the backwardness of those who don't.

I will not pretend that the concert at Richmond did not bear the marks of these hard conditions. It began short-handed, especially in the horn department. At the end of the overture a gentleman in irreproachable evening-dress, smiling, and carrying a black bag presenting the general outline of a French-horn, appeared and climbed up on the platform with a sort of 'Here I am, you see, safe and sound – never say die' air about him. As he mounted there was a crash of breaking wood, from which I gathered that he had succeeded in completing the sensation by shattering the platform. The conductor received him with grim patience, concealing all signs of the murderous thoughts that must have raged within him. Just imagine Mr Borsdorf, for instance, playing that trick on Richter! I wonder did it occur to the gentleman that money had been obtained from the public, with his consent, on the strength of his being in his place to play one of the horn parts in the overture. If it is too much to expect an ordinary English gentleman to be artistically conscientious, surely we may at least call on him to be commercially honest. However, justice forbids me to urge too harshly the offence of the man who came in after the overture, since I must perforce say nothing of the worse offenders who did not come at all. Almost immediately after the beginning of the Lohengrin prelude the band divided itself into two resolute factions, one maintaining that the bar in hand was the sixth bar, and the other equally convinced that it was the seventh. So they agreed to differ; and I listened with a drunken sensation of hearing the prelude double until the wind instruments rushed into the fray, and, mostly taking the side which the conductor had supported from the first, made the opposition waver and finally come over one by one, the fortissimo being played with almost entire unanimity. In the accompaniment to O star of eve! (Tannhäuser) the tremolando to the words Da scheinest du, etc., was ruined by the shirking of some lady-violinists, who, with faces expressive of the most shameful irresolution, and fear of being heard, rested their bows helplessly on the strings and sat quivering – an exceedingly amateur way of tremolandoing. But in spite of these and similar mishaps, I felt throughout that the thing was well worth doing. . . .

(*Music in London 1890–4*)

CECIL TORR

The waits are the worst

For many years I wasted time in trying to play the piano, until at last I saw that I should never play effectively, and then I gave it up. Curiously, my grandfather went through this process with the flute, though I never knew it till I found a letter of his just now: – 2 April 1843, 'I once had a great wish to learn the flute, and attended to it, and learnt all that was necessary, but could not make any advancement for want of an ear for it. I could play a tune by notes, but not give it that pleasing air that others could, for want of an ear. Therefore I considered it was time badly spent, and dropt it.' I think the fault was with the fingers more than with the ear. Had the ear been altogether bad, our bad playing might have pleased us . . .

He writes on 26 December 1847, 'The church singers by their inveteracy have rather disturbed the neighbourhood both Friday night and last night. [They used to bring the church bass-viol and violin and flute.] I order them not to come near, but unfortunately I am surrounded by a road, and they will pass near me: which my dogs notice.'

A friend of my father's writes to him from Moreton, 13 November 1843, 'We are going to have a ringing match here tomorrow. There has been nothing else but this noise the last three or four days.' Blunt's Use and Abuse of the Church Bells, 1846, gives a pretty picture of it all. 'Towards the latter half of the last century the ringing of the church bells became a fashionable amusement among the yeomanry and gentry, and was degraded to the level on which the hurdle-race and steeple-chase now stand. This amusement, however, at any rate in most parts of the country, has long ago "become vulgar"; and "gone out of fashion"; till at last our belfries are left in a state of filthy dilapidation, receptacles for dirt and rubbish of all kinds, and every frequently the drinking-place of the most profane and profligate persons of the parish, who ring the bells for their amusement.'

(*Small Talk at Wreyland*)

" *First of all we'll list the people who'll pay us to go away.*"

LADY LAURA TROUBRIDGE

Wait until you're asked twice

The amateur musician, unless asked to do so, does not bring his music or his instrument or offer to perform at a party. If asked to give a performance, he leaves music or instrument in the cloakroom or hall, whence he fetches it, or the hostess sends for it when the time comes. Such a guest should be careful not to continue to play or sing after one performance unless asked to continue. When asked to play or sing, he should do so without any fuss, showing neither conceit nor undue humility.

(*The Book of Etiquette*)

REBECCA WEST

An eventide home for bad musicians?

Cordelia had no idea that she was not musical. When Mamma had stopped giving her piano lessons, a little girl in the house next door was having violin lessons, and she had insisted on learning too, and had ever since then shown an extreme and mistaken industry. She had a true ear, indeed she had absolute pitch, which neither Mamma nor Mary nor I had, which was a terrible waste, and she had supple fingers, she could bend them right back to the wrist, and she could read anything at sight. But Mamma's face crumpled, first with rage, and then, just in time, with pity, every time she heard Cordelia laying the bow over the strings. Her tone was horribly greasy, and her phrasing always sounded like a stupid grown-up explaining something to a child. Also she did not know good music from bad, as we did, as we had always done.

It was not Cordelia's fault that she was unmusical. Mamma had often explained that to us. Children were like their father's family or their mother's, and Cordelia had taken her inheritance from Papa. That gave her some advantages, it did indeed. Mary had black hair and I had brown, and so had many other little girls. But though Papa was so dark there was red hair in his family, and Cordelia's head was covered with short red-gold curls, which shone in the light and made people turn round in the street. There was something more to that than mere heredity, too, which made it harder to bear. It was at Papa's insistence that Mamma kept Cordelia's hair short at a time when that was a long-forgotten fashion, not to be renewed for years. At his home in Ireland there had been a portrait of his Aunt Lucy, who went to Paris just after the Napoleonic wars and had herself painted by

Baron Gérard in a chiton and a leopard-skin, with her hair dressed in the fashion known as *à la Bacchante*, and as Cordelia was very like her he got Mamma to get her curls cut in as nearly the same style as puzzled hairdressers in South Africa and Edinburgh could manage.

Mary and I were not pleased about this. It made us feel that Cordelia was not only closer to Papa than we were, owing to an unfair decision of Nature, but that she was also an object on which he had worked to bring her up to the standards of his taste. He had not done that to us. Nor were we worked on by anybody else. With all this piano-playing, Mary and I had no time, and Mamma had no time either, to subject us to any process which would turn us into finished articles, we were raw material. It really was cruel that we had to play the piano as well as do so much, that Mamma had to go shopping and help with the housework and deal with Papa's worries so that she was never composed and dressed like other Mammas, that we had to go to school and always struck our teachers as careless and hurried. Yet it was piano-playing that set our accounts right. For though there was red hair in Papa's family, there was not a shred of musical talent, and we would rather be musical with Mamma than have red-gold curls and make utter fools of ourselves by playing the violin as Cordelia did. We were sorry for Cordelia, particularly now, when Papa, from whom she derived such interest as she possessed, had gone away for six weeks. But all the same she was an ass to think she could play the violin, it was as if Mary and I thought we had red-gold curls. . . .

Mary came out of the stable and looked across the yard and . . . joined us. She said, 'Mamma, do not wait for the post, it is Tuesday, nothing nice ever happens on a Tuesday,' and then stopped. Cordelia had begun to practise in her bedroom. We all three listened in silence while she played some scales. Then she broke off and repeated some bars of a melody. 'It isn't even like cats,' said Mary. 'Cats don't scoop.'

'Oh, children, children,' said Mamma. 'You should not be so impatient with your poor sister. It might have been far worse, she might have been born deaf or blind.'

'That would not have been worse even for her,' said Mary; 'she never would have known what was wrong with her, any more than she does now, and she would have gone to one of those big places with gardens for the deaf and blind one sees out of trains, and she would have been looked after by people who like being kind to the deaf and the blind. But there are no homes for bad violinists.'

'Homes for bad musicians, what a terrible idea,' said Mamma. 'The home for bad contraltos would be the worst. People would be afraid to go near it at night, the sounds coming from it would be so terrible, particularly when the moon was full. And you children are unnecessarily unkind about your sister, really if I did not know you I would think you were spiteful. And really she is not so bad. She is not bad at all, this afternoon. She is much better than she used to be. Heavens, how horrible that was! This is intolerable, I must go and try to help her, the poor child.'

She rushed up the garden path towards the farmhouse, wringing her hands. A stranger would have supposed that so distraught a mother had just realised that her baby had been left alone in a room with an unguarded fire or a dangerous dog. Mary and I sat down on the dyke...

'Listen, it is too silly,' said Mary coldly. There was sometimes nothing to listen to; Mamma could not play the violin, so she had to talk or sing her precepts. Between these patches of silence came Cordelia's repetitions of her melody, always without improvement, but each time offering instead a new variation of error. 'How can you laugh?' asked Mary through her teeth.

'Of course I'm laughing,' I said. 'It's funny when someone keeps on falling down on the ice, and this doesn't even hurt Cordelia.'...

'Yes, Mamma,' said Cordelia. 'Miss Beevor has been teaching me a piece to play to you. We have been working so hard to get it right so that even you would like it.'

'You see, I have been giving Cordelia quite a lot of lessons,' said Miss Beevor. 'Usually,' the poor woman added, stroking Cordelia's hair, so that the force of her rebuke should be directed solely on my mother and not be thought to extend to her favourite, 'an extra. But I am proud to make my lessons a gift to your daughter.'

My mother was silent for a second. She had drooped beneath the same lassitude she sometimes showed when she had to deal with a dunning tradesman, or a nail in the sole of one of our shoes. She got the tradesman to go away, the nail was hammered down or prised out, but one felt that however much she rested after this ordeal she would never get back to what she had been before. 'How wonderfully kind,' she said. 'You must forgive me for not recognising you, Christmas is such a rush for me that I lose my wits. So you have been teaching Cordelia and have taught her a solo?' She stooped and kissed Cordelia very tenderly. 'Now let us go to the sitting-room and hear it,' she said, and held the door open for Miss Beevor, turning her head to give me the penetrating look which we knew was her signal that she at once expected us to behave well and recognised that it would be difficult for us to do so....

...Mamma waved Miss Beevor to the piano, and sat down in a chair which she had moved so that her face would be hidden from the two performers. Then Miss Beevor ran her hands over the keys in a profusion of what Mary and I scornfully called collywobbles, and Cordelia stepped out into the space beside the piano, her eye running unhappily round the room. She was wishing that our dolls' house had been put away and hoping that Miss Beevor would not think her a baby for having one. I sank down on the floor, and Cordelia frowned at me and jerked her bow at me, to show that she wanted me to get up and sit in a chair, but I took no notice. She would have liked us to be tidied away as well as the toys.

After Cordelia turned to the piano and got the note, she set her chin down and raised her bow, but, smiling as if at some intimate and ridiculous memory, lowered it again. Turning back to Miss Beevor, she said, with the simper she always assumed when talking to a teacher, 'They all know this quite well, even the children, there was a poor old man who used to play it in the street in Edinburgh.'

My mother leaned forward in her chair and said, 'You do not mean the old man who always played outside our flat on Friday nights?'

'Yes, Mamma,' smiled Cordelia.

My mother turned her face away. The old man had been a violinist of great talent, who had once been second violin in the Scottish Orchestra, who had, as she delicately put it, 'come to grief' and lost his position, and come down to the gutter. When he played under our windows Mamma would lean out into the darkness, nodding in sad joy as she sniffed up the music, muttering, 'Poor wretch, his phrasing is as pure as ever,' and calling to our servant to take him out coffee and a sandwich. Cordelia began to play the composition he had never omitted from his serenade, Bach's 'Air on the G string.' That meant that she had heard it played exquisitely, time after time; she made it a juicy whine. My mother twisted round in her chair and glared at Mary and me, threatening us with her full rage if we, then or afterwards, mocked our sister's musical idiocy, which was now plainer than ever before, for Miss Beevor had made her playing at once much better and much worse, by giving her resolute fingers greater power to express her misunderstanding of sound. We glared back, trying to convey to her how much we thought she was to blame for having been so weak with Cordelia for not having forbidden her long ago to touch the violin. Then suddenly we were afraid, for she began to laugh. We watched in terror while she and her laughter contended like two desperate people wrestling on the edge of an abyss, for Cordelia and Miss Beevor really did not deserve that, nobody deserved that. She won just in time to be able to turn slowly as the last note sounded and say in an unhurried voice, 'Cordelia, what a lovely Christmas present,' and meet Miss Beevor's triumphant smile, while Cordelia clattered up to her for a kiss.

'And that,' began Miss Beevor, only to break off to wipe her eyes. 'And that,' she went on choking, 'isn't all. She's learned a lovely new piece called "Meditation" from an opera called *Thais*, by a French composer called Massenet. She learned it so easily. Oh, it's so wonderful to teach her. She is the pupil I have waited for all my life.'

(*The Fountain Overflows*)

298

NOTES ON CONTRIBUTORS

Aiken, Conrad (1889–1973) *Collected Poems* (Oxford University Press, New York, 2nd edn, 1970).

Amis, Kingsley (1922–) *Collected Poems* 1944–79 (Hutchinson, 1979); *Lucky Jim* (Gollancz, 1954). See editorial commentary.

Anon. 'An elegy on Anacreon' (6th century BC), in *Palatine Anthology*.

Anon. ('K.M.S.') 'Amateur rehearsal: Der fussy Clarinetist'. *Die Allerschonste Lengevitch* (Crown Publishers Inc., New York, n.d.).

Austen, Jane (1775–1817) *Mansfield Park* (1814); *Letters*, ed. R.W. Chapman (Oxford University Press, 1932). See editorial commentary.

Bowen, Catherine Drinker (fl. early 20th century) *Friends and Fiddlers* (Little, Brown, 1935; J.M. Dent, 1936). Unable to trace the author's family in New England, I hope that the warmth of her book may stir old memories.

Brazil, Angela (1868–1947) *The New Girl at St Chad's* (1911). See Arthur Marshall's appreciation in the *Dictionary of National Biography* and Gillian Freeman's biography *The Schoolgirl Ethic* (Allen Lane, 1976).

Buñuel, Luis (1900–83) Film-maker. His sister Conchita Portoles is quoted in Freddy Buache *The Cinema of Luis Buñuel*, trans. Peter Graham (Tantivy Press, 1975).

Burdett, Osbert (1885–1936) *Art of Pleasure* (Eyre & Spottiswoode, 1933). Essayist, biographer and cheese fancier.

Burney, Dr Charles (1726–1814) Musicologist, historian and diarist. His travels in France, Germany, Italy and the Low Countries were edited posthumously from his manuscripts, notably by Percy Scholes (Oxford University Press, 1959) and H. Edmund Poole (*Music, Men, and Manners*, Folio Society, 1969).

Burney, Fanny (Mme d'Arblay) (1752–1840) *Diary and Letters* (1778–1840). The daughter of Dr Burney (*q.v.*) and the author of *Evelina* (1778), she spent her early youth in the circle which included Dr Johnson, Garrick and Burke.

Byrd, William (1543–1623) 'To perswade every one to learne to sing', in *Psalmes, Sonets & Songs of Sadnes and Pietie* (1588).

Cardus, Sir Neville (1889–1975) *Second Innings* (Collins, 1950). Music and cricket critic for the (*Manchester*) *Guardian* from 1919/20.

Cary, Tristram (1925–) Composer. From *Adam* international review (1988), an issue devoted to his father, the novelist Joyce Cary.

Casanova, Jacques (1725–98) *History of My Life* [1725–48], transl. and ed. Willard R. Trask (Longman, 1987). See editorial commentary.

Chaucer, Geoffrey (*c.* 1345–1400) From *The Romaunt of the Rose* (*c.* 1370) and from *The Hous of Fame* (*c.* 1380).

Chesterfield, Lord (Philip Dormer Stanhope) (1694–1773) *Letters to his Son*, ed. Bonamy Dobree (1932).

Chopin, Fryderyk (1809–49) *Selected Correspondence*, transl. and ed. Arthur Hedley (Heinemann, 1962). In 1848, mortally ill, Chopin consented to visit Edinburgh, where his devoted pupil Jane Stirling supported him financially, and London. What with the philistines and the fogs, he could not wait to return to Paris.

Chopin, Kate (1850–1904) *The Awakening* (1899). See editorial commentary.

Clare, John (1793–1864) From 'Summer images' in *Poems* (Oxford University Press, 1935).

Coates, Eric (1886–1957) *Suite in Movements* (Heinemann, 1953). Violist and composer ('The Dam Busters March', etc.).

Cosman, Milein. Artist. Two informal drawings, done at the Haydn Quartet Marathon in 1987 to raise funds for Music Aid, of the Panic Quartet and of the editor. Her late husband, Hans Keller, is the author of *The Great Haydn Quartets* (Dent, 1986).

'Curio' (anon., but probably Richard Holmes). 'The Wiggins's musical party', in *Sketches* (1855).

Daniel, The Book of. *Authorized Version of the Bible* (1611). For another view, see also Britten, *The Burning Fiery Furnace* (church parable, 1966).

Davies, D.R. (1889–1958) *In Search of Myself* (Bles, 1961). Born in Pontycymmer, Glamorgan, Davies was successively miner, tramp, Congregational minister, Socialist preacher for the miners' cause, 'New Britain' campaigner, Socialist Leaguer and at last, Anglican priest.

Dickens, Charles (1812–70) *David Copperfield* (1849–50). Dicken's own instrument was the accordion.

Dolmetsch, Mabel (1874–1963) *Personal Recollections of Arnold Dolmetsch* (Routledge & Kegan Paul, 1957). In the extract, 'Elodie' was Dolmetsch's second wife. Mabel became his third.

Driver, Christopher (1932–) Extracts reprinted from *The Guardian* and *The Listener*. For this anthology the writer is grateful for numerous suggestions and advice from William Amos, Hugo Cole, Julia Reynell, Fritz Spiegl and more friends and acquaintances too numerous to list; also for the entire project germinated with Anna Hodson of J.M. Dent at a viola desk during a rehearsal break.

Elgar, Sir Edward (1857–1934) and Dr Charles Buck (1852–1932) *Letters of a Lifetime*, ed. J.N. Moore (Clarendon Press, 1990).

Eliot, George (1819–80) *Daniel Deronda* (1874–6); *Middlemarch* (1871–2). See also Evans, Marian and Lewes, G.H. (1817–78), *Correspondence*, ed. Gordon S. Haight (7 vols, Oxford University Press, 1954–6; 2 vols, Yale University Press, 1978); and editorial commentary.

Evans, George Ewart (1909–88) *The Strength of the Hills* (Faber, 1983). Author of *Ask the Fellows who Cut the Hay* and other books.

Evelyn, John (1620–1706) *Kalendarium* (Diary), ed. E.S. de Beer (Clarendon Press, 1950).

Flaubert, Gustave (1821–80) *Madame Bovary* (1857), transl. Francis Steegmuller.

Forster, E.M. (1879–1970) *A Room with a View* (William Blackwood, 1908).

Fothergill, Jessie (1841–81) *The First Violin* (1877). The novel, set in the Rhineland and long-forgotten, corresponds closely with some of the musical and emotional preoccupations in George Eliot's two heroines in *Daniel Deronda* (*q.v.*), which had been serialized (1874–6).

Fuller, John (1937–) 'Trio', in *Waiting for the Music* (Salamander Press, 1982).

Gainsborough, Thomas (1727–88) From *Letters*, ed. M. Woodall (Cupid Press, 1963). See also 'The Music Party' (illustration). William Jackson, his fellow-painter and correspondent, once remarked: 'Gainsborough's profession was painting, and music was his amusement, yet there were times when music seemed to be his employment and painting his diversion.' His own circle included C.F. Abel, the cellist, and J.C. Fischer, the oboist who was briefly married to his daughter Mary. Both Gainsborough and Romney played the violin and were enraptured by the playing of Giardini. On other instruments Gainsborough was less successful, by the account of J.C. Bach, 'the London Bach', who found him playing the bassoon and shouted, 'Pote it away, man; pote it away; do you want to burst yourself, like the frog in the fable?'

Gilbert, Sir William Schwenck (1836–1911) 'The Bandolier', in *Bab Ballads* (1869).

Grossmith, George and Weedon (1817–1912 and 1852–1919) *The Diary of a Nobody* (1892).

Hardy, Thomas (1840–1928) 'Absent-mindedness in a parish choir', in *Life's Little Ironies* (1894); 'At the railway station, Upway; 'A musical incident'; 'In the nuptial chamber', in *Collected Poems* (Macmillan, 1930). See editorial commentary.

Heath-Stubbs, John (1918–) 'The watchman's flute', *Selected Poems* (Carcanet, 1990).

Herbert, Dorothy (1770–1829) *Retrospections of Dorothy Herbert*, ed. 'G.F.M.' (Gerald Howe, 1929).

Hoffnung, Annetta, *Gerard Hoffnung* (Gordon Fraser, 1988). She is the widow of the illustrator Gerard Hoffnung (1925–59).

Hopkins, Gerard Manley (1844–89) 'Fallen rain' (composition). Humphrey House and Graham Storey, eds. *Journals and Papers* (Oxford University Press, 1959). See editorial commentary and instrumental accompaniment.

Huxley, Aldous (1894–1963) *Beyond the Mexique Bay* (Chatto, 1934).

Jennings, Paul (1918–89) From *Classical Music* magazine.

Jewel, John, Bishop of Salisbury (1522–71).

Joyce, James (1882–1941) 'Dead', in *Dubliners* (Jonathan Cape, 1914). See editorial commentary.

Lascelles, David (1944–) Staff banking correspondent, reprinted from *The Financial Times* (2 August 1986).

Lawrence, David Herbert (1885–1930) 'The piano', in *Collected Poems* (Martin Secker, 1928).

Leech, John (1817–64) Illustration 'Mr Honeyman at home', in W.M. Thackeray, *The Newcomes, q.v.*

Lee, Laurie (1914–) *Cider with Rosie* (Hogarth, 1959).

Livings, Henry (1929–) *That the Medals and the Baton be Put on View: the story of a village band 1875–1975* (David & Charles, 1975). Playwright. Lists in *Who's Who* 'Clubs: Dobcross Band, Delph Band'.

Lurie, Alison (1926–) *Love and Friendship* (Heinemann, 1962). Her first novel, written while she was on the English staff at Cornell.

Mackenzie, Compton (1883–1972) *Extraordinary Women* (Martin Secker, 1928). See editorial commentary.

Melly, George (1926–) *Owning Up* (Weidenfeld & Nicolson, 1965).

Mendelssohn, Felix (1809–47) Letter to his mother, transl. in Sidney Lee, *Queen Victoria* (1902).

Middleton, Stanley (1919–) *Ends and Means* (Hutchinson, 1977).

Mills, W. Haslam (1874–1930) *Grey Pastures* (Chatto & Windus, 1924). See editorial commentary.

Montagu, Lady Mary Wortley (1689–1762) Lord Wharncliffe ed. *Letters and Works* (1837) and numerous editions.

Nansen, Frijdtof (1861–1930) Reported in *The Musical Times* (March 1897), quoted in Percy Scholes, *The Mirror of Music* (Novello, Oxford University Press, 1947).

North, The Hon. Roger (1651–1734) *The Musicall Grammarian* (1728), in A. Jessopp, ed. *The Lives of the Norths* (1890); for modern editions, see also J. Wilson, ed. *Roger North on Music* (1959).

Nyren, John (1764–1837) *The Cricketers of My Time* (1833). See also E.V. Lucas in *The Hambledon Men* (Henry Frowde, 1907).

Partridge, Frances (1900–) The late-flowering diarist of Bloomsbury – and after, beginning at the age of 78. When asked permission in 1992 for extracts in this book, she replied, 'What a delightful sort of anthology! I should be honoured to figure in it, for I owe amateur music some of the happiest times in my life.' *A Pacifist's Diary* (Hogarth, 1978); *Everything To Lose* (Gollancz, 1985); *Hanging On* (Collins, 1990).

Pasternak, Boris (1890–1960) *An Essay in Autobiography*, transl. Manya Harari (Collins Harvill, 1959).

Peacham, Henry (?1576–?1643) *The Complete Gentleman* (1622).

Pepys, Samuel (1633–1703) *Diary* (Bell & Hyman, 1970–83). See editorial commentary.

Searle, Ronald (1920–) Illustration, in *Back to the Slaughterhouse* (Macdonald, 1951).

Shakespeare, William (1564–1616) *The Taming of the Shrew* (1594); *Sonnets* (1609). Commentary would be presumptuous – except to note the precision of the sustained harpsichord imagery in the sonnet. For the gamut imagery (and Pepys's problems with the same notation) see *The Oxford Companion to Music*.

Shaw, George Bernard (1856–1950) *Major Barbara* (Constable, 1905); *Music in London 1890–4* (Constable, 1932).

Shelley, Percy Bysshe (1792–1822) 'For Jane', in *Collected Poems* (Oxford University Press, 1905). See editorial commentary.

Shephard, Ernest H. (1879–1976) 'The Toy Symphony', in *Drawn from Memory* (Methuen, 1957).

Sime, Georgina (1880–?) *Brave Spirits* (privately printed, 1952). Born in Scotland, she studied music in Berlin, worked as a journalist in London and settled in Montreal, where she was described as one of the first writers to bring realism (and feminism) to the Canadian novel. She returned to England in 1945.

Sparks, Allister. From *The Observer* (14 June 1992).

Spiegl, Fritz (1926–) From *CD Magazine*.

Steinberg, Jonathan. From *New Society* (13 September 1979) and his postscript.

Tennyson, Alfred (1809–92) From *Maud: a Monodrama* (1855).

Thackeray, W.M. (1811–63) Novelist and illustrator. *Christmas Books* (1857); *The Newcomes* (1853–5): for the plot in this and many other classic novels, see *The Oxford Companion to English Literature*.

Trollope, Anthony (1815–82) *The Warden* (1855).

Troubridge, Lady Laura (1858–1929) *Etiquette* (2 vols, Associated Bookbuyers' Co., 1926). The author of romantic novels, she was the wife of Sir Thomas Troubridge Bt, hence often confused with her much more interesting sister-in-law, Lady Una Troubridge, the sculptor, estranged wife of Admiral Sir Ernest Troubridge and the lifelong partner of Radclyffe Hall, the poet and author of *The Well of Loneliness*. Ironically, Una Troubridge played the piano, had a trained voice and sang in public in Malta as an opera singer, after her marriage. But there was no love lost between two sides of the Troubridge family. As she wrote to her agent about her byline as a translator, ' . . . the "Una" must be in because otherwise there will be confusion with my foul sister-in-law!' See Richard Ormrod's biography of Una Troubridge (Jonathan Cape, 1984).

Torr, Cecil (1857–1928) *Small Talk at Wreyland* (Cambridge University Press, 1918–23).

Ward, Ned (1667–1731) *London Spy* (1698).

Welty, Eudora (1909–) Novelist of the American South. *Delta Wedding* (Bodley Head, 1947).

West, Rebecca (1892–1983) *The Fountain Overflows* (Macmillan, 1957).

Wright, David (1920–) 'The musician', in *Selected Poems* (Carcanet, 1988). The poet has been profoundly deaf since childhood.

Wynne, Betsey (1778–1857) *The Wynne Diaries*, ed. Anne Fremantle (Oxford University Press, 1936–40). See commentary.

INDEX OF INSTRUMENTS

[Instruments with many references have the principal references shown in **bold***]*.